How to Analyze
Businesses, Financial Statements,
and the Quality of Earnings

Joel G. Siegel, Ph.D., CPA

How to Analyze Businesses, Financial Statements, and the Quality of Earnings

Second Edition

PRENTICE HALL
Englewood Cliffs, New Jersey 07632

Prentice-Hall International (UK) Limited, *London*
Prentice-Hall of Australia Pty. Limited, *Sydney*
Prentice-Hall Canada, Inc., *Toronto*
Prentice-Hall Hispanoamericana, S.A., *Mexico*
Prentice-Hall of India Private Limited, *New Delhi*
Prentice-Hall of Japan, Inc., *Tokyo*
Simon & Schuster Asia Pte. Ltd., *Singapore*
Editora Prentice-Hall do Brasil, Ltda., *Rio de Janeiro*

© 1982, 1991 *by*

Prentice Hall, Inc.
Englewood Cliffs, New Jersey 07632

10 9 8 7 6 5 4 3 2 1

This publication is designed to provide accurate and
authoritative information in regard to the subject matter
covered. It is sold with the understanding that the publisher is
not engaged in rendering legal, accounting, or other
professional service. If legal advice or other expert assistance
is required, the services of a competent professional person
should be sought.
. . . *From the Declaration of Principles jointly adopted by a*
Committee of the American Bar Association and a Committee of
Publishers and Associations.

Library of Congress Cataloging-in-Publication Data

Siegel, Joel G.
    How to analyze businesses, financial statements, and the quality
of earnings/Joel G. Siegel.
        p.   cm.
    Includes bibliographical references and index.
    ISBN 0-13-400995-9
    1. Financial statements.   2. Industrial management.   I. Title.
HF5681.B2S4875   1991
657'.3—dc20   91–7532
                                                                   CIP

ISBN 0-13-400995-9

PRENTICE HALL
BUSINESS & PROFESSIONAL DIVISION
A division of Simon & Schuster
Englewood Cliffs, New Jersey 07632

Printed in the United States of America

About the Author

JOEL G. SIEGEL, Ph.D., CPA, is Professor of Accounting and Finance at Queens College of the City University of New York.

He was previously employed by Coopers and Lybrand, CPAs, and Arthur Andersen, CPAs. Dr. Siegel has acted as a consultant in accounting and finance to many organizations including Citicorp, International Telephone and Telegraph, United Technologies, American Institute of CPAs, and Person-Wolinsky Associates.

Dr. Siegel is the author of 32 books and about 200 articles on accounting and financial topics. His books have been published by Prentice Hall, McGraw-Hill, Harper and Row, John Wiley, Barron's, Macmillan, and the American Institute of CPAs.

He has been published in many accounting and financial journals including *The Financial Analysts Journal, Financial Executive, The CPA Journal, Practical Accountant*, and the *National Public Accountant*.

In 1972, he was the recipient of the Outstanding Educator of America Award. Dr. Siegel is listed in *Who's Where Among Writers* and *Who's Who in the World*.

Acknowledgments

I would like to express my deep appreciation to Ronald Cohen for his outstanding editorial work. It is an author's delight to work with such a talented editor. Thanks also goes to Joan Hiam and Barbara O'Brien for their valuable input in the production editorial process.

Distinguished Professor and Consultant Leopold A. Bernstein, a dear and wonderful friend, to whom this book is affectionately dedicated, has provided his thoughts and suggestions on the "quality of earnings" topic. I am indeed fortunate to be acquainted with this well-known and respected expert in financial statement analysis.

I wish to express my deepest appreciation to my wife, Roberta, whose sacrifice, devotion, inspiration, and typing have made this book possible.

Special gratitude goes to Professor David Hawkins of Harvard University who assisted me in my survey on earnings quality.

My colleagues at the City University of New York, Adrian Fitzsimmons and Abraham J. Simon, have contributed valuable suggestions.

In the field of professional accountancy I wish to express appreciation to Leon Lebensbaum, own account; Ed Lewis formerly of Deloitte, Haskins & Sells; James MacNeill formerly of the American Institute of CPAs; and Bob Roussey of Arthur Andersen for their valuable comments.

J.G.S.

What This Book Will Do for You

This revised edition encompasses all of the latest developments in accounting. It includes coverage of the analytical implications of the Statement of Cash Flows now required by FASB No. 95. In addition, FASB No. 87 made sweeping changes in pension plan reporting. This requires a modified analytical approach. Finally, foreign currency translation and transaction gains and losses are evaluated according to FASB. No. 52. Beside covering the latest FASB Statements, the book incorporates recent Statements on Auditing Standards applicable to the audit report.

This new edition also includes the latest references to financial analysis in practice and in the literature. The update will keep readers who bought the earlier edition current on recent developments. Thus, continued success in the neverending job of financial analysis may be assured. Readers buying this book for the first time will benefit from not only the earlier body of information but also from the ever-changing environment. A knowledge of the content of this book will give you the "right answers" when analyzing a company. You can not afford to make a mistake when recommending an investment or giving credit. What appears to be a good company may in fact be a poor financial risk!

A new chapter (7) has been added dealing with the very important topic of valuing a business. It presents a clear and comprehensive discussion of the earnings and asset-oriented valuation methods. Step-by-step instructions are provided to show how to determine how much a business is worth.

There are many features in this updated edition that will keep readers abreast with recent analytical trends, approaches, and techniques. The coverage of asset utilization and rates of return on assets has been expanded. There are new sections dealing with the analysis of cash flows, stockholders' equity, book value per share, and how to avoid business failure. Further, the discussion of many ratios has been elaborated on to achieve greater application and significance.

The latest requirements dealing with the preparation of the audit report are provided. Hence, the analyst must now base his analytical conclusions on present audit rules.

References to authoritative pronouncements that were superseded have been deleted. Authoritative pronouncements issued since the earlier edition have been incorporated along with their analytical implications. These recent pronouncements include FASB 52 (Foreign Currency Translation and Transactions), FASB 87 (Pension Plans), FASB 95 (Statement of Cash Flows), and FASB 105 (Financial Instruments).

What we have now is the most up-to-date, comprehensive work on financial statement analysis filled with the how to's and whys. By using the analytical techniques and "rules of thumb," you will be able to learn what is really going on in a company.

This book is a practical reference that contains proven approaches and techniques for diagnosing the financial and operating health of businesses. The content of the book applies equally to large, medium, and small companies. It is a working guide that will pinpoint what to look for, what to watch out for, what to do and how to do it when appraising a company's strengths and weaknesses, financial position, and earnings quality. The book studies the favorable and unfavorable characteristics associated with a firm, including an analysis of its income statement, balance sheet, and statement of cash flows.

The benefits of the book are that it:

1. Enables you to look behind reported financial statement figures and disclosures to get at the real financial position and performance of the entity.
2. Presents the techniques to measure and evaluate earnings and balance sheet posture that can be usefully applied in practice.
3. Highlights good or poor quality of earnings indicators.
4. Explores the meaning and boundaries of the "quality of earnings."
5. Provides the techniques involved in adjusting net income to an earnings figure that is more relevant to your needs.
6. Evaluates the realism of the accounting policies employed.
7. Uncovers attempts to artificially overstate or understate reported earnings.
8. Spots the improper reduction in discretionary costs.
9. Evaluates the degree to which earnings are backed up by cash.
10. Appraises the reliability and verifiability of reported earnings.
11. Notes the degree of uncertainty surrounding net income.
12. Provides approaches in appraising the stability of income statement components.
13. Measures the degree of earnings stability.
14. Specifies the means to measure and evaluate an entity's earning power

15. Considers the effect of inflation on the company's operating results and financial position.
16. Identifies overstated or understated assets and liabilities.
17. Evaluates the risk in assets.
18. Offers techniques to derive realistic values for balance sheet accounts.
19. Lists "red flags" indicating the improper maintenance of capital.
20. Evaluates the adequacy of the sources and uses of funds.
21. Appraises liquidity and solvency position.
22. Enumerates signs of future business failure.
23. Recommends means to correct for financial sickness.
24. Identifies areas of excessive business risk and recommends ways to minimize such risk.
25. Offers ways in which corporate return may be maximized.
26. Discusses the impact of economic and political factors upon the firm's financial position.
27. Evaluates the effects of industry characteristics on earnings quality.
28. Lists the financial and operating strengths and weaknesses of companies.

In short, the book assists investors in making optimal portfolio decisions, creditors in assuring repayment of loans and payables, auditors in evaluating the financial soundness of clients, and management in scrutinizing and correcting areas of inefficiency and risk.

HOW TO USE THIS BOOK

Illustrations and step-by-step instructions are provided on what to watch out for and how to do it. This enables you to see how the techniques and procedures are applied. The illustrations are primarily designed to show how income statement and balance sheet accounts are adjusted to come up with more realistic financial statement numbers that are indicative of the firm's financial strength and operating performance. Real life examples are given of the analytical points made. Checklists, summarizing the major areas discussed, are provided. In the index, a specific area of interest may easily be found.

Joel G. Siegel

Contents

CHAPTER ONE

How to Analyze Earnings Quality

This chapter covers the application of quality of earnings analysis. Recommendations are given to analysts, accountants, and management on using the quality of earnings approach. The meaning and boundaries of the concept "quality of earnings" are presented. Favorable and unfavorable characteristics in earnings are identified. Also, warning signs of business failure are noted and means to counteract such prospective failure are given.

101 / HOW TO USE THE QUALITY OF EARNINGS APPROACH

Earnings quality is relative rather than absolute; it refers to comparing the attributes of reported earnings among companies in an industry. The determination of an absolute figure representing a given firm's earnings quality is impossible, since analysts will differ as to their adjustments to reported results. Therefore, in appraising the quality of earnings, we are concerned with determining the degree to which a company's net income is of higher or lower quality than that of another.

Some points that should be borne in mind are:

First. The "quality of earnings" term encompasses much more than the mere understatement or overstatement of net income; it refers also to such factors as the stability of income statement components, the realization risk of

1

assets, and the maintenance of capital. For example, poor quality of earnings may be indicated when a firm has not properly maintained assets, or when its income statement elements are highly erratic. Although net income has not been manipulated, earnings quality is still poor.

Second. Quality of earnings is basically an analytical tool. It affects the P/E ratio in equity decisions. The marketplace assigns lower multiples to lower quality of earnings. In lending decisions, the quality of earnings bears upon the effective interest rate. When earnings quality deteriorates, lenders request higher interest rates and/or compensating balances. If the deterioration is acute, the more desirable sources of current financing may be unavailable to the firm. A company may find it necessary, for example, to borrow from finance companies because bank loans are suddenly not available. A company's bond rating may also be affected by its quality of earnings. For example, a high degree of earnings instability may result in lower bond ratings being assigned to the firm by such services as Standard and Poors. As a result, the market price of its bonds may decline. It should be remembered that changes in P/E ratios, effective financing costs, or bond ratings are *outcomes* rather than causes of the quality of earnings.

Third. Earnings quality relates to the nature of *currently* reported results. The term should not be used with reference to *intangible* characteristics relating to future performance as the ability to introduce new products. These have nothing to do with present earnings.

Fourth. Quality of earnings involves those factors that would influence investors or their surrogates considering investments in firms exhibiting the same reported earnings. Specifically, two firms in a given industry may report identical earnings but may be quite dissimilar in terms of operational performance. This is because identical earnings may possess different degrees of quality. For example, company A and company B may report the same earnings but company A may have exaggerated its net income by income manipulation and by the arbitrary reduction of discretionary costs. In addition, company A may have very liberal accounting policies compared to company B, which uses realistic accounting policies. Under these circumstances, company A has lower quality of earnings *relative* to company B. The key to evaluating a company's earnings quality is to *compare* its earnings profile (the mixture and the degree of favorable and unfavorable characteristics associated with reported results) with the earnings profile of other companies in the same industry. Analysts attempt to assess earnings quality in order to render the earnings comparable, and to determine what valuation should be placed upon those earnings.

101.1 / Spotting Desirable Characteristics in Earnings

Given the state of the art and the different analytical objectives, reported net income is only a starting point for analysts in assessing the quality of reported results. Consideration must be given to positive and negative attributes in earnings. Such attributes may exist in different proportions and intensities in the earnings profiles of various companies within an industry.

Although all analysts should be in basic agreement as to the desirable characteristics in earnings, subjective—and therefore varying—weights will be assigned to them by the different analysts. The desirable characteristics in earnings cannot be quantified objectively, and there is no *number* that all security analysts will agree on as representing the magnitude of a specific quality of earnings element. However, there should be a pattern in the ranking process, indicating which characteristics are more important and leading to a general consensus as to which factors are "strong" or "weak" in a particular profile of earnings.

The evaluation of reported results is a complex and time-consuming task. There are no commonly accepted guidelines or yardsticks to follow in rating the significance individually or cumulatively of the factors bearing on the quality of earnings. Further, the significance of certain quality of earnings factors, e.g., business risk, to the analyst can change as his preference for risk shifts.

Analysts must address the problem of evaluating earnings of competitive companies that report substantially different net incomes. The earnings quality of the firm reporting higher net income may in fact be inferior if the firm is burdened with more undesirable characteristics in earnings than its low-income-reporting competitor.

The recognition of desirable characteristics is important if the ability to distinguish between high and low quality of reported earnings is to be improved. Much of the book has been directed toward isolating those factors that should be considered in appraising quality. Although clear-cut answers do not exist for every case, the book will assist analysts in making finer distinctions between the earnings qualities of the different business enterprises.

101.2 / Restating Net Income for Comparative Purposes

When two competitive companies use alternative accounting policies, the analyst should attempt to adjust their net incomes to a common basis in order to reduce the diversity in accounting that exists. Information provided in footnotes may assist in this restatement process—there may be disclosure of what the earnings effect would have been if another method of accounting had been used. For example, some companies using LIFO for inventory valuation disclose what their earnings would have been under FIFO. The best basis for adjusting earnings for comparative purposes is to derive net income figures assuming that *realistic* accounting policies were used.

———— 102 / WORKING APPROACHES TO THE DESCRIPTION AND EVALUATION OF THE QUALITY OF EARNINGS ————

A variety of techniques exists to measure and describe a company's quality of earnings. Some of these approaches are quantitative; others are not. The approaches will provide analysts with a feeling about a company's earnings quality. For example, in appraising net income we can employ quantitative techniques, such as ratio analysis, as measuring instruments of the individual elements of the quality of earnings. We can therefore arrive at an overall conclusion concerning the quality of earnings reported by the firm.

We cannot arrive at a single quality of earnings figure independently. However, with proper adjustments, we can come up with a fairly close range of numbers that more accurately reflect a company's real earnings than does net income. We are converting net income into what the *analyst* considers "relevant" net income. The quality of earnings thus depends upon *relevance* and point of view. The adjustments made by the analysts are designed to derive the earning power of the firm.

A discussion of earnings quality characteristics follows. These are subsumed under the broader topics to which they relate: (1) Nature of Accounting Policies; (2) Discretionary Costs; (3) Degree of Certainty of Accounting Estimates; (4) Unreliability in Reported Earnings; (5) Cash Flow; (6) Realization Risk in Assets; (7) Maintenance of Capital; (8) Taxable Income; (9) Residual Income; (10) Stability of Earnings; (11) Growth Rate; (12) Off-Balance Sheet Liabilities; and (13) Unrecorded Assets.

102.1 / Watch the High Accounting Risk Company

Analysts must watch with a careful eye the accounting policies of a "high accounting risk" company. Such a company has one or more of the following attributes:

1. It is a "glamour" company known for its earnings growth.
2. It is highly visible—under the "public eye" and/or governmental regulation, as are oil companies.
3. It is having difficulty obtaining credit.
4. It is a risk maximizer.
5. It is subject to high risk because of the nature of its business operations (i.e., single product firm).
6. It is known for its liberal accounting policies.
7. It continually turns over its auditors.
8. It has significant insider transactions.

9. It has significant transactions with affiliates.
10. It is known to have engaged in dishonest activities—payoffs, for example.
11. It is headed by a headstrong individual.
12. It is entering a new line of business that is unproven.

In a questionnaire survey undertaken by the author,[1] a financial vice-president wrote:

> There needs to be a more precise definition of GAAP inasmuch as every year in our firm we have discretionary decisions that can affect reported results 15%. Our company nets $30 million of income.

102.2 / How to Check for Realistic Accounting Policies

Economic reality will impinge upon many financial statement elements, and if the reality is improperly recognized, the reported data will, of necessity, lead to lower earnings quality, and will make conclusions about a firm's earning power that much more difficult to render.

Analysts should determine what the impact on earnings would have been if a firm used realistic accounting policies (i.e., based on AICPA Industry Audit Guides and Statements of Position) instead of the accounting policies followed. If the employment of realistic policies would have resulted in substantially lower earnings, the quality of reported results is lower.

SEC Release No. 33–5427 states: "If a company's accounting principles vary with prevailing practices within the industry, the dollar effect on earnings should be disclosed . . . The disclosures set forth are necessary for a proper assessment of the quality of earnings of a registrant." Analysts may wish to determine what the effect on net income would have been if a firm had used for its stockholder reporting the accounting practices prevailing within the industry. If the use of such practices would have resulted in substantially lower earnings, the quality of reported net income may be lower.

102.3 / Are Accounting Changes Justified?

If accounting changes are unjustified, they will not reflect appropriately the economic substance of transactions. Reduction of bad debt provision as a percent of sales even though shipments are being made to more marginal customers, and nominal increases in the sales allowance account even though

---

[1] J. Siegel, "The Quality of Earnings' Concept—A Survey," *Financial Analysts Journal*, (March/April, 1982), pp. 60–68.

sales and corresponding returns have increased significantly, are examples of such changes.

Inconsistency in the application of accounting policies and changes made to bolster earnings will render results less meaningful and will create difficulty in predicting future income.

If improper accounting changes were made during the reporting period, analysts should restate earnings as they would have been reported originally had no unrealistic accounting changes (principles or estimates) been made. The dollar effect of these accounting changes on reported results should be isolated.

102.4 / How Accrual of Expenses Can Misstate Earnings

The overaccrual or underaccrual of expenses results in earnings misstatement. The analyst should revise net income for the difference between the recorded expense provision and what the normal expense provision should have been.

102.5 / Watch for the Accounting Cushion

A company that provides for an "accounting cushion" understates net income, thus lowering the quality of earnings. For example, a company's allowance for bad debts to accounts receivable may substantially increase even though the company's bad debt write-off experience has become much better. In this case, the overstatement of bad debt expense unjustifiably understates earnings. The analyst should upwardly adjust net income for the improper accounting cushion established.

102.6 / How Income Smoothing Works

Any form of income manipulation will result in earnings that reflect the economic results not as they are but rather as the firm wishes them to be. This masks the inherent cyclical irregularities that are part of the reality of the firm's experience and, therefore, lowers earnings quality. Further, a company's taking a "financial bath" results in lowering current period net income while relieving future income of these charges. Improper recognition of revenue, either prematurely or belatedly, lowers the quality of earnings. For example, the recognition of revenue before it is reasonably assured to be collectible may result in the reporting of earnings in one year and its reversal, and a resultant loss, in a subsequent year. Net income is improperly stated for both periods. Recognizing revenue without an adequate provision for future losses also lowers earnings quality. For example, interest should not be accrued on loans that may not be recoverable.

The analyst should restate net income for profit increases or decreases due to income smoothing attempts.

In conclusion, the quality of net income depends on the degree to which earnings stand on their own for the current period, as well as on the degree to which they borrow from the future or benefit from the past. Earnings are of lower quality if they do not portray the economic performance of the business entity for the period.

102.7 / Analyzing Discretionary Costs

A reduction in discretionary costs may cause a deterioration in earnings quality because management is starving the firm of some needed input. The result will be a negative impact on future performance. Analysts should examine trends in discretionary expenses (e.g., advertising, training) as a percent of net sales. Declining trends may indicate lower quality of earnings.

Analysts should also examine the relationship between discretionary costs and the assets with which they are associated. For example, a declining trend in repairs and maintenance as a percent of fixed assets may indicate future equipment malfunctioning.

If the trend in the ratio of discretionary costs to sales and/or assets is a vacillating one, it may be a sign that the firm is managing income by altering these costs.

The quality of earnings impact can be approximated by removing from reported earnings any increments or reductions arising from unjustified changes in discretionary costs. For example, if an unjustified decrease in advertising as a percent of net sales resulted in a per share gain, such gain should be subtracted from reported earnings per share.

It should be noted, however, that a reduction in discretionary costs may be justified if they were too high in prior years. For example, the reduction may be designed to eliminate waste and inefficiency.

102.8 / How Certain Are Accounting Estimates?

Within a framework of periodic income determinations, material uncertainties as to accounting estimates present a serious problem of revenue and expense determination. Consequently, if many estimates are involved in the income measurement process (e.g., the lives of fixed assets in a highly technological industry), the reported income figure may have a high degree of uncertainty attached to it. Analysts should, therefore, distinguish between factual and interpretive information affecting profit determination. This involves isolation of income statement elements representing cash and near-cash transactions from those involving subjective interpretations.

102.9 / How to Check Accounting Estimates

Analysts may wish to determine the variance between a company's estimated reserves and its actual losses for *previous years*. A company that has experi-

enced substantial deviation between the two may have lower earnings quality. For example, a firm's warranty reserve provision could be compared to its
actual warranty costs. A wide variance between the two figures, whether on
the high or the low side, may indicate that the company's overall accounting
estimates have been unreliable and uncertain, or that the firm has failed to
make proper provision for future losses.

The inherent characteristics of certain companies require that they
make numerous subjective accounting estimates. Companies engaged in long-
term business activites (e.g., construction companies using the percentage-of-
completion method) must determine the extent of partial completion of contract work. Companies engaged in risky business activities (such as manufacturers of explosives) may have difficulty in determining reserve provisions.
Insurance companies specializing in medical malpractice coverage may also
have difficulty in estimating future costs. Inflation and a changing social
atmosphere make it difficult for companies to accurately estimate future
malpractice awards.

102.10 / Spotting Firms that Use Questionable
Accounting Policies

A firm with poor internal control and/or high incidence of previous accounting errors has an unreliable financial reporting system. A lack of management honesty, such as that evidenced by bribes and covering up low
quality products, may infer a lack of management integrity in reporting
earnings. The analyst should look at financial publications that cite companies known to use questionable accounting policies.

102.11 / How to Analyze Cash Flow

When subjective evaluations are an important factor in the determination of
net income, management has more leeway in revising its estimates in order to
influence earnings. Therefore, accounting policies that do not track cash flow
have more subjectivity associated with them.

The recording of revenue or expense that is close to cash recognition
usually has "harder" evidence supporting the transaction. On the other hand,
revenue or expense recognition that is far removed from cash flow requires
more interpretation. This may result in an uncertain earnings figure—one of
lower quality from an analytical point of view. Income statement items
recognized close to the point of cash receipt and payment constitute a
desirable earnings characteristic. An example of such an item is sales that
immediately convert to cash after being recorded.

The analyst should compute the ratio of cash flow to net income. A high
ratio indicates good earnings quality since net income is backed up by cash.
Further, the ratios of (1) cash expenses to total expenses and (2) cash revenues
to total revenues should be determined. High ratios are indicative of better
earnings quality.

102.12 / Classifying Assets According to Risk

The quality of assets is lower if they have high realization risk in cash. Overstated assets lead to the overstatement of net income since reported earnings do not include necessary charges to write down assets to their appropriate amounts. The analyst should classify assets according to their degree of risk. Realization risk ratios should be computed, such as the ratio of intangible assets and deferred charges to total assets. Also, assets lacking separable value, such as work-in-process inventory, should be identified since they are not readily salable.

102.13 / How to Check Maintenance of Capital

The improper maintenance of property, plant, and equipment lowers earnings quality, since the company has not provided for the sustenance of its earnings stream. The analyst should compute the trends in the following ratios: repairs and maintenance to fixed assets, repairs and maintenance to sales, fixed asset acquisitions to total assets, net income to fixed assets, and sales to fixed assets. Footnote disclosure should be examined for any mention of inactive assets. The analyst should also compare the historical cost of the fixed asset to the replacement cost. He should then evaluate the firm's cash flow position to make needed replacements.

102.14 / What to Look for with Taxable Income

If book income substantially exceeds taxable income, it may mean that the firm's accounting policies for shareholder reporting are too liberal. The analyst can evaluate the trend in the discrepancy between the two by looking at the trend in the deferred income tax credit account.

102.15 / What to Look for with Residual Income

A residual income that is less than reported earnings indicates lower earnings quality. Residual income is an economic profit since the minimum return on total assets is deducted from net income. The trend in the ratio of residual income to net income should be examined by the analyst.

102.16 / How to Chart Stability of Earnings

Earnings quality depends upon the stability and growth trend in earnings as well as the predictability of factors that affects its future level. The analyst must watch out for abnormal and erratic income statement elements. He or she should arrive at normal earnings by adjusting net income for the earnings effect of these distortive items. The analyst should measure a company's stability of earnings over a period of years by the following methods: average reported earnings, average pessimistic earnings, standard deviation, coefficient of variation, instability index, and beta.

102.17 / Check Growth Rate

The growth rate of a firm may be expressed as the ratio of net income minus dividends to common stockholders' equity. A high ratio reflects a firm's ability to generate internal funds and thus it does not have to rely on external sources.

102.18 / Off-Balance Sheet Liabilities to Guard Against

The analyst must be on guard against unrecorded liabilities. Footnote disclosure must be searched for such items as unfunded past service pension expense, noncapitalized leases, litigation, and future guarantees. A determination must be made of the dollar magnitude of such off-balance sheet liabilities.

The analyst cannot always take at face value the disclosures provided. He or she may wish to ask further questions based upon the information given. For example, a contingency footnote may inadequately reflect the potential legal liability exposure.

Illustration ────────────────────────────────────

The Company is a defendant or co-defendant in a substantial number of lawsuits brought by present or former workers . . . and other persons alleging damage to their health from exposure to dust from asbestos fiber or asbestos-containing products manufactured or sold by the Company and, in most cases, by certain other defendants. The majority of these claims allege that the Company and other defendants failed in their duty to warn of the hazards of inhalation of asbestos fiber and dust originating from asbestos-containing products. In the opinion of Management, the Company has substantial defenses to these legal actions. . .

It is the Company's belief that the claims and lawsuits pending and which may arise in the future relate to events and conditions existing in prior years. More specifically, it is the Company's opinion, based on the following factors and assumptions, that since at least prior to the period covered by these financial statements, no significant new potential liabilities have been created for the Company with respect to diseases known to be related to asbestos and arising from asbestos fiber and/or asbestos-containing products manufactured or sold by the Company . . .

As of December 31, 19Y0, the Company was a defendant or co-defendant in 5,087 asbestos/health suits brought by approximately 9,300 individual plaintiffs. This represents a substantial increase from the December 31, 19X9 level of 2,707 cases (brought by approximately 4,100 plaintiffs) and the December 31, 19X8 level of 1,181 cases (brought by approximately 1,500 plaintiffs). During 19X9, the Company was named as a defendant in an average of 141 cases per month (brought by an average of 196 plaintiffs) as compared with an average of 65 cases per month (brought by an average of 83 plaintiffs) in 19X8. During the first three quarters of 19X0, the Company was named as a defendant in an average of 194 cases per month (brought by an average of 382 plaintiffs); this rate increased to an average of 304 cases per month (brought by an average of 403 plaintiffs) in the fourth quarter of 19Y0. During 19Y0, the Company disposed of 402 claims at an average disposition cost (excluding legal expenses) of $23,000, substantially all of which was paid by applicable insurance. This level of disposition cost represents a significant growth from the pre-19Y0 level of approximately $13,000 per claim. The growth in these two areas has significantly increased the uncertainties as to the future number of similar claims that the Company may receive, and the future disposition costs of these claims. . .

Because of the uncertainties associated with the litigation, and in spite of the substantial defenses the Company believes it has with respect to these claims, the eventual outcome of the litigation cannot be predicted and the ultimate liability after application of available insurance cannot be estimated with any degree of reliability. Under present GAAP, any future liability would be recorded at that future time. No reasonable estimate of loss, if any, can be made and no liability has been recorded in the financial statements. Depending on how and when these uncertainties are resolved, the cost to the Company could be substantial.

The footnote may be inadequate for the following reasons.

1. No amount or range is given, although the word "substantial" is used.

2. What is meant by disposition? Does this mean trial or settlement?

3. Why didn't the company accrue at least the lower end of the range, —the $23,000 average disposition cost? Is there any reason to believe the future disposition costs will change significantly? If so, why wasn't the reason stated?

4. How long are these cases pending? What is their current status? Are settlements to be on a case-by-case basis or do they fall into clauses generally?

5. The footnote states that the contingency is based upon *management's* opinion. It does not refer to the opinion of outside counsel.

6. It is not clear where insurance coverage ends and the company's liability begins.

7. What about unasserted claims? It is apparent that the number of claims is on the rise. Shouldn't some cognizance be made and adequate thought given to an accrual for unasserted claims? The footnote does not indicate whether the plaintiffs are seeking punitive damages.

The company received a qualified opinion from its auditors for the year-end 19Y0 because of the uncertainties surrounding the asbestos/health legal actions.

102.19 / Examples of Unrecorded Assets

Improved financial strength is indicated when an entity has unrecorded and/ or undervalued assets. Examples include a tax loss carry forward benefit, a purchase commitment where the contract price is lower than the current price, and research and development costs.

102.20 / Quality of Earnings Characteristics Summarized

"Quality of earnings" can be defined only in terms of accounting and financial characteristics that have an impact on the earning power of a firm as shown in its net income figure. These characteristics are complex and interrelated, and are subject to wide varieties of interpretation by analysts depending upon their own analytical objectives. Furthermore, measurements of some of the characteristics may be extremely difficult, elusive, and perhaps impossible. Nevertheless analysts cannot avoid sorting through the characteristics to determine which of them are favorable in terms of earnings quality and which are unfavorable, and to determine the degree to which they exist. They are then in a position to rank the relative quality of earnings of companies in an industry as well as to restate companies' net incomes.

102.21 / Five Favorable Characteristics of Earnings Quality

1. The degree to which the accounting policies employed reflect the economic reality of a company's transactions.
2. The degree of realism used to develop estimates of current and future conditions, referring here to the degree of risk attached to estimates or assumptions that may ultimately prove overoptimistic or unwarranted.
3. The degree to which sufficient provision has been made for the maintenance of assets and for the maintenance and enhancement of present and future earning power.
4. The degree of earnings stability associated with a firm. This refers also to the degree to which income statement components are recurring in nature.
5. The stability and growth trend of earnings as well as the predictability of factors that may affect their future levels.

102.22 / Twelve Unfavorable Characteristics of Earnings Quality

1. The degree to which accounting changes that are inconsistent with economic reality have been made.
2. The degree to which income manipulation exists.

3. The degree to which unrealistic deferrals of costs exist.

4. The degree to which a company has underaccrued or overaccrued its expenses.

5. The degree to which a company has recognized revenue prematurely or belatedly.

6. The degree to which unjustified reductions in discretionary costs have been made. Such reductions may deprive the business of expenditures needed for future growth.

7. The degree to which highly subjective and uncertain accounting estimates are associated with the recognition of revenue and expense items. In general, the further revenue and expense recognition is from the point of cash receipt and payment, the less objective the transaction and the more subjective the interpretations involved.

8. The degree to which assets are overstated and liabilities are understated.

9. The degree of risk attached to the probability of future realization of different types of assets.

10. The degree of operating leverage associated with the firm.

11. The degree to which a firm is susceptible to the business cycle.

12. The degree to which inflationary profits are included in net income.

It is apparent from the foregoing that the quality of the earnings figure of any given company for any particular time period is a matter of the degree to which favorable and unfavorable characteristics exist, and that the significance of the characteristics depends upon their relevance to, and the point of view of, the individual analyst.

— 103 / INDICATORS OF PROSPECTIVE BUSINESS FAILURE —

Security and credit analysts must watch out for signs of possible corporate failure so that they will not enter into relationships with companies they have not dealt with before or divorce themselves from firms they are currently associated with. Signs of potential failure may be indicated in ratio trends as well as in the financial and operating status of the business. The danger of an entity's default on its obligations is more pronounced today as a result of the inflationary and recessionary environment.

103.1 / Analyzing Financial Distress Ratios

The analyst should look at the trend in the following ratios in evaluating the entity's exposure to failure:

1. Current ratio.
2. Quick ratio.
3. Working capital to total assets
4. Working capital to sales.
5. Debt to equity.
6. Fixed assets to stockholders' equity.
7. Retained earnings to total assets.
8. Net income to sales.
9. Net income to total assets.
10. Cash flow from operations to total liabilities.
11. Sales to total assets.
12. Interest coverage.

Other possible signs include:

1. Significant decline in market price of stock.
2. Material drop-off in earnings and/or cash flow from operations.
3. Decline in total assets.
4. Deficient "Z-score."
5. Unfavorable "gambler's ruin."
6. A company in an industry having a high probability of failure (apparel and furniture manufacturers).
7. Young company.
8. Small company.
9. Significant cutback in dividends.

103.2. / Diagnosing Financial and Operating Deficiencies

Various financial and operating deficiencies may point to business distress:

1. Unstable earnings.
2. Inability to satisfy prior obligations and/or to obtain further financing from sources that have provided it in the past.
3. Difficulty in selling bonds.
4. Deficient financial reporting system.
5. Poor management quality such as one-individual rule, poor planning, and an inexperienced management team.
6. Expansion into areas unrelated to the company's basic business and beyond management's expertise.

7. Management's failure to keep abreast of current market conditions, such as that indicated by Chrysler's near failure because of its inability to recognize the shift in demand to small, economical cars.
8. Material restrictions in loan agreements.
9. Inability to control costs.
10. High energy dependence.
11. Ease of entry into the industry.
12. Excessive business risk such as where the product line is both elastic and positively correlated.

103.3 / Auditor Implications

The auditor is *required* to recognize and report on potential corporate failure in the audit report. If the company is going out of business, its assets must be valued on a liquidation basis.[2] A going-concern problem may be indicated by solvency and/or operational difficulties. Solvency troubles are indicated by, among others, continued operating losses, working capital inadequacy, and the denial of customary trade credit. Operating problems include the loss of key management personnel and strikes.

103.4 / Steps to Counteract Prospective Business Failure

Management must recognize the "red flags" of impending business failure and take appropriate action to *reverse* the tide. Possible steps include:

1. Enter into arrangements for bank lines of credit.
2. Identify and dispose of unprofitable divisions and product lines.
3. Diversify operations.
4. Practice good asset management.
5. Improve marketing strategy and policy—put sales quotas on high profit-margin merchandise.
6. Reduce personnel costs—give incentives for early retirement.
7. Improve cost and productivity control, such as by computing and analyzing variances by operation and department.
8. Reduce cost of data processing by taking advantage of service bureaus and time-sharing arrangements.

---

[2] J. Siegel, "Auditor Involvement Concerning A Client's Continued Existence," *The Ohio CPA*, (Autumn, 1983), pp. 177-180.

CHAPTER TWO

Strategies for Analyzing the Balance Sheet

201 / BALANCE SHEET ANALYSIS

Balance sheet analysis provides a check on the validity of reported earnings, and supplies the basis for analyzing the sources of earnings. If assets are overstated, earnings will be overstated also because the earnings will not include those charges required to reduce the assets to their proper valuations. The same condition may exist on the liabilities side. When liabilities are understated, earnings will not include those charges required to reflect the proper valuation of liabilities and earnings will be overstated in consequence.

201.1 / How to Use Realistic Values in Balance Sheet Analysis

For ratio computations, where possible, the analyst should attempt to use the realistic values associated with balance sheet accounts. Hence, understated and overstated assets and liabilities should be noted and adjusted for.

Illustration

Company A has total assets of $10,000,000, total liabilities of $4,000,000, and stockholders' equity of $6,000,000. The balances of specific accounts follow:

Assets

Long-term investments (lower of cost or market)	$ 500,000
Goodwill	300,000

Liabilities

Deferred pension liability	$ 100,000

Footnote disclosures provide the following information:

1. Long-term investments have a market value of $600,000.
2. The company has been found quilty by the government of selling defective merchandise. (The analyst thus concludes that the Goodwill on the books is worthless).
3. The unfunded past pension liability is $500,000.

The restated total assets to be used in ratios should be:

Reported total assets	$10,000,000
Increase in total assets due to the excess of market value over cost of long-term investments ($600,000–$500,000)	100,000
Decrease in total assets due to worthless Goodwill	(300,000)
Realistic total assets	$ 9,800,000

The restated total liabilities to be used in ratios should be:

Reported total liabilities	$ 4,000,000
Increase in total liabilities due to the unfunded past pension liability	500,000
Realistic liabilities	$ 4,500,000

201.2 / Factors Affecting the Quality of Assets

The quality of assets relates to the degree of certainty associated with the amount and timing of the *realization* of such assets. Asset quality may be affected by several factors, such as changes in industry and economic conditions, and changes in the nature or operations of the business entity. A change in asset quality—a change in realization—will signal a change in profits and in cash flow. A decline in the accounts receivable turnover, for example, may indicate future write-offs of customer balances.

Analysts can evaluate and measure the quality of earnings by analyzing assets according to risk category. The greater the dollar frequency of a company's assets in the high-risk category, the lower is its quality of earnings. Useful ratios here are the percentage of high-risk assets to total assets and to sales. High asset-realization risk indicates poor earnings quality because of possible future charge-offs. For example, the future realization of accounts receivable has a higher degree of probability than the future realization of goodwill.

Illustration _____

Company B reports total assets of $9,000,000 and sales of $10,000,000. Included in the former are the following assets which the analyst deems to be of high risk:

Deferred moving costs	$ 400,000
Deferred plant rearrangement costs	200,000
Receivables for claims under a government contract	$ 100,000
Goodwill	300,000

Relevant ratios follow:

High-risk assets to total assets $\dfrac{\$\ 1,000,000}{\$\ 9,000,000} = 11.1\%$

High-risk assets to sales $\dfrac{\$\ 1,000,000}{\$10,000,000} = 10\%$

The realization risk of each major asset category should also be evaluated.

Illustration _____

Company C reports receivables of $4,000,000. Included therein are the following high-risk receivables:

Notes receivable arising from extensions of unpaid balances from delinquent customers	$100,000
Advances to politically and economically unstable foreign governments	200,000

Thus, $300,000 or 7.5% of the receivables reported in the balance sheet are of dubious quality.

Multipurpose assets are considered to be of higher quality than single-purpose assets because of *readier salability*.

Interdependency of assets may cause a problem because the sale, discarding, or malfunctioning of one may adversely affect the profitability of the remaining related assets. For example, if a financially troubled company must sell a machine to raise needed funds there may be a resulting negative impact on the assembly process.

It is better when there is market price stability in assets. For example, if the market prices of assets vacillate, this may inhibit selling an asset to raise needed funds when the asset is at its lowest market price in the cycle.

In evaluating asset realization risk, analysts must also consider the impact of changing government policies on the company. There is a new and greater exposure to risk for companies because of the increasing number of decisions of regulatory bodies that certain products, e.g., those containing cyclamates or other chemical ingredients, are hazardous to human health. For the affected firms, substantial inventories may have to be written off as unsalable. Concern about the ecology has brought some pollution-causing industries under stricter control. The discontinuance of a product line or the costs of meeting antipollution standards could cause a manufacturing plant to be wholly or partially abandoned.

201.3 / Judging Assets With Separable Value

Assets that have no separable value and cannot be sold easily have low realizability and high risk. Such assets include intangibles and work-in-process. Further, the investment of cash into assets relating to the development and marketing of a new product involves significant risk as to the recovery of such commitment. On the other hand, investments represent solid realization assets and are therefore of higher quality.

201.4 / Considerations in Evaluating Balance Sheet Accounts: A Checklist

☐ The overstatement or understatement of assets and liabilities

☐ Determining realistic values for balance sheet accounts

☐ The effect of changing political, economic, industry, and corporate conditions on balance sheet valuations

☐ The realization risk of each major asset category

☐ The percentage of high-risk assets to total assets

☐ Salability of assets

☐ Multipurpose vs. single-purpose assets

☐ Impact of changing governmental policies on the realizability of assets

201.5 / How to Rate Riskiness in Assets

Type of Asset Component	Realization Risk
1. Cash	None
2. Receivables from trade customers	Low
3. Receivables from a company in a problem industry	High
4. Work-in-process	High
5. Finished goods	Low
6. Investment portfolio of development companies	High

7. Diversified investment portfolio	Low
8. Real estate	Moderate
9. Specialized machinery for a faddish product	High
10. Goodwill	High
11. Patents on successful products	None
12. Deferred charges	High

—— 202 / HOW TO ANALYZE THE CASH ACCOUNT ——

In evaluating the cash account, the analyst should note whether a portion is unavailable for use or restricted. For example, a compensating balance does not represent "free" cash. (Also, interest is not earned on it.) Similarly, cash held in a politically unstable foreign country, cash that cannot presently be remitted, is restricted. Certain foreign countries such as Spain, Brazil, and India have restrictions on cash remissions back to the United States. Cash held as a time deposit or in a temporary escrow account is also not available.

Illustration ————

Company D reports cash of $1,000,000. Related footnotes state the following:

1. The company is obligated under a $3,000,000 bank loan of which 10% represents a compensating balance.

2. Cash held of $50,000 in a foreign country's bank has now been expropriated by the foreign government.

Thus, of the cash reported of $1,000,000, $350,000 or 35% is unavailable for use and hence cannot be used to meet the cash needs of the business.

———— 203 / HOW TO ANALYZE RECEIVABLES ————

The realization risk of receivables may be evaluated by an analysis of the *nature* of the receivable balance. Receivables that have high realization risk should be identified. These include:

1. Receivables emanating from loose agreements with customers arising from a "push sale" policy.
2. Receivables relating to product components sold to a customer where collection is contingent upon the customer's receiving approval from the government to make the final product under federal specifications.

3. Receivables with offset provisions, such as when the vendor will not collect if something happens—if the seller must render further services or financing.

Firms dependent upon one or two customers are in a somewhat more vulnerable position than those with a large number of (equally important) accounts.

Generally receivables due from another corporate entity are safer than those due from consumers. Fair trade laws may protect consumers and force vendor adjustments to sales prices.

The factoring of accounts receivable may mean that the firm has a liquidity problem because it must make use of a higher cost financing source.

One must note that the assignment of accounts receivable with recourse does not transfer the ownership risk to another. The analyst must be on guard for any accounting treatment that implies that the risk has been passed on. In such a case, there is more than a mere footnoted contingent liability for the seller.

When a company's sales are lagging, it may attempt to improve profits by loading customers up with unneeded products via generous credit terms. Sales created in this fashion are a fiction. Warning signs of such a practice include: (1) a sharp boost in sales in the last quarter of the current year; (2) a significant amount of sales returns in the first quarter of the following year; and (3) a sharp drop in sales for the first quarter of the following year.

203.1 / Spotting Risky Receivables: A Checklist

☐ Amounts due from politically and economically unstable foreign governments

☐ Notes receivable involving an extension given delinquent customers

☐ Receivables from consignment sales

☐ Amounts subject to right-of-return provisions

☐ Receivables subject to offset provisions

☐ Receivables emanating from related customers

☐ Receivables from a selected few customers

203.2 / Measures of Realization Risk in Accounts Receivable

The degree of realization risk in accounts receivable can be partly determined by the calculation of the accounts receivable turnover ratio. This is equal to the annual credit sales divided by the average accounts receivable. In determining the turnover ratio, notes receivable emanating from normal sales and discounted notes receivable should be included with accounts receivable. However, one must note that if sales vary greatly during the year, this ratio can become distorted unless proper averaging takes place. In such a case, monthly or quarterly sales figures should be used.

In general, the higher the accounts receivable turnover, the better since the company is collecting quickly from customers and these funds can then be invested. However, an excessively high ratio may indicate that the company's credit policy is too stringent, with the company not tapping the potential for profit through sales to customers in higher risk classes. Note that here, too, before changing its credit policy a company has to weigh the profit potential against the risk inherent in selling to more marginal customers.

The collection period of accounts receivable should also be determined. The longer the receivables are outstanding beyond the expected payment date and relative to industry norm, the lower will be the probability of collection. Separate collection periods should be calculated by type of customer, major product line, and market territory. An aging schedule would be helpful here. However, it should be noted that in some cases a longer collection period may be justified. For example, the company may have extended its credit terms in connection with the introduction of a new product, or to meet unusual competition in the industry.

The quality of receivables may also be appraised by referring to customer ratings given by credit agencies.

A sharp rise in accounts receivable relative to the previous year may infer higher realization risk. Perhaps the company is selling to more marginal credit customers. The trends in both accounts receivable to total assets and accounts receivable to sales should be examined.

Illustration

Company E reports the following data for the years ended December 31, 19A and December 31, 19B:

	19A	19B
Sales	$400,000	$500,000
Total assets	600,000	650,000
Accounts receivable	50,000	90,000

On January 1, 19A, accounts receivable was $45,000.

Relevant ratios follow:

	19A	19B
Accounts receivable turnover (sales/average accounts receivable)	$\dfrac{\$400,000}{\$47,500}$	$\dfrac{\$500,000}{\$70,000}$
	8.42x	7.14x
Collection period (365/turnover)	$\dfrac{365}{8.42}$	$\dfrac{365}{7.14}$
	43 days	51 days
Accounts receivable to total assets	$\dfrac{\$50,000}{\$600,000}$	$\dfrac{\$90,000}{\$650,000}$
	8.3%	13.8%

The realization risk in accounts receivable is higher in 19B as evidenced by a lower turnover rate, longer collection period, and a higher ratio of accounts receivable to total assets.

203.3 / Evaluating the Bad Debt Provision

Analysts should examine trends in the ratios of (1) bad debts to accounts receivable and (2) bad debts to net sales. Unwarranted reductions in bad debt provisions lower the quality of earnings. This can occur when there is a reduction in bad debts even though the company is selling to less credit-worthy customers and/or actual bad debt losses are on the rise.

Firms that intentionally overstate bad debt provisions to establish accounting cushions will report understated earnings.

• In 19X3, company A increased its allowance for bad debts by $1,397,000 compared with $496,000 in the previous year. Earnings were thereby reduced by $0.04 per share. Actual bad debt write-offs, however, were only $133,000 in 19X3 as against $421,000 in 19X2. In fiscal 19X3 then, the company established an accounting cushion for future doubtful items.

Firms providing for substantial bad debt provisions in the current year because inadequate provisions were made in previous years distort their earnings trends.

• Company B had difficulty with slow and delinquent customers for a number of years. The company, therefore, made an addition of $6.5 million to its bad debt provision in fiscal 19X3. This substantial and unusual increase in its provision was necessary because the firm was remiss in adequately providing for bad debts in prior years.

Firms that make sudden and substantial accounts receivable write-offs may have previously understated expense provisions.

• Company C discloses that "in 19X4, the firm wrote off $92 million in accounts receivable."

A company may attempt to manage its earnings by first increasing and then lowering its bad debt provision.

• Company D discloses: "The firm's 19X3 provision for doubtful accounts was increased by 174%. In 19X4, the company's provision decreased 91% from the prior year's allowance based on the fact that the reserve level established in 19X3 was deemed adequate for the present level and risk of trade receivables."

Illustration _____

Company F reports the following financial data:

	19A	19B
Sales	$100,000	$130,000
Accounts receivable	30,000	40,000
Bad debt provision	2,000	2,200

The analyst concludes that the company is selling to more risky customers in 19B relative in 19A.

Relevant ratios follow:

	19A	19B
Bad debt provision to sales	2.0%	1.7%
Bad debt provision to accounts receivable	6.7%	5.5%

Since the firm is selling to more risky customers, its bad debt provision should rise in 19B. However, the ratios of (1) bad debt provision to sales and (2) bad debt provision to accounts receivable actually went down. The effect of understating the bad debt provision is to overstate net income and accounts receivable. Hence, net income should be reduced for the incremental earnings arising from the unrealistic lowering of bad debts. If the analyst decides that a realistic bad debt percentage to accounts receivable is 6.5%, then the bad debt expense should be $2,600 ($40,000 × 6.5%). Net income should thus be reduced by $400 ($2,600 less $2,200).

203.4 / Appraising Sales Returns and Allowances

The amount of sales returns and allowances is frequently a good index of the quality of the merchandise sold to customers.

A material reduction in a company's sales allowance account as a percent of sales is not consistent with economic reality when the firm has greater liability for dealer returns. The resulting earnings increment is of low quality.

Illustration _____

An analysis of company G's sales and sales allowance accounts for the period 19X3–19X5 reveals the following:

	19X3	19X4	19X5
Balance in sales allowance account at year-end	$1,657	$3,967	$1,973
Sales	$99,028	$213,398	$235,457
Percentage of sales allowance to sales	1.67%	1.86%	.84%

A reduction in the reserve as a percent of sales benefited fiscal 19X5 earnings by $0.11 per share. Between 19X3 and 19X5, sales increased 138%, whereas the reserve increased by only 19%. This imbalance is inconsistent with economic reality when one considers the added liability for dealer returns and credits on the expanded sales base.

203.5 / Evaluating Risk in the Loan Portfolio

A diversified loan portfolio generally has lower realization risk.

• Bank A discloses that "commercial and industrial loans, which account for the largest part of the loan portfolio, represent a broad diversity of industries and corporations which are regional, national and international in scope."

Failure to establish an adequate loss reserve on a loan portfolio results in lower quality of earnings. A bank with a conservative loan loss provision generally has higher earnings quality than one utilizing a liberal formula.

• Bank B discloses: "In 19X4, the provision for loan losses of $4.5 million was $1.5 million greater than the amount required under the formula of the regulatory authorities. The valuation reserve, that portion of the total reserve for loan losses which is available for loan charge-offs, amounted to 1.11% of total loans outstanding at December 31, 19X4. Each year since 19X0, the provision charged to earnings has exceeded our net loan losses."

203.6 / Factors to Consider When Appraising Receivables: A Checklist

☐ Accounts receivable turnover ratio
☐ Collection period
☐ Accounts receivable to total assets
☐ Bad debts to accounts receivable
☐ Bad debts to sales
☐ Sudden write-off of accounts receivable
☐ Sales returns and allowances to sales
☐ Ratings given by credit agencies
☐ Diversification in the loan portfolio

———— 204 / HOW TO DIAGNOSE INVENTORY ————

Buildup of inventory may indicate that the amounts carried in inventory are uncertain with respect to future realization. This buildup may be at the plant, wholesalers, or retailers. If a company is holding excess inventory, it means that funds which could be invested elsewhere are being tied up in inventory. In addition, there will be high carrying cost for storing goods, as well as obsolescence risk. A buildup is indicated when inventory increases at a rate much greater than the rate of increase in sales.

- Company H stated that "as of June 30, 19X3, the company's finished goods inventory account increased by 54% while total inventory increased by 40% and revenues by only 19%."

A decline in raw materials coupled with an increase in work-in-process and finished goods may be indicative of a future production slowdown.

Illustration ————

Company G reports the following makeup of its inventory account:

	19X1	19X2
Raw materials	$92,000	$81,000
Work-in-process	70,000	115,000
Finished goods	17,000	33,000

The company had a significant inventory component divergence between 19X1 and 19X2. Raw materials declined by 12.0% ($11,000/$92,000) while work-in-process increased by 64.3% ($45,000/$70,000) and finished goods advanced by 94.1% ($16,000/$17,000). This inconsistent trend between raw materials vs. work-in-process and finished goods strongly infers an upcoming slowdown in the level of production. It may also indicate a high probability of obsolescence with regard to the work-in-process and finished goods inventories as evidenced by the significant buildups.

The analyst should also appraise a company's ability to manage its inventory. Proper inventory management will lead to maximum return at minimum risk. A favorable indicator is seen when the advance in sales materially exceeds the increase in inventory.

Illustration ──────────────────────────────

Company H provides the following data regarding inventory:

	19X1	19X2
Sales	$200,000	$290,000
Total inventories	40,000	43,000

The percentage increase in sales was 45% while the advance in total inventories was only 7.5%. Good inventory control is thus indicated.

──

The turnover rate for each major inventory category as well as by department should be ascertained. A low turnover rate may point to: (1) overstocking, (2) obsolescence, and (3) deficiencies in the product line or marketing effort. However, in some instances a low rate may be appropriate, such as where higher inventory levels occur in anticipation of rapidly rising prices (e.g., oil), or when a new product line has been introduced for which the advertising effects have not been felt yet. A high turnover rate may indicate inadequate inventory levels, which may lead to a loss in business. Also, the turnover rate may be unrepresentatively high when the firm uses its "natural year-end" since at that time the inventory balance will be exceptionally low.

The number of days inventory is held should also be computed. The age of inventory should be compared to the industry norm as well as the past experience of the firm.

If we add the age of inventory to the collection period for receivables, we obtain the operating cycle of the business. A shorter operating cycle is desirable since it means cash is received faster.

Illustration ──────────────────────────────

Company I reports the following data relative to its finished goods inventory:

	Dec. 31, 19X1	Dec. 31, 19X2
Finished goods	$10,000	$15,000
Cost of goods sold	70,000	80,000

As of January 1, 19X1, finished goods inventory was $9,000.

The inventory turnover and the number of days inventory is held are indicated below.

	19X1	19X2
Inventory turnover (cost of sales/average inventory)		
	$70,000	$80,000
	$ 9,500	$12,500
	7.4X	6.4X
Number of days inventory is held (365/turnover)		
	365	365
	7.4	6.4
	49 days	57 days

Greater realization risk in inventory is indicated in 19X2 because of the lower turnover rate and increase in inventory age.

Higher realization risk is associated with merchandise that is susceptible to sharp variability in price or is of a faddish, specialized, or perishable nature. On the other hand, low realization risk exists in the case of standardized, staple, and necessity items since such goods are highly salable.

Inventory of raw material is generally safer than that of finished products because raw material has greater universal and multipurpose use.

Inventory secured to creditors on loans may have great realization risk. Inability to obtain adequate insurance because of high crime rate locations is another problem.

Inventory may be subject to political risk. The enormous jump in the price of gasoline, for example, has reduced the demand for gas-guzzling cars.

204.1 / Spotting Signs and Measures of Inventory Risk: A Checklist

- ☐ Buildup at plant, wholesaler, or retailer
- ☐ Ratio of inventory to sales
- ☐ Inventory turnover rate
- ☐ Number of days inventory is held
- ☐ Comparing the change in raw materials to the change in work-in-process to the change in finished goods
- ☐ Inventory subject to significant variability in price
- ☐ Inventory consisting of faddish, specialized, perishable, and luxury items

☐ Collateralized inventory

☐ Inadequately insured inventory

☐ Inventory susceptible to political risk

204.2 / Checking Questionable Costs in Inventory

Careful evaluation should be made of the types of costs included in inventory. Unusual costs, such as "learning curve" expenditures associated with the early phases of the production cycle, are questionable.

Firms may increase income by treating as inventory overhead costs that had been treated as period expenses in prior years. Such a situation may be indicated when the *ratio of cost of goods sold to sales declines substantially.*

• Iykes Youngstown discloses that "refractory brick and other supplies previously expensed upon purchase were included in raw materials and supplies inventories at December 31, 19X2, thereby increasing net income by $1,361,000."

Illustration _____

Company J reports the following for 19X1:

Ending inventory	$80,000
Net income	124,000

The analyst concludes, after evaluating the components included in company J's inventory account, that $11,000 are questionable and should have more appropriately been expensed. Hence, the restated net income is $113,000 ($124,000 less $11,000).

204.3 / Switching Inventory Methods

The appropriateness of a change in inventory method must be carefully noted. Specifically, a determination must be made whether the new method detracts from economic reality, and whether the change results in illusory earnings growth.

• S Company's annual report discloses: the LIFO method of inventory valuation was discontinued. It was replaced with the current cost or market method. If this change had not been made, it is estimated that net earnings for 19X2 would have been $6.7 million or $.55 per share less than the amount reported.

In recent years, which have shown a recessionary environment, some companies have switched from FIFO to LIFO. This is a sound move since the use of LIFO with its matching of current costs to current revenue results in lower taxable income, thus improving the firm's cash flow. Some companies are reluctant to switch to LIFO because it will also lower book income and make the firm appear less profitable to stockholders. But when the business environment is bleak, companies must not sacrifice the receipt of needed cash flow for artificial profits.

204.4 / Look at Unusual Fourth-Quarter Inventory Trends

Management possesses wide latitude when it comes to inventory. Cost of goods sold might be altered by changing the timing of purchases. Firms using LIFO, for example, can increase cost of goods sold by making substantial purchases at year-end. Firms could also bolster earnings by intentionally allowing LIFO inventories to become depleted. The analyst should look at the fourth-quarter financials to see if there are any unusual changes relating to inventory, such as significant purchases being made or substantial inventory declines. Further, management has flexibility in assigning values to unsalable and obsolete items.

204.5 / How to Spot Overstated Inventory

Overstatement in inventory may arise from errors in quantities, costing, pricing, or valuation of work-in-process. The more technical the product and the more dependent the valuation is on internally developed cost records, the more susceptible are the cost estimates to misstatement.

Sudden write-offs of inventory should make the analyst suspicious of a company's deferral policy. It may mean that prior years' earnings were overstated because of the failure to write-down low quality inventory and that the current year's earnings are understated because they must absorb charges more properly belonging to previous years.

204.6 / Is Inventory Undervalued?

The analyst should note that inventory may be undervalued. Since inventory is reflected at the lower of cost or market value, its carrying value may be lower than its worth. For instance, in inflationary periods, original cost usually is less than replacement cost. However, it should be recognized that the liquidity associated with inventory is often overstated since most items could not be liquidated within one year.

204.7 / Inflationary Effects on Inventory Profit

During periods of rapid inflation FIFO results in exaggerated earnings. Inventory profit is indicated when cost of sales is significantly less than what cost of sales would be on a replacement cost basis. Also, since FIFO incorporates inventory gains and losses, it usually causes profits to be more erratic during the business cycle. However, LIFO may not be a remedy to inflation accounting, because if LIFO inventories are depleted, costs incurred in prior years will find their way into the measurement of cost of sales, and distort the meaningfulness of net income. Further, when inventories include products subject to wide price fluctuations and/or shortages, the use of LIFO may still cause erratic earnings.

204.8 / Signs of Inventory Problems with Speculative Companies

A company that speculates in the futures market without protecting itself by hedging in inventory will tend to have lower earnings quality because it may be affected by a downturn in realizable values.

204.9 / Red Flags in Inventory Analysis: A Checklist

☐ Unusual costs included in inventory
☐ A change in inventory method that bolsters profits
☐ Fourth-quarter adjustments that materially affect the valuations of inventory and cost of sales
☐ Technologically oriented inventory items
☐ Inventory valuation that is significantly dependent on internally developed cost records
☐ Sudden write-offs of inventory
☐ Illusory inventory profits
☐ Losses on purchase commitments disclosed in the footnotes
☐ Inventory speculation in the futures market without hedging

———— 205 / HOW TO ANALYZE PREPAID EXPENSES ————

Since prepaid expenses are usually nominal in amount, they require only superficial analysis. The basic concern is whether items that should have been expensed are included in the prepaid category. A significant increase in prepaid expenses represents a "red flag" to be further investigated.

    • C Company reported in its prepaid expense category $96.8 million in 19X8 and $166.9 million in 19X9.

_____ 206 / ANALYZING INVESTMENTS _____

FASB Statement No. 12 (Accounting for Investments) requires reporting of an investment portfolio at the lower of *aggregate* cost or market value. In the case of marketable securities (current assets), the decline in value is shown as an unrealized loss in the income statement. For long-term investments (noncurrent assets), the reduction in value is reflected as a contra to stock-holders' equity in the balance sheet, thus bypassing the income statement. While a transfer of a security between categories requires it to be transferred at the lower of cost or market value with a realized loss being recognized in the income statement, category switching still permits corporate flexibility in reporting future earnings. The analyst must be on guard for frequent and dubious reclassifications since the quality of earnings may be adversely affected.

Illustration _____

On October 5, 19X1, company K reclassified a security from current to noncurrent that had a cost of $20,000 and a market value of $19,000. It thus reported a realized loss of $1,000.

If the analyst concludes that the *real* motivation behind the switch was to avoid reflecting anticipated future unrealized losses against income, he should downwardly adjust reported earnings in future years for such decline even though such losses are reported as a contra to stockholders' equity.

An investment portfolio that has a market value in excess of cost represents an undervalued asset.

• If a portfolio has a cost of $100,000 and a market value of $130,000, it will be reflected in the balance sheet at $100,000. However, the realistic value of the investment account is $130,000.

The analyst should be on the lookout for decreases in portfolio market values that may not be entirely reflected in the accounts. A clue to the fair value of investments may be the revenue (dividend income, interest income) generated by them. *A declining trend in the percentage of earnings derived from such investments to their carrying value may indicate higher realization risk in assets.* Also, it should be noted that debt securities may be reflected at cost, even though the cost exceeds market value, if management construes the decline to be "temporary." What is considered "temporary" is of course subjective. Furthermore, the analyst should examine the footnotes for *subsequent event* disclosure regarding any unrealized losses that have taken place on the securities' portfolio. The analyst may then wish to downwardly adjust the realizability of the investment account for such declines.

Illustration ────────────────────────────────

Company L reports the following data for the calender years ended 19X1 and 19X2:

	19X1	19X2
Investments	$30,000	$33,000
Income from investments	4,000	3,200
(dividends and interest)		

The 19X2 annual report has a footnote titled "Subsequent Events" which indicates that there was a $5,000 decline in the investment portfolio as of February 28, 19X3.

The ratio of investment income to total investments declined from 13.3% ($4,000/$30,000) in 19X1 to 9.7% ($3,200/$33,000) in 19X2, indicating higher realization risk in the portfolio. Further, the post balance sheet disclosure of a decline in value of $5,000 in the portfolio should prompt the analyst to downwardly adjust the realizability of the year-end portfolio.

───

206.1 / Diagnosing Problems in the Makeup of the Investment Portfolio

A company with an investment portfolio of volatile securities has higher realization risk than one with an investment portfolio diversified by industry and economic sector. However, the former company's portfolio can be more profitable in a bull market. *The analyst should evaluate the degree of diversification and stability associated with a company's portfolio.* Securities with negative correlations to each other add more market price stability to the portfolio than securities with positive correlations. In the case of the former, some securities will increase in market value at the same time that others decrease. In the case of the latter, the price changes of the securities will move in the same direction.

• R Company discloses: During the five years and nine months ended September 30, 19X4, the difference between cost and market on the equity investments of the affiliated insurance companies at their fiscal reporting dates has fluctuated between a cumulative market value over cost of $211.3 million at December 31, 19X2 and a cumulative cost over market of $498 million at September 30, 19X4.

The risk of an investment portfolio can be measured by determining the standard deviation of its rate of return.

By scrutinizing the investment portfolio one may see signs of a company's attempt to gain a controlling interest in another company. Such expansion may have positive or negative implications depending on the reader's viewpoint. For example, expansion for diversification purposes tends to curtail operating risk.

206.2 / Key Considerations in Evaluating Investments: A Checklist

- ☐ Constant switching between current and noncurrent categories
- ☐ A portfolio with a market value in excess of cost
- ☐ The ratio of investment income to total investments
- ☐ Debt securities which have a cost greater than market value
- ☐ Subsequent-event disclosure indicating a decline in the realizability of investments
- ☐ A portfolio of volatile and positively correlated securities
- ☐ A portfolio of high investment risk securities such as "junk" bonds
- ☐ Buying up securities in order to obtain control of a risky business

———— 207 / EVALUATING PROPERTY, PLANT, AND EQUIPMENT ————

Earnings quality depends on the extent to which adequate provision has been made for the maintenance of productive assets and for the maintenance and improvement of present and future earning power. Failure to replace obsolete fixed assets with new and more efficient equipment, and failure to perform necessary repairs on existing equipment, will result ultimately in decreased operational efficiency and breakdowns.

Analysts should ascertain the age and condition of each major asset category, as well as the replacement costs of the category's component parts. Further, they should examine the trend in the dollar amount of *fixed asset acquisitions to total gross assets.* This trend is especially important to note for technologically oriented companies. A substantial decline in the trend indicates that older machinery is not being replaced rapidly enough. Analysts should thus examine footnote disclosure for any mention of inactive or unproductive assets. The efficiency of assets may be checked by considering output levels, logged downtime, and temporary discontinuances. A higher ratio of fixed assets to stockholders' equity may mean a buildup in inactive fixed assets resulting in excessive costs such as taxes, insurance, maintenance, and storage. These increased costs will raise the break-even point. Assets not being used for a long period must be written down if economic reality is to be reflected.

• I Company had to establish a $39.6 million reserve for expected close-downs of obsolete facilities (88 years old) in 19X0 due to new pollution control requirements.

Appropriations of retained earnings for future plant acquisitions is a positive sign.

Illustration ───

Company M shows the following data relative to its fixed assets:

	19X1	19X2
Fixed assets	$100,000	$90,000
Repairs and maintenance	4,000	2,000
Replacement cost	180,000	210,000

Improper maintenance of capital is indicated by (1) the decline in the ratio of repairs and maintenance to fixed assets from 4% in 19X1 to 2.2% in 19X2; (2) the significant difference between replacement cost and historical cost; and (3) the decline in fixed assets over the year.

If the analyst concludes that a normal ratio of repairs and maintenance to fixed assets is 4%, he would downwardly adjust reported earnings by the incremental 1.8% of the fixed assets (4.0% less 2.2%). This amounts to $1,620 (1.8% × $90,000).

───

It is better for a company when assets are mobile and/or can easily be modified since this affords the firm greater flexibility. If the assets are easily accessible, it will also be easier to repair them. The location of the assets is also important since that may affect their condition and security. The location will also effect property taxes, so a company may be able to save on taxes by having the plant located in a low tax area.

A high ratio of sales to floor space indicates the efficient utilization of space.

207.1 / Analyzing Return on Fixed Assets

In evaluating the degree of a company's maintenance of capital, we must consider the rate of return being earned on its assets. If the return is acceptable, then the proper investment decision is to maintain and improve production facilities. Similarly, if the return in the industry is high or if the industry is in the process of growth, new equipment should be acquired. Under these circumstances, the company's failure to keep its plant and equipment up-to-date will detract from its competitive position. On the other hand, if the rate of return being earned on corporate assets is unsatisfactory, the company would be justified in not maintaining capital. Similarly, if the industry is in a state of decline, equipment replacement and repair should be restricted. Under these circumstances, the rational investment decision is to defer maintaining capital. For example, a company would be justified in not improving production facilities at branch locations that are being phased out.

Analysts should determine whether a company's policy of not maintaining capital is of a short-term or long-term nature. If it is a temporary policy, it may mean that the firm is presently short of cash and wishes to maintain its profit levels. If it is a permanent decision, it has serious implications. It means that management does not want to invest further in the business since it views the company as being in a state of liquidation.

The turnover in fixed assets should be determined. This is equal to sales divided by average fixed assets. The ratio is helpful in evaluating a company's ability to use its asset base effectively to generate revenue. A low ratio may be due to many factors, and it is important to identify the underlying reasons. For example, is investment in assets excessive when compared to the value of the output produced? If so, the company might want to consolidate its present operation, perhaps by selling some of its assets and investing the proceeds for a higher return or using them to expand into a more profitable area.

Another useful ratio is the operating assets ratio, which equals total operating assets divided by total assets. This ratio concentrates on those assets *actively employed in current operations*. Operating assets exclude (1) past-oriented assets and (2) future-oriented assets. Past-oriented assets arise from prior errors, inefficiencies, or losses because of competitive factors or changes in business plans. These assets have not yet been formally recognized in the accounts. Examples are obsolete goods, idle plants, receivables under litigation, delinquent receivables, and nonperforming loans (no interest being recognized). Future-oriented assets are acquired for corporate growth or generating future sales. Examples are land held for speculation and factories under construction. Nonoperating assets reduce profits and return on investment because no benefit to current operations occurs. They neither generate sales nor reduce costs. Rather, they are a "drain" on the company and may require financing.

207.2 / How to Determine the Nature of Fixed Assets

Analysts should examine the nature of a company's fixed assets. For example, in a prior year, Burroughs' rental-machines account included obsolete systems that were neither on rent nor being depreciated. Failure to write down such equipment resulted in overstated earnings.

A firm with specialized or risky fixed assets is more vulnerable to asset obsolescence. Examples are equipment used to make specialized products (missiles that are dependent on governmental spending policies) and faddish items (passion rings).

It may be beneficial for companies to lease rather than purchase assets where high technology that may cause rapid obsolescence is involved. An example is computer hardware.

207.3 / Considerations in Evaluating Fixed Assets: A Checklist

☐ Maintenance of capital investment

☐ Ratio of repairs and maintenance to fixed assets

☐ Ratio of fixed asset acquisitions to total gross assets

☐ Ratio of sales to fixed assets

☐ Ratio of net income to fixed assets

☐ Age and condition of equipment

☐ Technology within the industry

☐ Output levels and downtime

☐ Specialized or risky fixed assets

☐ Equipment subject to stringent pollution standards

—— 208 / HOW TO ANALYZE DEPRECIATION METHODS ——

In evaluating the quality of a company's earnings, analysts should consider the depreciation method used and the period over which fixed assets are depreciated. That depreciation method which results in the highest quality of earnings is the one in which the depreciation rate used best approximates the expiration of the asset's usefulness. Different types of assets require different depreciation methods. The units-of-production method may provide the most realistic depreciation charge for machinery because its service potential declines as it is used in production activities. On the other hand, accelerated depreciation may be the most appropriate measurement of the decline in value of automobiles.

208.1 / How to Measure Inadequate Depreciation Charges

In evaluating the adequacy of a company's depreciation rate, analysts should compare it with the industry norm. B. Graham, B. Dodd, and S. Cottle[1] believe that analysts should accept the tax basis of depreciation as the norm for the typical company, and they should adjust to this basis the earnings of most companies that use lower rates on their reports than on their tax returns.

The trend in depreciation expense as a percent of both fixed assets and net sales should be examined by the analyst. Declining trends may indicate inadequate depreciation charges for the possible obsolescence of assets.

---

[1] B. Graham, B. Dodd, and S. Cottle, *Security Analysis: Principles and Techniques* (New York: McGraw-Hill, 1962), p. 157.

• In 19X2, company N's average property, plant, and equipment rose by 52% while depreciation advanced by only 12%; $0.15 per share was fed into earnings.

Another possible indication of inadequate depreciation charges is a concurrent moderate increase in depreciation along with a significant increase in capital spending.

• In 19X4, company O's depreciation and depletion rose by 7.8%, the smallest annual gain in three years. At the same time, capital spending rose by 16.5%.

Illustration

Company N reports the following data:

	19X1	19X2
Fixed assets	$500,000	$570,000
Sales	600,000	700,000
Net Income	130,000	135,000
Depreciation expense per books	20,000	21,000
Depreciation expense per tax return	25,000	28,000
Relevant ratios follow:		
Depreciation expense to fixed assets	4.0%	3.7%
Depreciation expense to sales	3.3%	3.0%

The declining trends in depreciation expense to fixed assets and depreciation expense to sales may infer an inadequate provision for the deterioration in assets.

The percentage increase in fixed assets was 14% while the percentage increase in depreciation expense was only 5% This is a further indicator of inadequacy in depreciation.

If the analyst concludes that the depreciation reported on the tax return is more representative of the decline in the service potential of the fixed asset, a downward adjustment to 19X2's net income of $7,000 ($28,000–$21,000) for the additional depreciation can be made.

Significant declines in sales coupled with significant increases in capital expenditures may be inconsistent. It may reflect possible overexpansion and future write-offs of productive assets.

208.2 / Watch Accounting Changes in Depreciation

A decline in depreciation expense resulting from unwarranted changes in the lives or salvage values of fixed assets lowers the quality of earnings. In such a case, net income should be downwardly adjusted for the effect of such changes.

• In 19X0, company P extended the depreciable life of its Douglas DC-9 from 10 years to 12 years, and of its Boeing 727 from 10 years to 14 years. This lengthening of depreciable lives had the effect of lowering 19X0 depreciation expense by $8.7 million, and increasing net earnings by $4.4 million. Earnings per share was increased by $0.38. Because reported earnings per share for 19X0 was only $0.32, the effect of the change was to avoid reporting a loss of $0.06 per share.

Firms might classify newly acquired assets in different depreciation categories from those that are being replaced in order to manage earnings. For example, a company may depreciate new assets based on the straight-line method rather than the previously used double declining-balance method. Changes in classification to less appropriate depreciation categories will lower the quality of earnings. A.H. Robins's 1980 annual report discloses:

• In 1980, the method of computing depreciation on newly acquired assets of domestic companies was changed to the straight line method to more closely match depreciation with estimated consumption. The remainder is computed on the declining balance method. The change increased net earnings by $394,000, or $.02 per share.

Vacillating depreciation policies will violate the continuity in reported earnings.

208.3 / When Does Depreciation Start?

S. Hepworth writes:[2]

> An arbitrary method of affecting the income of a single accounting period through the medium of depreciation is in connection with the determination of the date upon which depreciation begins to accrue on new plant items.

208.4 / How to Eliminate the Effect of Underdepreciation

Analysts should eliminate the effect of underdepreciation. This can be accomplished by determining the difference between depreciation based on replacement cost and depreciation based on historical cost. Also, analysts should note that inflationary effects are reduced if there exists a high turnover rate in sales to property, plant, and equipment.

---

[2] S. Hepworth, "Smoothing Periodic Income," *Accounting Review* (January, 1953), pp. 32–39.

208.5 / Depreciation Policy—Indicators of Poor Earnings Quality: A Checklist

□ The depreciation method used does not realistically reflect the decline in service potential of the asset

□ The depreciation rate for stockholder reporting is significantly less than the depreciation rate for tax return

□ A declining trend in depreciation expense to fixed assets and to sales

□ A moderate increase in depreciation expense coupled with a significant boost in fixed asset expansion

□ A decline in sales concurrent with a significant increase in capital expenditures

□ An unjustified change in depreciation method or estimate

□ Using a less realistic depreciation method for new acquisitions

□ Depreciation expense per books is materially less than what depreciation expense would be on replacement cost and constant dollar bases.

209 / HOW TO ANALYZE SPECIAL TOOLS

Analysis is required of the special tools account in industries having constant changes in design, such as the auto industry. The adequacy of the expenditures made for special tools each period should be appraised by comparing such expenditures to sales and fixed assets. Also, the analyst should compute the ratios of (1) amortization expense of special tools to sales and (2) amortization expense of special tools to fixed assets.

Illustration

Company O provides the following data:

	19X1	19X2
Deferred special tool costs	$100,000	$120,000
Sales	950,000	1,280,000
Amortization expense of special tools	4,000	4,100

Relevant ratios are:

	19X1	19X2
Amortization expense to deferred special tools	4.0%	3.4%
Amortization expense to sales	.4%	.3%
Deferred special tools to sales	10.5%	9.4%

Since the ratios of (1) amortization expense to deferred special tools, (2) amortization expense to sales, and (3) deferred special tool costs to sales have declined, it appears that the company has not kept up-to-date in obtaining tools needed for design modifications.

If it is decided that the appropriate relationship between amortization expense and sales should be .4% in 19X2, net income should be downwardly adjusted for the incremental amortization expense of $1,020 ($5,120–$4,100).

210 / REVIEWING INTANGIBLE ASSETS

A high ratio of intangible assets to total assets or to net worth indicates an asset structure of high realization risk. The amounts recorded for intangibles may be overstated relative to their market value, or to their future income-generating capacity. Analysts should thus treat them with suspicion. For example, during business recessions a company's goodwill may be overstated, and perhaps worthless. Since APB Opionion No. 17 provides for a forty-year amortization period for intangibles, some firms tend to ignore economic reality by making only minimum amortization provisions. Further, intangibles acquired prior to the effective date of the Opinion are not even subject to such minimum amortization. For example, General Instrument discloses in its 1989 annual report that "for acquisitions made prior to November 1970, costs in excess of net assets acquired are not amortized."

Analysts should examine the relationship between the change in capitalized intangibles (e.g., patents) and the change in reported earnings. If a significant portion of the change arose from capitalization rather than expensing, this should be regarded as a red flag because net income may have been relieved of proper charges against it.[3]

Illustration

Company P provides the following data:

	19X1	19X2
Intangible assets	$ 50,000	$180,000
Total assets	500,000	520,000
Sales	600,000	615,000
Net income	100,000	125,000

Relevant ratios follow:

	19X1	19X2
Intangible assets to total assets	10.0%	34.6%
Intangible assets to sales	8.3%	29.3%

[3] D. Hawkins, "Accounting Dodos and Red Flags," *Financial Executive*, (May, 1974), p. 89.

The higher ratios of (1) intangible assets to total assets and (2) intangible assets to sales in 19X2 indicate a greater realization risk in intangibles. Further, the 260% increase in intangibles coupled with only a 25% increase in earnings may mean that net income has been overstated due to the failure to reflect items which should have been expensed rather than capitalized. Assuming the analyst concludes that $128,000 should more appropriately be expensed, net income should be downwardly adjusted for that amount.

Unwarranted changes in the amortization period for intangible assets will lower the quality of earnings. For example, a company may increase its amortization period for goodwill from 10 years to 30 years even though the company's reputation has been impaired because of political bribes and environmental violations.

It should be noted, however, that in some cases intangible assets may contribute in an important way to a business, and may in fact be undervalued. For example, the carrying value of patents is almost always less than the present value of future cash flows to be derived from them, but patented products are less valuable when they may easily be infringed upon by minor alteration or when they relate to high technologically oriented items. Also relevant is the financial soundness of a firm, since it may have to incur significant legal costs in defending patents. Furthermore, the analyst should carefully watch the expiration dates of the patents as well as whether the firm has impending patented products coming on stream.

As we all know, goodwill can be recorded only in a business combination accounted for under the purchase method when the cost to the acquirer exceeds the fair market value of the acquired company's assets. The analyst should appraise the value of the goodwill account by determining whether in fact the company has superior earning potential. If it does not, the goodwill recorded has no value since the company does not have excess earnings over other companies in the industry. It should be noted, however, that a company may have off-balance sheet goodwill that has been *internally* developed, such as McDonald's.

210.1 / Measures of Realization Risk in Intangible Assets: A Checklist

☐ Ratio of intangible assets to total assets

☐ Ratio of intangible assets to stockholders' equity

☐ Ratio of intangible assets to sales

☐ Ratio of intangible assets to net income

☐ Ratio of a specific, questionable intangible asset (goodwill) to total assets

☐ Ratio of the change in intangible assets to the change in reported earnings

☐ Determining whether superior earnings have been generated from purchased goodwill

———— 211 / KEY PROBLEMS TO WATCH FOR WITH DEFERRED CHARGES ————

Deferred expenses depend to a greater degree on estimates of future probabilities and developments than do other assets. These estimates are often overly optimistic; and the risk of failure to achieve expectations is relatively higher than with other assets. Firms may be deferring items that have no future economic benefit, merely to defer costs in order not to burden reported results. Also, deferred charges do not represent cash realizable assets and hence cannot be used to satisfy creditor claims. Examples of deferred charges that have dubious future benefit are moving expenses, start-up costs, plant rearrangement costs, merger expenses, and promotional costs. Numerous examples exist of dubious deferred costs including:

• Some computer manufacturers defer engineering costs for leased computer systems in their rental equipment accounts. These accounts will be overstated if there exists, to any major degree, a potential exposure of unexpected equipment returns. An example was company M's write-off of $90 million of previously capitalized costs in 19X4.

• In the extractive industries, the full cost method allows companies to defer unsuccessful exploration and drilling expenses. Under certain circumstances, this policy might result in the overstatement of assets because the total amounts capitalized as cost of reserves could substantially exceed the value of such reserves. In this case, the deferred account is overstated and not in accord with economic reality. Furthermore, some companies continue to retain capitalized costs on their books even though exploration activity has ceased. The failure to write-down such excess costs results in an overstatement of both assets and earnings.

In evaluating the realization risk associated with the deferred exploration cost account of petroleum refiners, analysts should examine the trend in the ratio of the *present value of reserves to capitalized costs*. A declining trend may indicate higher realization risk in assets. For example, from 1974 to 1976, Getty's gas reserves declined substantially while over the same period capitalized costs relating to exploration and production activities increased by 70%. The decline in the company's reserves per dollar of capitalized costs indicates that the deferred account was overstated in terms of its future economic benefit.

Firms may attempt to hide declining profitability by *deferring costs that were expensed in prior years*. One must be on the lookout for such a change in policy.

- In fiscal 19X4, S Company adopted the policy of capitalizing the carrying costs, real estate taxes, and interest of construction-in-process on land held for future use. The effect of the change was to increase earnings by $14.1 million ($0.09 per share).

- In 19X2, company Q started to defer questionable costs that were previously expensed, aggregating $30,000. For analytical purposes, deferred charges and net income should be reduced by such amount.

It should be noted, however, that in some cases an increase in deferred charges may be proper. For example, the deferral of start-up costs is justified where a company has begun a new operation in order to expand its market share.

211.1 / How to Measure Realization Risk of Deferred Costs

Analysts should determine the trend in deferred costs to net sales and/or to earnings, and the trend in the ratio of deferred costs (i.e., deferred promotion costs) to total expenditures (i.e., total promotion expenditures). Rising trends may indicate an unjustified change to a more liberal policy.

Illustration ——————————————————————————————

Company R shows the following data:

	19X1	19X2
Deferred costs	$ 50,000	$125,000
Total assets	600,000	670,000
Sales	700,000	740,000
Net income	200,000	220,000
Relevant ratios follow:		
Deferred costs to total assets	8.3%	18.7%
Deferred costs to sales	7.1%	16.9%
Deferred costs to net income	25.0%	56.8%

The higher ratios of deferred costs to (1) total assets, (2) sales, and (3) net income in 19X2 indicate greater realization risk in the asset structure. Also, 19X2's quality of earnings is lower since deferred charges probably include items that should have been expensed.

———

A high ratio of intangible assets and deferred charges to total assets indicates an asset structure of high realization risk. Assets with low realizability may be overstated, and as a result, require future write-off.

211.2 / Deferred Charges: A Suspicious Asset—Indicators of Low Earnings Quality: A Checklist

☐ Significant increase in deferred charges

☐ Deferring costs that were previously expensed

☐ Increasing trend in deferred costs to net sales and/or to net income

☐ Increasing trend in deferred costs to total expenditures

☐ Sudden write-off of deferred charges

☐ Increasing trend in intangible assets and deferred charges to total assets

———— 212 / WATCH WRITE-OFF OF ASSETS ————

The analyst should be on guard against the possibility that undisclosed losses are building up, such as unfulfillable sales contracts and losing ventures. In recession years, when earnings are already deficient, management may decide to "clean house" by making substantial write-offs. A high earnings growth rate and a neglect of sound operating procedures are indicators of possible unreported losses being piled up.

———— 213 / HOW TO ANALYZE LIABILITIES ————

Analysts must be particularly attuned to the existence of understated liabilities with a possible concurrent overstatement of earnings.

• In 19X6, R International reported that its accounts payable might be understated by as much as $1 million.

The SEC found that in 19X6 A Corporation in its 19X1 filing did not mention its obligation to pay royalty guarantees to record companies amounting to over $80 million. The company's understated loss provision applicable to returned tapes resulted in the overstatement of earnings in that year.

If because of financial difficulties, a company issues to a bank common stock in substitution of its loan payable, the existing common stockholders may suffer financially because the company will typically "sweeten the deal" for the bank. This occurred in the cases of Navistar and Chyrsler.

The maturity dates of debt should be staggered so they do not become due all at one time. The company may have a problem paying them all on one date, or the interest rates at the renewal date may be unusually high.

213.1 / Beware of the Estimated Liability

The use of estimated liabilities for future costs and losses may impair the significance of reported earnings and should be viewed with skepticism. According to FASB 5 (Accounting for Contingencies), estimated liabilities may be established for such things as warranties, litigation, and employee compensation. In appraising the adequacy of estimated liability accounts, the analyst must carefully examine footnote disclosures and familiarize himself or herself with the financial and accounting characteristics of the industry.

Arbitrary adjustments of estimated liabilities should be eliminated in determining a company's earning power. In other words, *analysts who find that reserves are used to manage earnings should add back the amounts charged to income, and deduct the amounts credited to income.* For example, earnings derived from a recoupment of prior year reserves may require elimination.

- In 19X8 H Company established an estimated liability for potential losses on its assets in a foreign country. The provision was reduced by $950,000 in 19X9, having a per share effect of $0.02.

Illustration _____

Company S reports the following data:

	19X1	19X2
Estimated liability	$ 50,000	$ 47,000
Net income	100,000	120,000

If the analyst concludes that the estimated liability established in 19X1 was intentionally overstated by $8,000, he should increase 19X1 net income to $108,000. If $3,000 of the $8,000 excessive reserve was drawn down in 19X2, net income for that year should be lowered to $117,000.

_____

A company that has an unrealistically low provision for future costs has lower earnings quality. For example, it may be inconsistent if a company lowers its warranty provision when prior experience indicates that the quality of the product is deficient.

- B Insurance Company increased its reserve for claims by a lower amount in 19X3 than in the previous year in spite of increased claim losses during this period and a rapid-inflation environment.

- In 19X0, I Company's percentage increase in its reserves for employees' indemnities and retirement plans was significantly less than in the years immediately prior.

Illustration _____

Company T reports the following information:

	19X1	19X2	19X3
Estimated liability for warranties	$ 30,000	$ 33,000	$ 40,000
Sales	100,000	130,000	190,000

From 19X1–19X3, the company reports that there has been a higher rate of defective merchandise that has to be repaired.

Relevant computations follow:

	19X1–19X2	19X2–19X3
Percentage increase in the estimated liability account	10.0%	21.2%
Percentage increase in sales	30.0%	46.2%

The percentage increase in the estimated liability account is significantly less than the percentage increase in sales. Since the firm is experiencing quality problems, it is clear that the estimated liability account is understated. Hence, net income is overstated because a sufficient provision for warranty expense has not been established.

_____

Overprovision of estimated liabilities is sometimes made when earnings are too high and management wishes to bring them down. This also has the effect of setting up a reserve for a "rainy day." An overprovision may also take place when earnings are already so bad that lowering them further by establishing a future cushion will not matter that much in the eyes of investors.

A lower earnings quality source may exist when more operating expenses and losses are being charged to reserve accounts relative to previous years.

Firms may also improve earnings by altering their reserve policies.

• Company G always charged losses to it catastrophe reserve in two ways: for individual casualties, and for cumulative wind and earthquake losses. Prior to 19X4, the company never had an occasion to use the cumulative part of the reserve. However, in 19X4 when this reserve element was affected, the company changed its accounting method of charging the reserve. The cutoff point for accruing losses was lowered from 1.25% to 0.90% of premiums earned. Thus, losses over 0.90% of premiums earned were charged to the catastrophe reserve. This change in rate represented a new accounting policy. It improved 19X4 pre-tax earnings by $4 million. This amount represented a decline of more than 25% from the $14 million accrual which would have been made had the rules not been altered.

213.2 / How Companies Offset Material Gains

Sometimes when a company realizes a material nonrecurring or extraordinary gain, it simultaneously provides for an estimated liability of the same amount or close to it in order to cancel out the effect. The objective is to remove from the earnings stream an unusual income increase that may be impossible to meet in the following year. It also provides a cushion against which the reserve account can be charged in order to improve the earnings trend, or it will enable a reserve provision that was impractical to provide previously.

213.3 / Questions to Be Asked with Regard to Estimated Liabilities: A Checklist

- ☐ Are reserve provisions understated or overstated?
- ☐ Do provisions conform to the reality of the situation?
- ☐ Has there been a recoupment of previous years' reserves in the current period?
- ☐ Has an estimated liability been established solely for a "rainy day"?
- ☐ Are more expenses and losses being charged to reserve accounts than in prior years?
- ☐ Have reserve estimates been altered?
- ☐ Has an estimated liability been established in order to offset a significant nonrecurring or extraordinary gain?

—————— 214 / STOCKHOLDERS' EQUITY ——————

If a company cuts back on its dividends or omits them, it may mean it is having financial problems. It is better when a company varies its dividends rather than paying constant dividends so it can more easily reduce them in troubled times. If stockholders are used to receiving constant dividends each time, it will be more difficult for the company to adjust such dividends without upsetting stockholders.

If a loan agreement places restrictions on the company, such as its ability to pay dividends, this inhibits management's freedom of action and is a negative sign.

The analyst should look negatively upon a company that has reacquired its stock for the sole purpose of artificially boosting its earnings per share. However, if treasury stock is acquired, the market price of the company's stock will rise because less shares will be on the market. If a company has previously purchased treasury stock at a cost significantly below the current market price, it is "sitting on" a significant potential increase in cash flow and paid-in-capital.

If a company has two classes of common stock, one voting and the other not, the potential investor must recognize that the voting common stock may be controlled by an "inside group" such as members of the founder's family and/or by management.

If a company issues preferred stock for the first time or if it issues substantial amounts of preferred stock in the current year, it may mean the company has problems with issuing its common stock. This is a negative sign since the investing public may be viewing its common stock as too risky.

If stock options issued to executives are excessive and not justified by managerial performance, this unfairly dilutes the stockholders' interest in the company. The analyst should look at the trend in the ratio of stock options to total shares outstanding. If the trend has increased but profitability has decreased, this may not be consistent.

If authorized shares significantly exceed issued shares, there exists the possibility of a substantial additional issuance of securities that may dilute stockholders' interest. If new shares are issued, the market price of the stock will drop.

If convertible bonds or convertible preferred stock are converted to common stock, this means that bondholders or preferred stockholders are optimistic about the company. However, this will result in a drop in the market price of common stock as more shares are issued. On the plus side, the company will be able to omit the interest payment on bonds and the dividend payment on preferred stock.

If stock is issued at a discount on the *original* issuance, the stockholder is legally liable for the difference if the company goes bankrupt.

Foreign translation gains and losses are reported as a separate item in the stockholders' equity section. However, for analytical purposes it should be reclassified as an income statement item and included in the net income figure because such gains and losses are a reflection of management's operating performance. For example, if the company did poorly in foreign exchange markets, that should effect its bottom-line.

While unrealized losses on long-term investments are reported as a separate item in the stockholders' equity section, they should also be reclassified for analytical purposes in the income statement. These unrealized losses on noncurrent investments show that management's investment performance has been poor and that the company is losing money. This holding loss adversely effects operating performance and more appropriately belongs in the income statement as a charge against earnings.

Corrections of errors which were made in previous years are reported as prior period adjustments which are shown as an adjustment to the beginning balance of retained earnings. Error corrections are an indication of a poor financial reporting system in the company.

An increasing trend in retained earnings means that the company has been profitable, while a high ratio of retained earnings to stockholders' equity is good because it indicates that capital financing is being achieved internally.

A high ratio of net income to preferred dividends is a positive sign since there is a greater amount left over for common stockholders.

Stockholders are interested in receiving dividends and prefer to see high ratios for the following:

- Dividend Yield = Dividends per share/Market price per share
- Dividend Payout = Dividends per share/Earnings per share

Obviously, a decline in these ratios signals a decline in the value of dividends and would cause concern on the part of stockholders.

_____ 215 / BOOK VALUE PER SHARE _____

Book value per share is net assets available to common stockholders divided by shares outstanding, where net assets is stockholders' equity less preferred stock.

$$\text{Book value per share} = \frac{\text{Total stockholders' equity} - \text{Preferred stock}}{\text{Shares Outstanding}}$$

Comparing book value per share with market price per share gives an indication of how investors regard the company. For example, if a company's market price of stock is currently $20 per share and the book value per share is $26, the stock is probably looked upon unfavorably by investors.

In computing book value per share, the value of the preferred stock is based on the liquidation value of the preferred stock outstanding plus preferred dividends in arrears. Care must be taken in computing the liquidation value of preferred stock. Some companies have preferred stock issues outstanding that give the right to significant liquidation premiums that substantially exceed the par value of such shares. The effect of such liquidation premiums on the book value of common stock can be quite material.

_____ 216 / SUMMARY CHECKLIST OF KEY POINTS _____

216.1 The overstatement of assets leads to the overstatement of earnings because net income will not include those charges necessary to reduce assets to their appropriate amounts. Conversely, the understatement of assets causes the understatement of current and future earnings.

216.2 The understatement of liabilities causes the overstatement of earnings since net income does not contain required charges to reflect the proper valuation of liabilities. Conversely, the overstatement of liabilities leads to the understatement of reported earnings.

216.3 In ratio determination and evaluation, analysts should attempt to use the realistic values of balance sheet accounts rather than the un-representative carrying values.

216.4 High realization risk can lurk almost anywhere in the balance sheet, and consequently affect the quality of earnings. The only certain rule that can be laid down for analysts is that each asset must be analyzed on its own as well as in relation to the body of assets belonging to the company.

216.5 / Low Quality of Earnings Indicators

1. Low Quality Assets

What to Watch Out For

☐ Asset valuations that are highly susceptible to changes in economic, political, industry, and corporate conditions

☐ Assets having high realization risk in cash

☐ Suspicious deferral of costs

☐ Single-purpose assets, since they lack alternative use

☐ Assets vulnerable to changing government policies (pollution standards for equipment, health standards for inventory)

☐ Assets lacking separable value since they are not readily salable (intangibles, work-in-process)

☐ Assets relating to the development and marketing of a new product that has a high risk of not succeeding

What to Do

☐ Determine the turnover rates for each major asset category.

    a. Sales to assets

    b. Net income to assets

☐ Classify assets according to the degree of their risk.

☐ Prepare ratios involving high risk assets.

    a. Intangible assets plus deferred charges to total assets

    b. Intangible assets plus deferred charges to sales

☐ Within each asset category (i.e., receivables), identify and classify the components according to their risk.

2. Unavailability of Cash

What to Watch Out For

☐ Cash that is restricted or not available
☐ Poor cash management policies

What to Do

☐ Determine the amount of compensating balances.
☐ Ascertain the amount of cash being *held* by an unfriendly foreign government.
☐ Compute the ratios of (1) sales to cash, (2) net income to cash, and (3) cash to total current assets.

3. Overstated Receivables

What to Watch Out For

☐ Receivables that may not be realized
   a. Advances to questionable foreign governments
   b. Notes receivable emanating from extensions of unpaid balances from delinquent customers
   c. Receivables from large customers having financial difficulties
   d. Receivables applicable to consignment sales
   e. Receivables having right-of-return privileges
   f. Receivables coming out of loose agreements with customers
   g. Receivables applicable to product components sold to customers where collection of the account is contingent upon the customer obtaining governmental approval to make the product under federal specifications
   h. Receivables containing offset provisions
   i. Receivables emanating from contra relationships
   j. Receivables from affiliated companies and officers
☐ Sudden write-offs of accounts receivable
☐ A high percentage of receivables from consumers relative to corporations
☐ The factoring of accounts receivable

What to Do

☐ Identify and determine the dollar amount of high realization risk receivables.

☐ Calculate and analyze the following ratios:

a. Accounts receivable turnover

b. Number of days accounts receivable are held

c. Accounts receivable to total assets

d. Accounts receivable to sales

☐ Look at customer ratings given by credit agencies (e.g., **Dun and Bradstreet**).

4. Loading Customers Up with Unneeded Merchandise

What to Do

☐ Determine if the last quarter's sales have been artificially raised by:

a. Comparing the sales of the last quarter to each of the previous quarters and to the last quarter of the prior year.

b. Ascertaining whether there is a significant boost in sales returns for the first quarter of the following year.

c. Spotting a sharp drop in sales for the first quarter of the following year.

☐ Reduce net income and receivables for incremental sales of unneeded merchandise that will likely be returned at the beginning of the next year.

5. Understatement of Bad Debts

What to Watch Out For

☐ The bad debt provision is reduced while at the same time the company is selling to more risky customers and/or actual bad-debt losses are increasing.

What to Do

☐ Determine the trend in the following ratios:

a. Bad debts to accounts receivable

b. Bad debts to sales

☐ Downwardly adjust net income for the incremental earnings arising from the unrealistic lowering of bad debts.

6. Overstatement of Bad Debts

What to Watch Out For

☐ Overstating the bad debt provision in order to establish an accounting cushion.

☐ A significant bad debt provision in the current year because of inadequate provisions in prior years.

What to Do

☐ Compare the percentage change in the allowance for bad debts account to the percentage change in sales.
☐ Restate net income as what it would have been if an appropriate bad debt provision (based on previous experience) had been made.

7. Understatement of Sales Returns and Allowances

What to Watch Out For

☐ Excessive returns
☐ Understatement of the sales returns and allowances account, such as when the provision decreases and at the same time there is a greater liability for dealer returns

What to Do

☐ Determine the trend in the ratio of the sales returns and allowances account to sales.

8. Realization Risk in Loans Receivable

What to Watch Out For

☐ A lack of diversification in the bank's loan portfolio
☐ An inadequate loss provision
☐ Interest is not being collected on loans or the interest rate has been modified.
☐ The collateral value of the loan is materially less than the principal of the loan.
☐ Loans to officers

What to Do

☐ Determine the trend in the loan loss provision to total loans outstanding.
☐ Compare the bank's loan loss provision rate to the minimum amount required by the regulatory agency.
☐ Compare over time the loan loss provision to the ultimate actual loan losses.
☐ Compute the ratios of (1) loans receivable to total assets and (2) loans receivable to stockholders' equity

9. Buildup of Inventory

What to Watch Out For

- ☐ Inventory buildup at the plant, wholesaler, or retailer
- ☐ Decline in raw materials with a concurrent increase in work-in-process and finished goods since a future production slowdown is indicated
- ☐ Too much work-in-process since this is a low realizable inventory component. In the event of liquidation, it cannot be sold readily.

What to Do

- ☐ Compare the change in inventory to the change in sales.
- ☐ Determine the percentage of work-in-process to total inventory.
- ☐ Determine inventory turnover rates by:
  - a. Category
  - b. Department
- ☐ Determine the number of days inventory is held.

10. Risky Inventory

What to Watch Out For

- ☐ Merchandise subject to sharp variability in price
- ☐ Inventory of a faddish, specialized, or perishable nature
- ☐ Merchandise secured to creditors under loan agreements
- ☐ Inadequately insured inventory
- ☐ Inventory subject to political risk (big cars—an oil embargo)

What to Do

- ☐ Determine the ratio of insurance expense to inventory.

11. Improper Costs Included in Inventory

What to Watch Out For

- ☐ Unusual costs included in the inventory account (learning curve expenditures)
- ☐ Costs included in inventory that used to be expensed

What to Do

- ☐ Determine the trend in the ratio of cost of sales to sales.

☐ Downwardly adjust net income for costs included in inventory that should have been expensed.

12. Unjustified Change in Inventory Method

What to Watch Out For

☐ A switch to an unrealistic inventory method
☐ A change in method that has the effect of bolstering earnings

13. Unusual Fourth-Quarter Inventory Trends

What to Watch Out For

☐ Changing the timing of purchases
☐ Depletion of LIFO inventories

What to Do

☐ Determine if there have been significant purchases or declines in inventory in the last quarter.

14. Misstatement of Inventory

What to Watch Out For

☐ Products that are difficult to cost because either they are of a technological nature or they are highly dependent upon internally developed cost records
☐ Sudden write-offs of inventory

What to Do

☐ Restate what the earnings trend would have been had overvalued inventory been written down in the years in which the items were really obsolete rather than being written down in the current period.

15. Inflationary Profits in Inventory

What to Watch Out For

☐ The use of the FIFO method, since it usually results in greater inflationary profits

What to Do

☐ Look at the footnote disclosure and study the difference between reported cost of sales and what it would be based on:

    a. Constant dollars (CPI adjusted)

    b. Replacement cost

16. Unfavorable Purchase Contracts

What to Watch Out For

☐ Losses on purchase commitments

☐ Speculating in the futures market

What to Do

☐ Review footnote disclosure relating to purchase commitments.

17. Improperly Valued Investments

What to Watch Out For

☐ Frequent or dubious reclassifications of securities

☐ Decreases in portfolio market values that have not been recorded in the accounts

☐ Debt securities that are reflected at cost, regardless of the fact that their cost exceeds market value

☐ A decline in market value occurring after year-end

What to Do

☐ Downwardly adjust net income for unrealized losses on noncurrent investments (reported as a contra to stockholders' equity) if there was in a prior year an unjustified switch from current to noncurrent classification.

☐ Determine the trend in the ratio of investment income to total investments.

☐ Examine the "subsequent event" footnote for any unrealized losses taking place on securities after the balance sheet date. Downwardly adjust the investment account for such declines.

18. Risky Investment Portfolio

What to Watch Out For

☐ A portfolio of volatile, positively correlated securities

☐ Buying up securities of a risky company in order to obtain a controlling interest

What to Do

☐ Determine the variation between cost and market value of the portfolio over the last five years.

☐ Determine the standard deviation in the rate of return of the portfolio.

19. Improper Maintenance of Property, Plant, and Equipment

What to Watch Out For

☐ Old and inefficient fixed assets

☐ Pollution-causing machinery, as government standards may require new machinery or expensive modifications in existing machinery

What to Do

☐ Determine the trends in the following ratios:
  a. Repairs and maintenance to fixed assets
  b. Repairs and maintenance to sales
  c. Fixed asset acquisitions to total assets
  d. Net income to fixed assets
  e. Sales to fixed assets

☐ Examine footnotes for any mention of inactive or unproductive assets.

20. Risky Fixed Assets

What to Watch Out For

☐ Specialized or risky fixed assets (machinery used to make a faddish item)

☐ Obsolete items

☐ A high-technology company

☐ Sudden write-offs of fixed assets

What to Do

☐ Determine what the earnings trend would have been if fixed assets were written down when they should have been.

21. Unrealistic Depreciation Method

What to Watch Out For

☐ A depreciation method that does not appropriately reflect the decline in service potential of the fixed asset

22. Inadequate Depreciation

What to Do

☐ Compare the depreciation rate for stockholder reporting to the depreciation rate for tax return purposes.
☐ Downwardly adjust net income for the difference between book depreciation and tax depreciation if the latter is deemed more appropriate.
☐ Determine the tend in:
   a. Depreciation expense to fixed assets
   b. Depreciation expense to sales
☐ Compare the increase in depreciation expense to the increase in capital spending.

23. Unjustified Change in Depreciation Policy

What to Watch Out For

☐ A switch to a less realistic depreciation method
☐ Unwarranted changes in the lives or salvage values of fixed assets

What to Do

☐ Downwardly adjust net income for incremental earnings due to unjustified changes in depreciation estimates.

24. The Use of a Less Realistic Depreciation Method, Such As Straight-Line for Newly Acquired Fixed Assets

25. Underdepreciation Due to Inflation

What to Do

☐ Determine the difference between reported depreciation and what depreciation would be on a constant dollar basis (using the CPI index) and on a replacement cost basis.

26. Inadequate Provision for Special Tools

What to Do

☐ Determine the trend over time in the ratios of:

    a. Amortization expense of special tools to fixed assets.

    b. Amortization expense of special tools to sales.

    c. Deferred special tools to sales.

27. Risky Intangible Assets

What to Watch Out For

☐ Intangibles that are overstated in terms of their market values or future income-generating potential (goodwill of a company that has been operating at continued losses)

☐ Unrealistically long amortization periods

☐ Intangible assets put on the books before APB Opinion 17 and the company decides not to amortize them

☐ Sudden write-offs of intangible assets

☐ Unwarranted increase in the amortization period for intangible assets

☐ Patented products that may easily be infringed upon by minor alteration or that apply to technological items

☐ Financial weakness of the firm to protect its patents in court, if need be

☐ Patents that will shortly expire; impending patented products are not forthcoming

What to Do

☐ Determine the trend over time in the following ratios:

    a. Intangible assets to total assets

    b. Intangible assets to stockholders' equity

    c. Intangible assets to sales

    d. Intangible assets to net income

☐ Compare the change in capitalized intangibles to the change in reported earnings.

☐ Downwardly adjust net income for:

    a. Items that were treated as intangible assets that should have more properly been expensed

    b. Incremental earnings arising from an unjustified increase in the amortization period of intangible assets

☐ Determine whether reported goodwill has value by ascertaining whether the company has "superior earning power."

    a. Compare the earnings growth rate of the firm to both (1) major competitors and (2) industry norms.

28. Overstated Deferred Charges

What to Watch Out For

☐ Deferral of costs that have no future economic benefit

☐ Deferral of costs that were expensed in prior years

☐ Deferral of costs for book purposes that are expensed for tax reporting

☐ Sudden write-offs of deferred charges

☐ The full cost method used in the extractive industry where unsuccessful exploration costs are deferred

☐ Deferred exploration costs exceeding the present value of the reserves

☐ The capitalization of increased fuel costs by a utility when it is doubtful that the regulatory commission will permit such costs to be passed on to consumers

What to Do

☐ Determine the trends in the following ratios:

    a. Deferred costs to sales

    b. Deferred costs to net income

    c. Deferred costs to total assets

    d. Deferred costs to total expenditures

☐ Reduce net income and deferred charges for items that have been deferred but should have been expensed.

☐ For companies in the extractive industry, look at the trend in the ratio of the present value of reserves to capitalized costs.

29. Improperly Stated Estimated Liabilities

What to Watch Out For

☐ Overstatement or understatement of estimated liability accounts (e.g., the warranty expense provision is lowered even though the quality of the company's product has deteriorated)

☐ Arbitrary adjustments to estimated liabilities

☐ More operating expenses and losses are being charged to reserve accounts relative to prior years

☐ Establishing an estimated liability in order to offset a material nonrecurring or extraordinary gain

What to Do

☐ Examine footnotes to become familiar with the particular financial and accounting attributes of the industry.

☐ Add back to net income overstated estimated liability provisions.

☐ Deduct from net income understated estimated liability provisions.

☐ Eliminate from net income:

  a. Earnings derived from a reserve provision solely designed to offset a material nonrecurring gain

  b. Earnings arising from the recoupment of prior year reserves

☐ Compare the percentage change in the estimated liability account to the percentage change in sales.

──── 217 / HIGH QUALITY OF EARNINGS INDICATORS ────

1. High Quality Assets

What to Watch Out For

☐ Mulitpurpose assets

☐ High realizable and salable assets (investments)

☐ Assets having market values that exceed their carrying amounts

☐ A loan portfolio that is diversified by industry as well as by geography

☐ Inventory that is standardized, a staple, or a necessity

☐ A high percentage of raw material inventory, since it is more universal and multipurpose in nature than finished goods and work-in-process

☐ An investment portfolio having a market value in excess of cost

☐ A diversified investment portfolio consisting of negatively correlated securities

☐ Undervalued intangible assets, as when the carrying value of patents is materially less than the present value of future cash flows to be obtained from them

What to Do

- ☐ Determine the excess of market value over book value of assets.
- ☐ Calculate the percent of raw material inventory to total inventory.

2. **Good Inventory Management, Such As When Advance Sales Significantly Exceed the Increase in Inventory**

3. **Internally Developed Goodwill**

CHAPTER THREE

Strategies for Analyzing the Income Statement

This chapter discusses the accounting factors that should be considered in gauging a company's quality of earnings. These factors relate to the nature of the accounting policies employed, degree of certainty of accounting estimates, discretionary costs, tax reporting, and the verifiability of earnings.

When evaluating a company, comparisons should be made to industry norms and financial figures of competing companies. In addition, we have to look at the trend in the accounts of a company over the years. A "red flag" is posted when distorted comparisons and/or trends exist. This requires further investigation. However, a lack of change does not always mean normalcy. Additional analysis may still be required. For example, manpower growth may be up but product/sales may be *static* or down. Hence, manpower costs may be disproportionate to operational activity.

— 301 / HOW MEANINGFUL ARE REAL EARNINGS FIGURES? —

An absolute measure of real earnings will *never* exist because in our complicated changing economic environment, it is almost impossible to distill an entire year's operations into a single absolute figure. Further, financial statements are general purpose in nature and are therefore designed to serve the needs of many users. Consequently, a single earnings figure cannot be meaningful to all financial readers. It is therefore the task of the analyst to adjust reported net income to arrive at an earnings figure that is most relevant to his or her needs. The issue of quality of earnings arises when the analyst attempts to determine the extent to which reported net income reflects what *he* or *she* considers to be actual earnings.

301.1 / Key Elements of Quality of Earnings

Quality of earnings is a *multifaceted* concept that embraces many *accounting and financial considerations*. Therefore, in describing the quality of earnings we must consider all of the elements that make up the definition of the term. These elements are of two types—quantitative and qualitative. Quantitative elements such as cash flow are subject to measurement. Qualitative elements such as quality of management cannot be measured objectively.

Some elements of the quality of earnings are inherent in an enterprise, such as the degree of recurrence in its earnings. Other elements are not inherent but are dependent on management choices such as the degree of maintenance of capital.

—— 302 / HOW TO EVALUATE ACCOUNTING POLICIES AND THE QUALITY OF EARNINGS ——

An evaluation of a company's accounting policies will discover clues to the quality of its earnings. *Measures of operating performance such as cash flow and taxable income may be compared to net income in order to obtain an evaluation of the quality of reported results.* We must be on the lookout, since there exist numerous ways in which accountants and management can deliberately show a desired earnings figure.

302.1 / Inspecting Quality of Conservative Accounting Policies

Net income that has been determined based on conservative accounting policies is generally considered to be of higher quality than comparable earnings based on liberal accounting policies. Analysts prefer to rely on a conservatively constructed income base as a guide to future income projections. They regard the risk of overstatement of income as greater than that of understatement. However, *ultraconservatism* may result in earnings that are both misleading to present investors and useless in predicting performance.

302.2 / Estimating Current and Future Conditions

Earnings quality also depends on the degree of conservatism with which the estimates of current and future conditions are made. This addresses the concern that estimates or assumptions may be overoptimistic or misleading.

• An example of a questionable estimate is when an airline depreciates a plane over 15 years with a salvage value of 20% while its competitors are depreciating the same model over 10 years with a salvage value of 15%. This is coupled with the fact that new technology in the industry usually makes a plane obsolete in about 10 years. In this case, the airline's accounting estimates are overoptimistic.

One indication of whether a company's estimates and assumptions are unwarranted may be when the company has misjudged the lives and salvage values of its assets in prior years. Thus, *if a company's prior estimates have been significantly different from what has actually occurred, one may question the reasonableness of the firm's estimates.*

• If a company had estimated a salvage value of $1,000,000 for a fleet of planes that were actually sold for $100,000 at the end of their lives, we could infer that the estimate was overly optimistic.

• Another possible indication of unwarranted assumptions is when a company's estimate of interest rate, mortality, etc. in connection with its pension plan is significantly different from actual experience. This may be evidenced when the company experiences significant amounts of actuarial gains and losses.

302.3 / Comparing with Industry Standards

A comparison may be made between the accounting policies employed by the firm and the standard accounting policies prevalent in the industry. If the company's accounting policies are considerably more liberal, its earnings quality may be lower. Hence, a security analyst might consider the company's timing of the recognition of revenue and the deferral of costs in relation to the prevailing policies in the industry and other industries and in comparison with his or her own concept of cash-flow-generating earnings (with emphasis on the substance rather than the form of transactions).

302.4 / What Is Economic Reality?

Earnings that reflect *economic reality* are of *higher quality.*[1] Economic reality means that the ups and downs of business conditions are recognized without artificial smoothing. Economic reality also means that the measurement standards used in determining net income are realistic in accounting for the *economic substance* of the company's transactions. The accounting principles and estimates used should reflect the underlying business and financial realities of the firm and industry. For example, the depreciation method selected

---

[1] *Economic Reality in Financial Reporting* (New York: Touche Ross & Co., 1976), p. 10.

for a fixed asset should be the one that most closely approximates the decline in service potential and usefulness of that asset.

• A company may fail to write down inventory during a recessionary period when its salability is doubtful. The economic reality of the industry may dictate such write-downs if it is highly susceptible to recessionary forces (e.g., the jewelry industry).

• Another example of a dubious deferral is failure of a company to write down goodwill even though it has been operating at substantial losses and its market share is evaporating.

• Firm A recently made a questionable deferral of costs. General and administrative expenses relating to long-term U.S. Government contracts capitalized in inventory amounted to $24.1 million at year-end 19X6 compared to $12.5 million at year-end 19X5. The increase amounted to $0.27 a share. Capitalized G&A expenses increased in spite of a substantial decline in inventories to $435.1 million at year-end 19X6 from $777.7 million at year-end 19X5.

302.5 / Getting a Realistic Picture of Earnings

"High quality earnings" defines earnings that relate as reasonably as possible in the circumstances to the business operations of a company within a period of time. It assumes that the most *realistic* accounting alternative was employed for each set of facts. Compliance with GAAP doesn't necessarily mean that a company has high quality earnings. For example, it may use the most liberal accounting policies rather than realistic ones in order to show the highest possible earnings figure. (This is supported by Judge Friendly's decision in the famous Continental Vending Case in which he held that conformity with GAAP is not necessarily a valid defense to a lawsuit against the appropriateness of a company's financial statements). Examples of realistic accounting policies are cited in the AICPA Industry Audit Guides and in accounting policy guides published by various CPA firms.

Analysts may wish to determine what the effect on net income would have been if a company used the most realistic accounting principles (e.g., as per the Audit Guides) rather than the accounting principles it selected. If the use of realistic principles would have resulted in a substantially lower profit, the quality of earnings is lower. For example, accelerated depreciation is more realistic than straight-line depreciation for an automobile.

Illustration ───

Company X defers and amortizes plant rearrangement costs over 10 years. However, a recommended policy for the industry is to expense such costs as incurred. If in 19X1, the costs were $100,000, the analyst should adjust net income downward by $90,000 computed as follows:

Amortization expense	$ 10,000
If expensed	100,000
Adjustment	$ 90,000

302.6 / Understanding the Economics of the Industry

Economic reality also refers to the economics of the industry in which the firm operates—seasonality, nature of product demand, and nature of costs. Corporate accounting policies must be compared with the economic reality of the industry to evaluate earnings quality.

• If an industry is highly seasonal, companies in that industry should take their inventory counts at the ebb of the season (e.g., June 30). Since the level of inventory items at the ebb is at a low point, there is less likelihood of estimation error. (Some examples of estimates made in inventory valuation are the allocation of costs and the determination of realizable value.) The use of another year-end date could have a distorting effect on operating results. For example, the taking of inventory at the height of the season could result in greater estimation error since the ending inventory will be much higher.

302.7 / Beware of the Accounting Change!

Accounting changes made to conform with new FASB Statements, AICPA Industry Audit Guides, and IRS Regulations are justifiable. However, an unjustified accounting change results in an earnings increment of low quality. Unwarranted changes may be made in accounting principles, estimates, and assumptions.

• A company may reduce its bad debt provision as a percent of sales and accounts receivable even though customer delinquencies are substantially on the rise and/or the company is selling to customers who pay more slowly.

• Another example is the reduction in pension expense resulting from an unjustified change in actuarial assumptions. For instance, a company may increase its estimated interest rate on its pension portfolio from 8% to 10% even though the company and its competitors have been earning only an 8% rate of return. This is coupled with a trend in the market place toward lower interest rates on the types of securities held by the firm.

• An airline in 19X5 changed its revenue recognition policies to avoid violating covenants in bank loan agreements.

• Company D changed its inventory valuation policy for a major subsidiary from LIFO to FIFO in 19X0, boosting before-tax profit by $13.8 mil-
lion.

The effect of accounting changes is often to increase reported profits,
resulting in illusory earnings growth. Further, if a company makes numerous
accounting changes, it will be more difficult for analysts to use current year's
earnings as a predictor for future earnings.

It should be noted, however, that certain types of changes in accounting
principles (LIFO to FIFO or change in accounting for construction contracts)
require retroactive restatement of prior years. In this case, there is no distorted earnings trend.

Illustration

An airline has experienced lawsuits against it because of a crash of its X-2 plane. The
cost of the fleet on 1/1/X1 was $10,000. The accumulated depreciation on 12/31/X3 is
$2,700. The planes have been depreciated for 3 years, had an original life of 10 years,
and a salvage value of $1,000. (Note that the accumulated depreciation was
computed by taking $900 per year for 3 years). On 1/4/X4, the airline decides that the
original life should have been 14 years with a salvage value of $2,000. Considering the
crash and the fact that the other airlines continue to use a 10-year life, the change in
estimate is unrealistic. The analyst should downwardly adjust 19X4 net income by
$418 computed as follows:

Depreciation expense after change in estimate		$482
Original cost	$10,000	
Less: accumulated depreciation	2,700	
Book value - 12/31/X3	$ 7,300	
New salvage value	2,000	
Amount to be depreciated	$ 5,300	
New life remaining (14-3)	11yrs.	
	$ 482	
Depreciation expense should be		900
Adjustment		$418

Illustration

The goodwill account and related amortization expense for company T follows:

	19X1	19X2
Goodwill	$200,000	$192,000
Amortization expense	10,000	8,000

The initial amortization period was 30 years and 10 years have been amortized. Thus, the original amount of goodwill had to be $300,000 ($200,000 plus $10,000 × 10) Company T presents the following information in two separate footnotes:

Footnote C—The remaining life of goodwill was increased beginning in 19X2 from 20 to 25 years.

Footnote G—In January 19X2, the company reached a settlement with the government in which it will furnish customer rebates because of the sale of defective goods.

An increase in the amortization period appears unrealistic in light of footnote G. A downward adjustment to net income of $2,000 is thus required for 19X2 computed as follows:

Amortization expense recorded	($200,000/25)	$ 8,000
Proper amortization expense		10,000
Adjustment		$ 2,000

302.8 / Management's Masking of Reality

Reported income may not accurately portray economic results as they are but rather in a way that *management wants them presented.* The artificial shifting of net income from one period to another results in lower quality of earnings. This involves bringing future revenue into the present (or its converse), shifting earnings from profitable years to bad years, or shifting expenses and losses among the years. It should be noted that the trend in earnings is more significant than absolute size.

302.9 / Look at Sales vs. Net Income

A weak functional relationship between sales and net income may be an indication that a company is managing its earnings.

Illustration ——————————————————————————

Company L's ratio of net income to sales was as follows for the period 19X1 to 19X4:

19X1	19X2	19X3	19X4
12%	3%	20%	(5)%

The above pattern indicates a weak association between net income and sales and hence the "manipulator" status may be inferred.

302.10 / Factors of Income Management to Consider

Income management may be accomplished in many ways. Some examples follow.

- A significant portion of the net income of company **A** is derived from the sale of used vehicles. The company has managed earnings through the timing of such sales. The company makes these resale profits possible by depreciating the vehicles faster than the actual decline in market value. When the autos are sold, the excess of market value over book value is recognized in earnings. In 19X9 when the company's regular business (leasing and rentals) was on the downturn, it increased its sales of used vehicles in order to achieve its profit goals.

- A housing company and an affiliated mortgage banking company can trade their portfolios of securities with each other. In so doing, each may be able to pick up earnings by trading low-cost securities that have higher market values.

- Companies in the electronic industry have different accounting policies to record the distribution of electronic components to independent distributors. Most firms have a "return privilege" in which the distributor can return the merchandise if the retail selling price declines. It is more conservative not to record the sale until the product is actually sold by the distributor. Some companies record the sale when the merchandise is shipped to the distributor and at the same time establish a reserve for possible returns (usually based on 20%–30% of selling price). They are able to manage earnings by changing the reserve estimate. If selling price declines occur, there will be substantial returns that may cause a company to reverse previously recorded sales. Companies may also have to book large write-offs on the undesirable merchandise.

- Timber companies can easily manage earnings by selling timber from a high-cost or low-cost timber area. They can also change cutting rates to influence their tax rate and, therefore, their profitability.

- Cosmetic companies can manage earnings by accelerating or deferring sales promotion activities. Many firms use spot TV in which advertising is booked in advance. If earnings are depressed in the current year, the company will elect to book TV commercials at the beginning of the following year rather than at the end of the current year.

- An agricultural company writes down good inventory in order to show a loss in years of excessive profits. In the following years, when profits are low, the lower valued inventory is sold at the regular selling price.

- Cabot, Cabot, and Forbes Trust disclosed: "The reduction of the investment adviser's fee resulted from the effects of a revision of the Advisory Contract. *Revisions* take place *periodically* which influence the amount of the advisory fee."

- A company that has deferred pre-opening costs will start to amortize them when a new facility opens. The company could accelerate or defer the opening date based on its desired earnings level. For example, if earnings are too low, the company will move the opening date from December to January in order to defer the initiation of amortization expense. There is also latitude in determining what constitutes an opening date (e.g., the day all employees are hired, the date the facility is first opened to the public).

• Another smoothing method involves the form in which employee benefits are declared. Bonuses paid in cash require a charge against earnings. However, if stock options are given, net income is not effected.

• The allocation of overhead for joint products enables a firm to manage its earnings. The joint cost is usually arbitrarily allocated to different items and the method of allocation can change for new products. Assume a manufacturer produces items 1 and 2. The company may increase the inventory cost of item 1 and decrease the inventory cost of item 2 by allocating a higher percentage of joint costs to item 1. This may be done to increase earnings when most of item 1 is still in inventory and item 2 has almost all been sold.

302.11 / Checking Revenue Recognition

According to P. Defilese,[2] it is possible under GAAP to *create profits* where in fact economic reality doesn't warrant them.

• An example prior to FASB 45 was the recording of franchise sales that stood a good chance of not being realized or even cancelled.

• Another example is the sale of bowling equipment to inexperienced operators which results in the recognition of the full profit on the equipment without adequate provision for bad debts.

Some companies immediately recognize revenue even though certain services are yet to be performed.

• A correspondence school or health spa that derives income from membership dues may be recognizing revenue when the advance cash payment is received. This method may overstate current year's earnings. It would be more appropriate to allocate the fee over the enrollment period.

• Some magazine publishers recognize subscription income immediately when the full cash payment is received from subscribers. Subscription income should not be included until the earnings cycle is complete.

A firm that unrealistically defers the recognition of revenue has poor earnings quality, since net income is unjustifiably understated.

• Company Y recorded franchise sales of $100,000 along with an estimated liability provision of $10,000. After analysis, the analyst concludes that

---

[2] P. Defilese, "What Makes Profits Look 'Obscene'," *Business Week*, (August 4, 1975), p. 10.

$25,000 would be a more adequate provision in light of the financially weak status of franchisees. A downward adjustment to net income of $15,000 is required. The estimated loss provision should be $25,000 rather than $10,000.

• A correspondence school receives an advance payment of $10,000 in 19X1 for a 4-year enrollment fee. It recognizes immediately as income the total fee of $10,000. A downward adjustment of $7,500 to net income is required ($10,000 less $2,500).

302.12 / How Companies Reverse Previously Recorded Profits

The reversal of previously recorded profits makes one suspicious of a company's revenue recognition policies.

• For example, company B makes the following disclosure in its 19X3 annual report: "The ship contract was recorded at a breakeven, resulting in the reversal of $718,000 income recorded in prior years."

Similarly, a company that reverses a prior write-off of an asset has a questionable accounting policy.

• For example, in 19X6, company C reversed an equipment write-off, originally made in 19X5, amounting to $885,000 in order to partially offset a $4.4 million exchange loss.

302.13 / Watch for Underaccrual or Overaccrual of Expenses

The underaccrual or overaccrual of expenses results in lower quality of earnings.

• An example of an underaccrued expense is failure of a computer manufacturer to provide normal maintenance service for rented computers because they are being used by lessees.
• Company D discloses: "Certain repair and maintenance expense which might otherwise have been incurred during 19X3 was postponed until 19X4 due to demands from lessees for continued utilization of covered hopper cars during a period of unprecedented volume of grain shipments." It appears that 19X3 earnings were overstated to the extent that these repair costs were not incurred.
• Another example is a firm's failure to have a sufficient warranty provision. For instance, a company may have sold defective products in the current period but failed to increase its normal provision.

• An example of an overaccrued expense is the decision of a company with excessively high earnings to accrue for possible sales returns that are highly unlikely to materialize.

Analysts should attempt to determine what these *normal charges* are and *adjust* reported net income accordingly.

• Company T shows an expense provision of $8,000 but the analyst concludes that an appropriate provision should be $13,000. Net income should be downwardly adjusted for $5,000 due to the underaccrued expense.

• Company L accrued a warranty provision of $6,000. The analyst concludes that such a provision was prompted by a desire to set up an accounting cushion and thus is too high. He believes that the normal provision should be $5,000. Net income should thus be upwardly adjusted by $1,000.

302.14 / Examples of Accounting Policies That Lower the Quality of Earnings

The following accounting policies lower the quality of earnings:

1. A company may reduce its expenses for expected recoveries of excess costs resulting from changes in government contracts. Exaggerated expectations may unjustifiably reduce expenses with the resultant overstatement of net income.

• For example, in fiscal 19X4, company E filed suits against governmental agencies for the recovery of excess costs resulting from delays and modifications in certain contracts. Accordingly, it reflected $800,000 in claim receivables and reduced its costs. The latter increased per share earnings by $0.21. Subsequent events showed that only about 65% of the claim was collected.

2. There may be an unrealistic decline in a company's percentage of sales allowances to sales.

• For example, sales may increase by 200% while sales allowances may increase by only 20%. This trend may not be consistent with economic reality, especially if dealer returns are substantially on the rise because of the larger sales base. In this case, earnings are overstated.

3. A company may make a substantial provision for future costs (warranties) in the current year because it was *remiss in making adequate provisions in prior years.*

• In 19X2, company F recognized a loss on the settlement of customer notes of $9.8 million. Was it not known in prior years that such notes were likely to become uncollectible?

4. A company may decide to take a "financial bath." This involves a cleanup of balance sheet accounts by writing down assets, and providing for estimated losses and expenses that may apply to the future. This results in lowering current period earnings while relieving future years' income of these charges.

5. A bank may renegotiate the terms of its loan with a financially weak borrower. This may involve a reduction of interest (e.g., 10% to 2%) along with a provision for contingent interest (e.g., 30% of earnings up to a maximum of 150% of prime). In accruing interest on these renegotiated debts, some banks include an estimate of the contingent interest. However, the earnings increment due to the contingent interest is of a lower quality. Some banks have provided overly optimistic accruals even though the principal of the loan has a high degree of collection risk.

6. The acquisition of a savings and loan association by another firm accounted for under the purchase method often results in lower quality earnings. Goodwill is recorded and amortized over 40 years. The firm acquires the mortgage portfolio, which is recorded at the present value of the mortgages. The present value is based on the current mortgage rate over the average remaining mortgage life (e.g., 7 years). The company increases its mortgage portfolio and credits income over the remaining 7 years in order to bring the portfolio to its maturity value. In effect, the company is front-loading income over 7 years while amortizing goodwill over 40 years.

7. A parent company with two consolidated subsidiaries operating independently can decide to transfer certain administrative costs from Sub. 1 to Sub. 2. Sub. 1 has expensed these costs as incurred. The company now decides to make Sub. 2 a cost center (therefore including the administrative costs transferred from Sub. 1). In so doing, the company has been able to increase its overall earnings since previously expensed costs are now included in inventory.

8. A company may decide to sell securities that have a market value in excess of cost to pick up a gain and then buy back the same securities after year-end at the higher price. Such a gain should be eliminated by the analyst from the reported earnings figure.

• In 19X3, company A sold $7.3 million of company B's stock at a $7.2 million gain, and two months later purchased $7.4 million of company B's shares.

9. Income creation can arise through extraordinary gains on the early extinguishment of debt. (If early extinguishment takes place in a sinking

fund, the gain is not extraordinary.) In some cases, companies have retired low-interest bonds only to issue in turn higher interest debt because of a desire to boost earnings. Of course, financially such a policy is unsound.

A change in corporate policy may result in profit distortion among reporting periods. For example, firm F discloses:

• A departure from normal policy renewal processing schedules caused written premiums in the amount of $5.8 million to be entered in the fourth quarter of 19X3 that normally would have been entered in the first quarter of 19X4.

302.15 / How to Analyze Income from Discontinued Operations

Income from discontinued operations shown in the income statement has significance in evaluating the quality of earnings. Such income is usually of a one-time nature and can be ignored in predicting future earnings. Thus, the net income reported for continuing operations offers the most representative earnings figure indicative of a company's current operating performance. The amount of income from discontinued operations also shows whether a business is in a state of contraction. Significant dispositions of segments may lead one to question the continued viability of the entity. It may also indicate prior poor management decisions on entering new types of business.[3]

302.16 / The Impact of Accounting Policies on the Quality of Earnings

Nature of Accounting Policy	Effect on Earnings Quality
1. Liberal	Negative
2. Ultraconservative	Negative
3. Reflects economic reality	Positive
4. Estimates differ materially from actual experience	Negative
5. Corporate accounting policies differ from standard policies employed in the industry	Negative
6. Deferral of expenses having high realization risk	Negative

---

[3] L. Savage and J. Siegel, "Disposal of a Segment of a Business," *The CPA Journal*, (September 1978), p. 32.

Nature of Accounting Policy	Effect on Earnings Quality
7. An accounting change which conforms to a required or recommended policy in a new FASB or AICPA Industry Audit Guide	Positive
8. An accounting change not justified according to the facts	Negative
9. Frequent accounting changes	Negative
10. Income smoothing	Negative
11. Net income borrows from the future or benefits from the past	Negative
12. Weak relationship between net income and sales	Negative
13. Recognizing revenue before significant services are performed	Negative
14. Revenue recognition is inappropriately deferred	Negative
15. Profits recognized in previous years are reversed in the current period	Negative
16. A prior write-off of an asset is reversed in the present period	Negative
17. An expense is underaccrued	Negative
18. An expense is overaccrued	Negative
19. A significant expense or future loss provision is made in the current period because the firm was remiss in making adequate provisions in prior periods	Negative
20. Taking a "financial bath" via extensive write-offs associated with new management taking over the firm	Negative

—— 303 / HOW TO DIAGNOSE DISCRETIONARY COSTS AND THE LOWERING OF EARNINGS QUALITY ——

Discretionary costs can be increased or decreased by management decision. They include advertising, repairs and maintenance, and research and development. Analysts should note whether the current level of discretionary expenses is consistent with the company's previous trends and with its present and future requirements. Index numbers may be used to compare current discretionary expenditures with base year expenditures.

Discretionary costs are often reduced when a firm is either in difficulty or desires to show a stable earnings trend. A reduction in discretionary costs may cause a deterioration in earnings quality since management is starving the firm of needed expenses.

• For example, the absence of expenditures for new designs by a textile firm lowers its future earning potential since it will not be able to keep up with competitors.

• A reduction in costs related to employee benefits, such as Christmas bonuses, may have an adverse effect on employee morale.

• A declining trend in training costs in a technologically oriented company may result in employees failing to keep-up-to-date with recent developments.

Analysts should determine the trend in discretionary costs as a percent of net sales. A declining trend may reflect a deterioration in earnings quality.

• For instance, a company with level sales volume coupled with a decline in the percentage of selling, general, and administrative costs to sales may be unjustifiably cutting back on needed costs, such as sales force.

• Company G has maintained its profit margins during 19X1–19X3 in part by curtailing advertising expenses as a percent of sales (2.3% in 19X1, 2.2% in 19X2, and 1.8% in 19X3).

• In fiscal 19X4 the Company's reduction in marketing expenditures as a percent of sales aided 19X4 incremental comparisons by $0.79 a share.

Analysts should also examine the relationship of discretionary costs to the assets with which they are associated.

• For example, a declining trend in repairs and maintenance as a percentage of fixed assets may indicate a company's failure to maintain capital.

Illustration

The following relationship exists between advertising and sales for the period 19X1 to 19X3:

	19X1	19X2	19X3
Sales	$100,000	$130,000	$90,000
Advertising	10,000	15,000	4,000

The base year (the most typical year) is 19X1.

After 19X4, it is anticipated that advertising effort will be a key ingredient for corporate success because of an anticipated increase in competition.

The ratios of advertising to sales are:

19X1	19X2	19X3
10%	11.5%	4.4%

In terms of base dollar analysis, 19X1 is assigned 100. In 19X2, the index number is 150 ($15,000/$10,000). For 19X3, the index number is 40 ($4,000/$10,000).

The above are negative signs with regard to 19X3. The company's level of advertising is lower than in prior years. In fact, it should have been higher because of anticipated increased future competition.

Illustration ————————————————————————————————

Company V presents the following data relative to its fixed assets:

	19X1	19X2
Fixed assets	$5,000	$5,200
Less: accumulated depreciation	3,200	3,500
Book value	$1,800	$1,700
Repairs and maintenance on fixed assets	$ 300	$ 230
Replacement cost of fixed assets	7,000	8,000
Price-level adjusted value of fixed assets (based on the Consumer Price Index)	7,500	8,300
Sales	40,000	45,000
Working capital	3,000	2,700
Cash	1,000	950
Total debt-to-stockholders' equity ratio	40%	65%
Downtime of equipment expressed as a percentage of capacity available	3.0%	4.5%

Repairs and maintenance to gross fixed assets from 19X1 to 19X2 went from 6% ($300/$5,000) to 4.4% ($230/$5,200). Similarly, over the same period, there was a decline in the ratio of repairs and maintenance to sales from .75% ($300/$40,000) to .5% ($230/$45,000).

Between 19X1 and 19X2 the gap widened between replacement cost and book value of fixed assets as well as between price-level adjusted value and book value. In 19X2, replacement cost exceeded book value by $6,300 and price-level adjusted value exceeded book value by $6,600.

Machinery downtime increased from 19X1 to 19X2, inferring more equipment failure.

Acquisitions of fixed assets in 19X2 are minimal, $200. In 19X2, the ratio of new acquisitions to the gross fixed asset base is 4% ($200/$5,000).

As evident from the above, company V's maintenance of equipment is poor. The ratio of repairs and maintenance to fixed assets and to sales, coupled with the failure to make an adequate level of replacements, most likely accounts for the increased downtime.

As indicated by the widening divergence between replacement cost and book value as well as that between price-level adjusted value and book value, the equipment is getting older. Long-term negative effects upon the production process may be forthcoming.

It will be difficult for the firm to replace fixed assets when needed as evidenced by the decline in the company's cash and working capital positions. The increased replacement cost points to a significant future drain on corporate liquidity. The problem is compounded because the high debt-to-equity ratio (65% in 19X2) may mean difficulty for the firm in obtaining suitable financing, especially in a tight money market.

Also look at the trend in the ratios of (1) sales to number of employees, and (2) sales to total payroll to determine the return on staff and productivity. This will help determine whether "fat" exists in the organization.

303.1 / Recognizing Legitimate Reductions in Discretionary Costs

It is important to recognize that one cannot automatically conclude that any reduction in discretionary expenditures relative to the prior year is unjustified. Such reductions may be necessary when the previous corporate strategy is found to be deficient and ill-conceived.

• A reduction in R&D would be justified if the firm's research program has been unsuccessful and management is now considering a new research strategy, which will shortly be implemented.

• A reduction in R&D and advertising may also be in order if the company suddenly becomes the market leader because its principal competitors have gone out of business.

• Another legitimate reason for a cutback in discretionary costs exists when management engages in a cost-cutting program that eliminates waste and thus makes the firm leaner and more efficient.

303.2 / Watch for a Jump in Discretionary Costs

A significant increase in discretionary costs may have a positive effect on a company's earning power and future growth.

• D Company's R&D expenses in 19X3 were more than double those in 19X2. However, it must be noted that if an increase in a given company's R&D expenditures was prompted by a desire to make up for a deficiency in its prior years' expenditures, then the firm's overall research activity may have remained static. In this case, the company is not necessarily in a growth stage.

303.3 / How Companies Smooth Earnings

A vacillating trend in discretionary costs as a percent of revenue may indicate that a firm is smoothing earnings by changing its discretionary costs.

> • Company J discloses: "Advertising expense decreased 22% from 19X2 to 19X3. Advertising expense increased 61% in 19X4, representing a return to a more normal relationship to sales dollars."

303.4 / How to Evaluate Discretionary Costs: A Checklist of Questions

Question	Answer	Indicator as to Earnings Quality
1. Is the level of discretionary costs in conformity with prior years?	No	Reduction
2. Is there a decline in the trend of discretionary costs as a percent of net sales and/or of the assets they relate to?	Yes	Reduction
3. Does the cost reduction program involve significant cuts in discretionary costs?	Yes	Reduction
4. Does the cost reduction program eliminate "fat" within the organization?	Yes	Improvement
5. Do discretionary costs relative to sales show fluctuation from year to year?	Yes	Reduction
6. Is there a sizable increase in discretionary costs?	Yes	Improvement

———— 304 / USING CASH FLOW INFORMATION ————

As reported in an article appearing in the February 2, 1981 issue of *Forbes*,[4] Harold Williams, then Chairman of the Securities and Exchange Commis-

---

[4] "Are More Chryslers in the Offing," *Forbes*, (February 2, 1981), pp. 69–73.

sion, stated that: "If I had to make a forced choice between having earnings information and having cash flow information, I would take the latter." Cash flow analysis is especially critical during inflationary times. The same article reports a useful analytical measure developed by Kidder, Peabody & Co. called "discretionary cash flow," which is the amount a firm has left over after deducting the cash needed to maintain its fixed assets and to pay dividends. For example, Kidder found that Union Carbide had a negative discretionary cash flow of $360.4 million in 1980. In effect, the company probably was paying dividends from borrowed money.

There have been instances where companies prior to failing were reporting steady earnings but showing negative cash flows from operations. A case in point was W.T. Grant.

In general, the greater the degree of a company's cash reinvestment into the business the better, because it indicates future corporate growth. "The cash reinvestment ratio is equal to cash employed (increases in gross plant and equipment plus increase in net working capital) divided by cash obtained (income after tax plus depreciation)."[5] The higher the ratio, the more cash used in the business.

304.1 / How to Use Cash Flow in Analyzing the Income Statement

Cash flow, which really refers to funds (i.e., working capital) flow, is equal to net income adjusted for income statement items not involving funds (depreciation, amortization).

Accordingly, earnings are of higher quality if they are backed up by cash. The trend in the ratio of cash flow from operations to net income should be thoroughly examined.

The greater the proximity of a recorded transaction to cash, the more objective is the evidence supporting revenue or expense recognition. As the proximity to cash becomes less, the less objective is the transaction and the more subjective are the interpretations involved. *High quality of earnings is associated with recording transactions that are close to cash realization.*

Illustration ─────────────────────────────────────

A condensed income statement for Charles Corporation follows:

Sales	$1,000,000
Less: Cost of sales	300,000
Gross margin	$ 700,000

---

[5] B. Gale and B. Branch, "Cash Flow Analysis; More Important Than Ever," *Harvard Business Review*, (July–August, 1981), p. 135.

Less: Operating expenses		
Salary	$100,000	
Rent	200,000	
Telephone	50,000	
Depreciation	80,000	
Amortization expense	60,000	
Total operating expenses		490,000
Income before other items		$ 210,000
Other revenue and expense		
Interest expense	$ 70,000	
Amortization of deferred credit	(40,000)	
Total other revenue and expense		30,000
Net income		$ 180,000

The ratio of cash flow from operations to net income is 1.55, calculated as follows:

Cash flow from operations		
Net income		$ 180,000
Add: Non-cash expenses		
Depreciation	$ 80,000	
Amortization expense	60,000	140,000
Less: Non-cash revenue		
Amortization of deferred credit		(40,000)
Cash flow from operations		$ 280,000

$$\frac{\text{Cash flow from operations}}{\text{Net income}} = \frac{\$280,000}{\$180,000} = 1.55$$

_____ 305 / KEY FACTORS TO CONSIDER WITH TAXABLE INCOME _____

If a firm reports substantial book income while it reports a substantial tax loss, the analyst may wish to scrutinize the quality of reported results.

• In 19X3, company K reported earnings of $207.7 million to stockholders, while reporting a $41.5 million loss to the IRS.

A company with a large deferred income tax credit account on the balance sheet has low quality of earnings because accrual earnings are greater than taxable earnings. An increasing trend in the "Deferred Tax Credit" account may mean that the firm is changing to more liberal accounting policies (revenue recognition, expense capitalization). As the liability for deferred taxes increases, so does the gap between book income and taxable income. Thus, the trend in the Deferred Tax Credit account must be closely scrutinized.

Taxable income is generally more conservatively determined than book income because companies must, or elect to, use more conservative accounting policies for tax reporting. Taxable income will usually be somewhat less than book income because of a firm's incentive to pay lower taxes.

Many companies report profits earned in low tax jurisdictions. Foreign earnings are usually not repatriated to the U.S., as they are subject to U.S. taxation. If profits are regarded as funds available to stockholders, the reported earnings are exaggerated. Drug companies are known for their tax shelters that accelerate earnings growth.

Illustration _____

Trans Corporation provides the following information:

	19X1	19X2	19X3
Deferred income tax credit	$105	$120	$310
Sales	$10,000	$11,000	$11,500
Net income	$ 4,000	$ 4,100	$ 3,700

The increase in the deferred income tax credit account in base dollars for 19X2 was 114 ($120/$105) and for 19X3 was 295 ($310/$105).

The ratios of deferred income tax credit to sales for the period were:

19X1	19X2	19X3
1%	1%	2.7%

The ratios of deferred income tax credit to net income for the period were:

19X1	19X2	19X3
2.6%	2.9%	8.4%

In 19X3, the deferred income tax credit account sharply increased, indicating a material difference between book income and taxable income for the year.

_____

305.1 / Analyzing the Effective Tax Rate

The effective tax rate is the relationship between the tax accrual and the pre-tax book income. It is influenced by permanent differences. However, temporary differences have no effect on the effective tax rate because of interperiod income tax allocation. The rate is calculated by dividing income tax expense by income before income taxes. As the tax rate drops, the gap between the growth rate of pre-tax earnings and that of net earnings widens.

A company with tax-sheltered income will have a lower effective tax rate. Earnings quality is lower when there is a high probability that such tax shelter will be abolished within the next few years.

A decline in the effective tax rate due to a nonrecurring source (a loss carryforward that will shortly expire) results in an earnings increment of low quality. These tax benefits will not continue in the future. On the other hand, the effective tax rate may be stable when it results from a recurring source (foreign tax credits, interest on municipal bonds).

305.2 / Check the Domestic International Sales Corporation (DISC) Tax Benefit

Flow-through accounting for DISC tax deferrals inflates current earnings. The method assumes the deferrals are either a reduction in the effective tax rate or a permanent difference. Under the method, if any past deferred taxes become payable, they are charged against current income. An alternative approach requires comprehensive tax allocation accounting and does not require tax deferrals in current earnings. It assumes the deferred taxes will be paid in the future. Consequently, these future tax payments are included in current tax expense to avoid the overstatement of earnings.

305.3 / Effects of Changes in the Tax Rate

Higher earnings quality exists if the earnings level and growth rate are not dependent on a reduction in the tax rate by means that may be susceptible to future changes in the tax law or that place adverse restrictions on the firm's use of its tax deferrals or savings.

305.4 / Low Earnings Quality Indicators: A Checklist

☐ Book income substantially exceeds taxable income

☐ There is an increasing trend in the deferred income tax credit account

☐ Increased earnings arise because of a tax benefit that will be discontinued or significantly curtailed in the future

☐ Changes in the tax law that will have adverse effects upon profitability are anticipated

☐ There exists a high percentage of foreign earnings that will not be repatriated to the U.S. for a long time

_____ **306 / EVALUATING RESIDUAL INCOME** _____

The quality of earnings may be evaluated by determining the trend in residual income to reported results. An increasing trend may indicate a stronger degree of profitability for the firm since it is earning enough to cover its imputed cost of capital. Residual income may easily be determined by deducting the imputed cost of capital (weighted average cost of capital times total assets) from net income.

Illustration _____

If a company's weighted average cost of capital was 10.5%, its net income was $1,000,000 and its total assets were $5,000,000, the firm's residual income would be:

Net income	$1,000,000
Less: Cost of capital × total assets	
10.5% × $5,000,000	525,000
Residual income	$ 475,000

The percentage of residual income to net income is 47.5% ($475,000/ $1,000,000).

Although in the above example the cost of capital rate is given, it almost always must be computed by the analyst based upon financial data available in the company's annual report. The weighted average cost of capital takes into account the cost of the various financing instruments as well as their weights in the capital structure. For instance, based on the following data we can compute the weighted average cost of capital for X Company.

Balance Sheet data:	
Bonds Payable-15%	$ 50 million
Preferred Stock-dividend rate	10
12%	
Common Stock	40
Total	$100 million

The dividend per share on common stock is $10 and the market price per share is $100. The tax rate is 30%.

The computation of the weighted average cost of capital follows:

Security	Percent in the Capital Structure	After-tax Cost of Capital	Weighted Average Cost of Capital
Bonds Payable	50%	10.5%	5.3%
Preferred Stock	10%	12 %	1.2%
Common Stock	40%	10 %	4.0%
Total	100%		10.5%

The cost of financing may also be based on the cost to replace capital, as that would reflect current prices. Using such a competition base would make company-to-company comparisons more meaningful.

307 / RETURN ON INVESTMENT

Return on investment (ROI) is a good measure of a company's performance. Although ROI shows the extent to which earnings are achieved on the investment made in the business, the actual value is generally somewhat distorted.

There are basically two ratios that evaluate the return on investment. One is the return on total assets, and the other is the return on owners' equity.

The return on total assets (ROA) indicates the efficiency with which management has used its available resources to generate income.

$$\text{Return on total assets} = \frac{\text{Net Income}}{\text{Average Total Assets}}$$

The Du Pont formula shows an important tie-in between the profit margin and the return on total assets. The relationship is:

Return on total assets = profit margin × total asset turnover
Therefore:

$$\frac{\text{Net Income}}{\text{Average Total Assets}} = \frac{\text{Net Income}}{\text{Net Sales}} \times \frac{\text{Net Sales}}{\text{Average Total Assets}}$$

As can be seen from this formula, the ROA can be raised by increasing either the profit margin or the asset turnover. The latter is to some extent industry dependent, with retailers and the like having a greater potential for raising the asset turnover ratio than do service and utility companies. However, the profit margin may vary greatly within an industry since it is subject to sales, cost controls, and pricing. The interrelationship shown in the Du Pont formula can therefore be useful to a company trying to raise its ROA since the area most sensitive to change can be targeted.

The return on common equity (ROE) measures the rate of return earned on the common stockholders' investment.

$$\text{Return on Common Equity} = \frac{\text{Earnings Available to Common Stockholders}}{\text{Average Stockholders' Equity}}$$

ROE and ROA are closely related through what is known as the equity multiplier (leverage, or debt ratio) as follows:

$$ROE = ROA \times \text{equity multiplier}$$

$$= ROA \times \frac{\text{Total Assets}}{\text{Common Equity}}$$

or

$$= \frac{ROA}{1 - \text{debt ratio}}$$

308 / RISK AND VARIABILITY

The analyst must consider the concept of "accounting risk" in the evaluation of reported results. This risk is inherent in the existence of alternative accounting policies, the flexible criteria that define them, and the resulting flexible standards applied in practice.

308.1 / Degree of Certainty of Accounting Estimates

The more that subjective accounting estimates and judgments are used in arriving at earnings, the more uncertain is the net income figure. This reflects unfavorably on the quality of earnings. For example, a company engaged in long-term activity (e.g., a ship-builder using the percentage-of-completion contract method) has greater uncertainty attached to income because of the material estimates involved.

Analysts may wish to ascertain the difference between a firm's estimated reserves and its actual losses for prior years. A substantial discrepancy between the two may indicate lower quality of earnings.

• A firm's warranty reserve provision could be compared to its actual warranty costs. A wide difference between the two figures, either way, may indicate that the company's overall accounting estimates have been incorrect and uncertain or that the firm has failed to make adequate provision for future losses.

If there is more uncertainty involved in arriving at estimated liability amounts, reported results are more uncertain.

Illustration

Company B makes a provision for expected sales returns of $100,000 in 19X1 and $130,000 in 19X2. The actual returns for 19X1 sales were finally determined to be $150,000 and for 19X2 sales $190,000. The unfavorable variance in sales returns attributable to 19X1 sales is $50,000, or 50% of the estimate ($50,000/$100,000). For 19X2 sales, there is an unfavorable variance of $60,000, or 46% of the estimate ($60,000/$130,000).

We do not have much faith in the company's estimation process. Further, the company's earnings in 19X1 and 19X2 are overstated, since the estimated expense provisions are understated.

Significant gains and losses on the sale of assets may be an indication that inaccurate depreciation estimates were originally used.

A higher percentage of assets subject to greater accounting estimates (intangible assets) means uncertain reported income.

308.2 / Look at Cash vs. Estimated Income Statement Components

The effects of quality of earnings could be identified by separating factual and interpretative information that enters income determination. That would involve isolation of revenue and expense items representing cash and near-cash transactions versus revenue and expense items that involve subjective estimates and interpretations. Analysts should attempt to *segregate cash expenses versus estimated expenses*. They may wish to determine trends in cash expenses to net sales and in estimated expenses to net sales.

Illustration _____

The analyst assembles the following data for Company G for the period 19X1 and 19X2:

	19X1	19X2
Cash and near-cash (conversion period to cash is short) revenue items	$100,000	$110,000
Non-cash revenue items (long-term receivables arising from credit sales to the government, revenue recognized under the percentage of completion method)	150,000	200,000
Total revenue	$250,000	$310,000
Cash and near-cash expenses (salaries, rent, telephone)	$ 40,000	$ 60,000
Non-cash expenses (depreciation, depletion, amortization, bad debts)	70,000	120,000
Total expenses	$110,000	$180,000
Net income	$140,000	$130,000

Estimated revenue items to total revenue was 60% ($150/$250) in 19X1 and 65% ($200/$310) in 19X2. Estimated revenue to net income was 107% ($150/$140) in 19X1 and 154% ($200/$130) in 19X2.

Estimated expense items to total expenses was 64% ($70/$110) in 19X1 and 67% ($120/$180) in 19X2. Estimated expenses to total revenue was 28% ($70/$250) in 19X1 and 39% ($120/$310) in 19X2. Estimated expenses to net income was 50% ($70/$140) in 19X1 and 92% ($120/$130) in 19X2.

Uncertainty exists with regard to the net incomes of 19X1 and 19X2 because of the high percentages of estimated income statement items. Further, a greater degree of estimation is associated with 19X2's income measurement process.

308.3 / Accounting Estimates and the Quality of Earnings

Signs of Uncertainty Involved in Formulating Accounting Estimates

1. Long-term activity such as construction work.
2. Need to establish significant estimated liabilities such as for medical malpractice insurance.
3. Material variance exists between estimated liabilities and actual losses.
4. Sharp deviation between estimates and actual experience. An example is material misjudgements in prior years of estimating the lives and salvage values of fixed assets as evidenced by unusual gains and losses on disposition.
5. A high percent of assets to total assets that require significant estimates.
6. A high percent of estimated expenses to (1) total expenses, (2) sales, and (3) net income.
7. A high percent of estimated revenue items to total revenue and to net income.

308.4 / How Is the Internal Control?

Poor internal control lowers earnings reliability. It may be very difficult to discover these errors if the client's audit trail is weak. Perhaps, if audit fees have substantially increased, additional audit time was required because of the client's poor internal control system.

Was the audit date extended and why?

• Company L's 19X2 annual report discloses: Restated financial statements for 19X1 are presented because it was determined during an audit for the first quarter of 19X2 that there was an overstatement of operating income of $182,000 ($0.04 per share) and of net income of $590,000 ($0.12 per share) for the year ended December 26, 19X1. Errors in compilation resulted in previously reported consolidated inventories of

$73,744,000 being overstated by $907,000 and the liability for product warranties of $11,404,000 being overstated by $453,000 at December 26, 19X1.

These errors cast doubt upon the company's financial reporting system and internal audit function.

308.5 / Has the Auditor Been Fired?

According to Accounting Series Release No. 165, firms must disclose in SEC Form 8-K whether a change in CPA resulted from a disagreement between the parties over a contemplated accounting change. If the new CPA firm agrees to the change, the company must disclose what the earnings would have been had the previous accounting policy been maintained. Analysts should compare reported results (using the new policy) to what earnings would have been had the accounting change not been made. Analysts should evaluate the appropriateness of the new method by referring to Industry Audit Guides. If the change resulted in substantially higher earnings, the quality of that increment may be suspect, and a downward adjustment to reported results may be required. Analysts may be wary of earnings increments when a company has fired auditors in prior years in order to obtain acceptance of accounting changes designed to increase earnings. Analysts may also question earnings increments when a firm is known to manage its net income and/or have liberal accounting policies.

For example, a few years ago, SEC reports revealed that four computer lessors fired their auditors because of disagreements about the value assigned to computer equipment. Major losses owing to new, lower valuations of the equipment followed.

——— 309 / INDEPENDENT AUDITOR'S REPORT ———

A company's reported earnings are usually deemed to be of higher quality if it has received an unqualified ("clean") opinion from its auditors rather than a qualified opinion, disclaimer, or adverse opinion.

When an auditor renders a qualified opinion, disclaimer, or adverse opinion on his client's financial statements, useful information is often revealed about the company's present and future financial health. In a qualified opinion, the CPA basically states that "except for" something, the financial statements fairly present the financial position and operating results of the firm. A disclaimer means that the auditor is unable to render an opinion for one of several possible reasons, such as he is unable to perform all necessary audit procedures. Certain qualifications or disclaimers may be so significant as to question the reliability of the financial statements. In an adverse opinion, which is rare, the CPA states that the financial statements do not fairly present the financial position. An adverse opinion generally results from a situation in which the auditor is unable to persuade his client to revise his financial statements so that they reflect what the auditor considers the outcome of the future event or in which the financial statements do not adhere to GAAP.

An "except for" qualification relates to limitation placed on the scope of the audit, which results in the independent CPA's failure to obtain sufficient objective and verifiable evidence in support of events that have occurred. Such an opinion may emanate from a lack of conformity of the financial statements to GAAP. It is issued when the auditor is not satisfied with the fairness of presentation of items in the financial statements. Therefore, the reader is put on alert that he must look behind the reported figures to determine what is really going on with the company. The question may arise: Is the client trying to hide something detrimental?

A separate paragraph in an unqualified opinion may be rendered when significant uncertainties affecting the company exist, such as lawsuits, tax matters, renegotiation proceedings, and possible expropriations of property by a foreign government. Uncertainties may also relate to the expected realization of assets in terms of cash. Such disclosed uncertainties are quite revealing to the financial statement user since they add to business risk and make the future recurrence in earnings more doubtful. Less earning power is attributable to firms having a high degree of corporate risk and uncertainty. When the nature of the uncertainties is extremely significant, an adverse opinion would be called for.

The auditor should be alert to circumstances that may jeopardize an entity's continued existence. A going-concern problem may be indicated when there are either solvency difficulties (recurring operating losses, negative cash flows, working capital deficiency, inability to obtain suitable financing, and violation of existing loan agreements) or operating problems (pronounced labor difficulties, loss of key personnel, uninsured casualty losses). The *severe* problems uncovered may have to be mentioned in the auditor's report. The auditor must specifically cite his reservations about the recoverability and classification of recorded assets and the amounts and classification of liabilities in light of that doubt. If a company is going to go out of business, its assets must be reflected at liquidation value.

There are guidelines for the auditor to follow in appraising management plans for staying solvent and improving operations. The auditor should review such plans and discuss them with management. Underlying assumptions in forecasts and budgets must be analyzed for reasonableness. The auditor, however, must look at such plans with a careful eye, as a troubled company would tend to be overoptimistic, and perhaps even distort the facts, to avoid admitting to prospective failure.

If the financial statements, including the related footnotes, fail to disclose material information, the auditor must provide such information in his report. Such disclosure should be carefully noted by the analyst since it may be something management wanted to sweep "under the rug." An example might be adverse governmental action, such as a ban on the firm's product line.

When a material event occurs subsequent to the date of the audit report but before the issuance of such report, the auditor may disclose the event in his report if the client does not wish to show it in a footnote. In such a case, a qualified opinion is rendered. Disclosure of subsequent events is highly informative because it may indicate current and future problems with regard to the entity. Examples include catastrophe losses, litigation, death of the president, and political bribe incidents.

If a related party transaction occurs (i.e., the president of the company is also on the board of directors of a supplier) and the auditor is unable to reach a conclusion as to the propriety thereof, he should provide a comment to that effect in his report. We must be wary of related party transactions since they may cause a distortion in the financial statements or be detrimental to the existing stockholders. Transactions with insiders of the company and affiliates may be biased—a way of "fooling around" with reported balance sheet and income statement figures.

—— 310 / EVALUATING MANAGEMENT'S INTEGRITY ——

Management's integrity has a bearing on the quality of earnings. Management's honesty can be evaluated by reviewing corporate actions. For example, recent disclosures of corporate bribes (which sometimes result in suits filed by governmental agencies and stockholders) taint management's image.

• Company M may be unable to engage in future business with Japan because it made payoffs to Japanese politicians.

There are examples of management's lack of forthrightness—Ford's Pinto and Firestone's "500" radial tires.

—— 311 / SUMMARY CHECKLIST OF KEY POINTS ——

311.1. No single "real" net income figure exists.

311.2. The analyst must adjust reported net income to an earnings figure that is relevant to him.

311.3. Earnings quality evaluation is important in investment, credit, audit, and management decision making.

311.4. Appraising the quality of earnings requires an examination of accounting, financial, economic, and political factors.

311.5. Earnings quality elements are both quantitative and qualitative.

311.6. / Low Quality of Earnings Indicators

1. **Unstable Income Statement Elements Unrelated to Normal Business Operations**

2. **Earnings that Reflect Dubious Adjustments to Estimated Liability Accounts**

3. **Earnings that have been determined using liberal accounting policies (methods and estimates) because of the resulting overstatement of net income. Such overstatement also results in the overstatement of future earnings projections**

   What to Do

   □ Compare the company's accounting policies to the prevalent accounting policies in the industry.

4. **Net income based on ultraconservative accounting policies since the resulting net income is misleading as a basis for predicting future earnings**

5. **Unreliable and Inaccurate Accounting Estimates**

   What to Watch Out For

   □ Prior estimates materially differ from actual experience, such as where the company's assumed interest rate on pension fund assets significantly differs from the actual interest rate earned, as reflected by significant actuarial gains and losses

   What to Do

   □ Restate net income as if realistic accounting estimates were used.

6. **Earnings That Have Been Artificially Smoothed or Managed**

   What to Watch Out For

   □ Revenue reflected earlier or later than the realistic time period
   □ Shifting of expenses among reporting periods
   □ Smoothly rising earnings trend

- ☐ Sharp increase or decrease in sales in the last quarter of the year as reflected in the 4th quarter income statement
- ☐ Trading of investment securities among affiliated companies
- ☐ Significant modification in estimated liability accounts in the last quarter
- ☐ Writing down a good asset (inventory) and selling it next year to show higher earnings
- ☐ The "financial bath," in which everything is written off in an already bad year so that it will be easier to show good profits in the following years. This sometimes occurs when new management takes over and wishes to blame old management for poor profits or when earnings are already so low that their further reduction may not have significant impact

What to Do

- ☐ Look at the functional relationship of sales and net income over time. An inconsistent relationship may be a manipulator indicator.
- ☐ Restate earnings by taking out profit increments or reductions due to income management ploys.

7. Deferral of Costs that Do Not Have Future Economic Benefit

What to Watch Out For

- ☐ Inventory of unsalable items in light of the current environment (big cars, with the oil shortage)
- ☐ Sudden write offs of inventory
- ☐ Goodwill on the balance sheet but the company has none (operating at losses, significant decline in market share, bad publicity like Firestone's defective tire experience)
- ☐ Costs that are currently capitalized when in prior years they were expensed (i.e., tooling costs in inventory)

What to Do

- ☐ Restate net income as if the unrealistic deferral had not been made.

8. Unjustified Changes in Accounting Principles and Estimates

What to Watch Out For

- ☐ A firm that has a past history of making frequent accounting changes

☐ Accounting changes that create earnings growth

☐ The company fires the auditor and hires another one because of a disagreement over a proposed accounting change. Note that in such a case, Accounting Series Release No. 165 requires the company to footnote the effect on net income as a result of making the accounting change

What to Do

☐ Determine whether the accounting change is justified by seeing if it conforms to requirements in new FASB Statements, Industry Audit Guides, and IRS regulations.

☐ Ascertain whether the accounting change is preferable, given the nature of the business (i.e., decreasing the life of a computer because of new technological advances in the industry).

☐ Does the change make sense? (Lowering bad debt expense as a percent of accounts receivable is not logical when customer defaults are on the rise.)

☐ If the accounting change results in increasing net income, restate earnings as they would have been if the old method had been retained.

9. Premature or Belated Revenue Recognition

What to Watch Out For

☐ Accruing unbilled sales

☐ Is there a sufficient provision for future losses in connection with the recognition of revenue (i.e., recognizing franchise revenue even though the franchisee is financially weak and risky)?

☐ Immediate revenue recognition of a five-year membership fee by a correspondence school even though course cancellations may require student reimbursement

☐ Improper deferral of revenue to a later period

☐ Reversal of previously recorded profits

What to Do

☐ Restate earnings as they would be if proper revenue recognition were made.

10. Underaccrual or Overaccrual of Expenses

What to Watch Out For

☐ Failure to incur necessary maintenance expenditures

☐ Inadequate warranty provision in light of quality problems with the company's products

☐ Setting up an accounting cushion for future years via the overaccrual of an expense provision (warranty provision, loan loss provision)

What to Do

☐ Adjust net income for the difference between the expense provided and the *normal* expense.

11. Improper Accounting Policies

What to Watch Out For

☐ The reduction of expenses for overly anticipated recoveries of excess costs due to modifications in governmental contracts

☐ A substantial provision for future costs in the present year (i.e., warranties) because the firm was remiss in making sufficient provisions in prior years

What to Do

☐ Restate the earnings of the years effected so that a proper earnings trend is determined.

12. Modification in Loan Agreements Due to Financially Weak Borrowers

What to Watch Out For

☐ A lowering of interest on the loan. In this case, not only is the interest income on the loan questionable but so is the principal.

What to Do

☐ Downwardly adjust net income for the inclusion of accrued interest income on risky loans.

13. Change in corporate policy for the current year, which impacts earnings (writing insurance renewal contracts in the fourth quarter of the current year rather than the first quarter of the next year)

14. Unjustified Cutback in Discretionary Costs

What to Watch Out For

☐ Declining trend in discretionary costs as a percent of net sales and/or the assets to which they apply

☐ Vacillation in the ratio of discretionary costs to sales and/or assets over the years, as this may infer the management of earnings

What to Do

☐ Determine the trend in discretionary costs over time through the use of index numbers.

☐ Determine the ratio of discretionary costs to sales and/or to assets over the last five years of each major item. An example is repairs and maintenance to sales and/or to fixed assets.

15. Book Income that Substantially Exceeds Taxable Income

What to Watch Out For

☐ A continual, significant rise in the deferred income tax credit account due to liberal accounting policies.

16. Residual Income that is Substantially Less than Net Income

What to Do

☐ Determine the ratio over time of residual income to net income.

17. A High Degree of Uncertainty Associated with Income Statement Components

What to Watch Out For

☐ A firm engaged in long-term activity requiring many estimates in the income measurement process

☐ Significant future loss provisions

☐ Estimates that have consistently been materially different from actual experience. An example is when significant gains or losses occur on the sale of assets

What to Do

☐ Compare over time a firm's estimated liability provisions with the actual losses eventually occurring. An example is looking at the warranty provided, with the actual warranty costs.

☐ Determine what percent of total assets are intangible assets, which by their nature require material estimates to be made.

18. Unreliably Reported Earnings

What to Watch Out For

☐ Poor system of internal control because it infers possible errors in the reporting system

☐ High turnover rate in auditors

☐ The company has a reputation for managing earnings and/or using liberal accounting policies

☐ Indications of a lack of management integrity as evidenced by such things as bribes and covering up the fact that a poor quality product exists

What to Do

☐ Determine the trend in audit fees over time.

☐ Examine for disclosure made by the company relating to adjustments due to prior years' accounting errors.

☐ Look at accounting, finance, and brokerage research publications that note and give examples of companies with questionable accounting policies.

311.7. High Quality of Earnings Indicators:

1. Net Income Backed Up by Cash

What to Do

☐ Determine distributable cash flow.

2. Net income not involving the inclusion of amortization costs related to questionable assets like deferred charges

3. Net Income that Reflects Economic Reality

What to Do

☐ Determine whether the measurement standards used are realistic in accounting for the *economic substance* of the firm's transactions. For example, is the depreciation method used an accurate reflection of the decline in usefulness of the fixed asset?

☐ See if the company's accounting policies are the same as those recommended in AICPA Industry Audit Guides, Industry Trade Publications, CPA Firm Publications, and in the accounting and financial literature (books, periodicals). When unrealistic policies have been employed, ascertain the dollar impact on net income and balance sheet position if the recommended accounting policies had been used.

☐ Determine whether the firm's accounting policies are in conformity with the realities of the industry. For example, if the firm is in a highly seasonal industry, its fiscal year-end should be the "ebb" of the season.

4. Income Statement Components that are Recognized Close to the Point of Cash Inflow and Cash Outflow

What to Do

☐ Determine the percent of cash expenses to sales and cash revenues to sales. The higher the ratios, the higher is the objectivity associated with income statement recognition.

———— 312 / RESTATING EARNINGS PER SHARE FOR LOW QUALITY OF EARNINGS ELEMENTS ————

Analysts can determine "relevant" earnings per share by making quantitative adjustments to reported earnings per share, with the revised figure reflecting more realistically the earning power of a company. The conversion process will result in a higher quality of earnings figure.

Analysts can determine more "relevant" or "acceptable" quality EPS by adjusting reported EPS for low quality items. An illustration of a suggested adjustment process follows.

Assume a company's reported EPS of $10.00 includes numerous low quality components. These items are listed below as deductions from reported EPS. (Items that must be deducted from EPS in order to arrive at an "acceptable" quality EPS were chosen with a view toward developing an approach that allows for a clearer understanding of the adjustment process. In reality, of course, reported EPS would be adjusted upward or downward for various reconciling items. An example of an upward adjustment would be the adding back to EPS of the effect of an unjustified accounting cushion arising from overestimated warranty provisions or bad debt provisions.)

Reported EPS   **$10.00**

Deductions from reported EPS in order to arrive at an "acceptable quality" EPS

• Unjustified cutbacks in discretionary costs (e.g., advertising) as a percent of sales.   .02

- A decline in the ratio of bad debts to sales that is not warranted by experience.   .03
- One-time gains (gain on the sale of land) that are not expected to recur over the long run.   .04
- Income derived from the sale of acquired assets that were recorded at suppressed amounts at the time of a pooling transaction.   .05
- Inventory profits.   .06
- Accounting changes designed to bolster earnings (LIFO to FIFO).   .07
- Lower pension expense arising from an unrealistic change in pension assumptions (increase in the acturially assumed interest rate).   .08
- Increase in deferred expenditures that do not have future economic benefit.   .09
- Items included in inventory which were previously expensed (labor, interest, administrative costs), assuming such items have no future utility.   .02
- Items included in plant and equipment that were previously expensed (e.g., maintenance costs).   .03
- Lower provision (relative to prior years) for cost overruns on long-term construction contracts. (For example, company A reduced income by $1.6 million in 19X4 and $12.9 million in 19X3 in connection with its provisions for cost overruns. The lower 19X4 provision aided earnings comparisons by $0.33 a share).   .04
- Increase in expenses (relative to prior years) charged to reserve accounts.   .05
- Unjustified reduction in reserve accounts.   .06
- Incremental capitalized interest relative to prior year. (For example, in spite of a reduction in sales volume, B Company capitalized $17.4 million of interest in fiscal 19X5 versus $12.4 million in fiscal 19X4. The company disclosed the following: "Had the company continually expensed interest as incurred, net earnings would have been reduced by $0.40 a share in fiscal 19X5 and $0.26 a share in 19X4").   .07
- Amount of underaccrual of expenses (or reserve provision).   .08
- One-time earnings increment arising from a change in revenue recognition policy. (For example, in 19X4, company C adopted the policy of accruing estimated unbilled revenues. This change in accounting treatment resulted in net income from

19X4 increasing by $16,531,000, of which the cumulative effect of the change to January 1, 19X4 was $12,353,000.)   .09

- Lower effective tax rate arising from a one-time tax benefit, such as a foreign tax credit that now becomes prohibited.   .02

"Acceptable Quality" EPS $ 9.10

CHAPTER FOUR

Evaluating the Financial Structure of the Firm

This chapter discusses characteristic conditions that relate to earnings quality and are inherent in industries and companies. An example is income stability that facilitates the prediction of future earnings and stock prices. There are numerous reasons why earnings may not be stable, such as the existence of a high degree of operating leverage inherent in a company's operations and the susceptibility of the firm and industry to the business cycle. Also discussed here are factors that enhance a company's future earning potential. Proper maintenance of capital will ensure the plant and equipment will be efficient and productive in future years. A good quality management will ensure the continued effective running of a business.

401 / ANALYZING STABILITY OF EARNINGS

Since analysts rely on the repetitiveness of occurrence in *projecting* future earnings, they separate stable elements of income and expense from those that are random and erratic. Analysts consider earnings derived from recurring transactions related to the basic business of the firm to be of higher quality than those resulting from isolated transactions.[1]

---

[1] J. Siegel, "The Evaluation of Earnings Stability," *University of Michigan Business Review*, (May, 1979), pp. 30–32, 36.

401.1 / Determining Abnormal and Erratic Income Statement Elements

Analysts should determine the extent to which earnings reflect one-time gains and losses that are *not* part of the basic business of the firm. This is because erratic and abnormal income statement elements distort the current year's income as a predictor of future earnings. For example, a one-time gain will result in a higher than normal level of earnings for the year. As a result, such items are often eliminated from net income by the analyst in determining relevant earnings. The following are some examples of erratic income statement items:

1. A gain on the sale of administrative offices.
2. The receipt of a "once-and-for-all" extraordinarily large order from a customer, resulting in a one-shot increase in sales.
3. An uninsured casualty loss that is not within the normal risk category of the firm.
4. Collection of the proceeds of a life insurance policy on a decreased corporate executive.

Whenever a company starts selling off what appears to be part of its capital assets and running the profits through income, investors should look upon the earnings increment as suspect. For example, company A's 19X3 third quarter showed increased land sale profits amounting to 243% of the quarterly comparative gain in share earnings.

Illustration ——————————————————————————————

Company B's income statement for the year ended December 31, 19X1 reveals:

Operating Income	$4,000,000
Nonrecurring, nonoperating gain	500,000
Income before extraordinary item	$4,500,000
Extraordinary loss	300,000
Net income	$4,200,000

To determine the *normal* amount of earnings for the year, the following adjustment to net income is required:

Net income	$4,200,000
Adjustments to net income:	
Nonrecurring, nonoperating gain	(500,000)
Extraordinary loss	300,000
Relevant earnings	$4,000,000

To determine the extent to which net income is affected by distortive elements, the percent of one-time gains and losses to net income and to sales should be computed.

Illustration ————————————————————————————————————

The following figures are extracted from company C's comparative income statements:

	19X0	19X1	19X2
Sales	$100,000	$105,000	$113,000
Net income	20,000	22,000	27,000
Net one-time gains (one-time gains less one-time losses	5,000	7,000	10,000

The percent of net one-time gains to sales and to net income are:

	19X0	19X1	19X2
Net one-time gains to sales	5.0%	6.7%	8.8%
Net one-time gains to net income	25.0%	31.8%	37.0%

The rising percentage of net one-time gains to sales and to net income indicates a deterioration in earnings quality.

401.2 / Evaluating Quality of Operating Income vs. Nonoperating Income

Some financial managers believe that operating income is *always* of higher quality than nonoperating income because it represents the earnings generated from the selling activities of the firm.[2] However, other income may be a highly stable earnings source (royalty income under long-term contracts with financially secure parties, rental income under long-term leases, and financial income such as dividend income). These are some instances of nonoperating income being more stable than sales. If such is the case, nonoperating income is of higher quality than operating income.

• IBM's lease income is more repetitive in nature than is its income from sales of computers. This occurs because revenue derived from leases is assured to be collected uniformly over the long run, while sales of computers occur more sporadically depending upon the state of the economy.

---

[2] J. Siegel, "The Quality of Earnings Concept—A Survey," *The Financial Analysts Journal*, (March/April, 1982), pp. 60–68.

Analysts should evaluate nonoperating income to determine the extent to which it is recurring and acts as a cushion to the stability of total income.

401.3 / Possible Stable Nonoperating Sources of Earnings

- Rental Income
- Royalty Income
- Franchise Income
- Dividend Income
- Interest Income

In appraising earnings quality, the analyst should determine the trends in operating income sources (sales) and nonoperating income sources (lease income, royalty income) over the last five years. He or she should also look at the current environment to see if any changes in demand for the company's products or services are anticipated. In the event that the analyst concludes that greater recurrence and dependability is indicated by one or more nonoperating income sources he or she should look at the trend in the percent of such nonoperating items to sales and to net income. Rising trends are reflective of higher earnings quality.

Illustration ───

Company D shows the following pattern of sales, lease income, and franchise income.

	19X0	**19X1**	**19X2**
Sales	$300,000	$307,000	$280,000
Lease income	70,000	71,000	74,000
Franchise income	40,000	42,000	43,000
Net income	25,000	26,000	24,000

From the above, it is clear that the nonoperating sources of income show more stability than sales.

The relationship of nonoperating income (lease income plus franchise income) to sales and to net income follows:

	19X0	**19X1**	**19X2**
Nonoperating income to sales	36.7%	36.8%	41.8%
Nonoperating income to net income	4.4x	4.3x	4.9x

Improved earnings stability is indicated because the trend in nonoperating income to sales and to net income has been upward between 19X0 and 19X2.

401.4 / Management's Desire to Show a Stable Earnings Trend

Management desires to show a stable, upwardly rising earnings trend because it infers corporate stability, which, of course, is desirable to security analysts and creditors. We must be cautious and verify that such stability actually exists and has not been intentionally portrayed. Warning signs of artificial stability must be recognized, such as:

1. Management's compensation plan is *closely* tied into the "bottom line."
2. The company is closely regulated and declining earnings may prompt new regulatory reporting requirements because of a perceived corporate crisis.
3. The company is a monopoly and rapidly rising earnings may imply that the public is being taken advantage of.
4. The company is under public scrutiny (such as a petroleum refiner that society suspects is taking advantage of an oil shortage to unfairly boost prices).

401.5 / Using Measures of Earnings Stability

In evaluating the nature and riskiness of a company as well as the quality of its management, it is important to examine the stability of the earnings trend. Of course, the trend in income is considerably more significant than its absolute size.

Earnings stability can be measured by: (1) average reported earnings; (2) average pessimistic earnings; (3) standard deviation; (4) coefficient of variation; (5) instability index; and (6) beta. When using these techniques, the earnings trend should be looked at over a long time period (ranging from five to ten years). The greater the variation in earnings for a company as indicated by these measures, the lower is the quality of earnings of that company.

1. Average Reported Earnings. The average earnings (in five years) will smooth out abnormal and erratic income statement components as well as cyclical effects upon the firm. Thus, the average earnings figure results in a better measure of earning power than that of net income for a particular year.

2. Average Pessimistic Earnings. This is the average earnings based on the *worst* possible business activity of the firm. Such minimum earnings are only useful in situations where the company is quite risky and the credit analyst wishes to fully provide for such risk.

The first step of course is to restate the reported earnings to minimum earnings for each year. Then, the minimum earnings for all years are totaled and finally divided by the number of years involved.

3. Standard Deviation. $\text{S.D.} = \sqrt{\dfrac{\Sigma(y - \bar{y})^2}{n}}$

where y = reported earnings for period t,
$\bar{y}$ = average earnings,
n = number of years.

A high standard deviation indicates poor earnings quality.

4. Coefficient of Variation. $\text{C.V.} = \dfrac{\text{S.D.}}{\bar{y}}$

The coefficient of variation can be used to evaluate relative instability in earnings among companies. The higher the coefficient of variation in earnings of a company, the higher the risk associated with its earnings stream.

5. Instability Index of Earnings. $\text{I} = \sqrt{\dfrac{\Sigma(y - y^T)^2}{n}}$

where y^T = trend earnings for period t, and is calculated by:

$y^T = a + bt$
where a = dollar intercept,
b = slope of trend line,
t = time period.

A simple trend equation solved by computer is used to determine trend income. The index reflects the deviation between actual income and trend income. The higher the index, the lower the quality of earnings associated with the firm.

6. Beta. Beta is determined via a computer run by the following equation:

$r_{jt} = \alpha_j + B_j r_{Mt} + E_{jt}$
where r_{jt} = return on security j for period t,
α_j = constant,
B_j = beta for security j,
r_{Mt} = return on a market index such as the New York Stock Exchange Index,
E_{jt} = error term.

Beta is a measure of systematic or undiversifiable risk of a stock. A high beta means that the company's stock price has shown more variability than that of the change in the market index, indicating that it is a risky security.

High variability in stock price may indicate greater business risk associated with the firm, instability in its past earnings trend, or lower quality of reported results. For example, a beta of 1.6 means that the firm's stock price rises or falls 60 percent more than the market. Beta values for individual companies can be obtained from various services such as Standard and Poor's.

Over time, a company's stock may have had a positive beta in some years and a negative beta in other years. The analyst should ask himself the following questions. If the market moves up, will the stock move up more or less than the general market? If the market moves down, will the stock move down faster or slower than the general market? Most stocks do not have equal up and down betas. IBM, for example, over the past 10 years has reacted in a worse way than the general market. It moves up slower in an up market (beta less than 1) and moves down faster in a down market (beta more than 1).

Illustration

Company D shows the following trend in reported earnings:

19X0	$100,000
19X1	110,000
19X2	80,000
19X3	120,000
19X4	140,000

The standard deviation in earnings is:

$$\text{Standard Deviation} = \sqrt{\frac{\Sigma(y - \bar{y})^2}{n}}$$

$$\bar{y} = \Sigma\frac{y}{n} = \frac{100,000 + 110,000 + 80,000 + 120,000 + 140,000}{5}$$

$$= \frac{550,000}{5} = 110,000$$

Year	$(y - \bar{y})$	$(y - \bar{y})^2$
19X0	−10,000	100,000,000
19X1	0	0
19X2	−30,000	900,000,000
19X3	+10,000	100,000,000
19X4	+30,000	900,000,000
Total		2,000,000,000

$$\text{Standard Deviation} = \sqrt{\frac{2,000,000,000}{5}}$$
$$= \sqrt{400,000,000}$$
$$= 20,000$$

The coefficient of variation in earnings is:

$$\text{Coefficient of Variation} = \frac{\text{Standard Deviation}}{\bar{y}}$$

$$\frac{20,000}{110,000} = 18.2\%$$

Illustration ───────────────────────────────

Company F's trend in beta determined by comparing its stock market price to the Dow Jones Industrial Index follows:

19X0	**19X1**	**19X2**	**19X3**
.7	1.2	1.6	2.1

In 19X0, the company's stock price fluctuated less than the market index. However, there has been an upward trend in riskiness of the company's stock as indicated by the rising trend in beta. For the years 19X1 to 19X3, the stock price has risen or fallen to a greater degree than the market index.

401.6 / Measures of Earnings Vacillation: A Checklist

☐ Average Reported Earnings
☐ Average Pessimistic Earnings
☐ Standard Deviation
☐ Coefficient of Variation
☐ Instability Index
☐ Beta

─── 402 / EVALUATING GROWTH RATE OF THE FIRM ───

In evaluating earnings quality, analysts may wish to determine a company's implied growth rate. This rate represents the change in retained earnings divided by the beginning net worth (stockholders' equity). The growth rate in earnings per share may also be calculated:

$$\frac{\text{EPS (end of period)} - \text{EPS (beginning of period)}}{\text{EPS (beginning of period)}}$$

Of course, the same approach may be used in computing the growth rate in dividends per share. Other measures of growth may also be used, such as the change in sales and total assets.

——— 403 / LOOK AT THE GROSS PROFIT PERCENTAGE ———

A high gross profit percentage is a favorable quality of earnings characteristic since it indicates that the firm is able to control its manufacturing costs. These costs are very difficult to control, as they relate to external factors that are often out of the company's control (such as steel prices to an auto manufacturer). SG&A expenses are easier to control, as they are internal to the organization and are therefore subject to cost reduction programs.

An increase in the ratio of gross profit to sales may mean the company was able to increase its sales volume or selling price, or to reduce its cost of sales. In general, manufacturers have higher gross profit rates than merchandisers.

——— 404 / EVALUATE OPERATING LEVERAGE ———

In evaluating a company's earnings quality, the analyst should consider the degree of its operating leverage. Operating leverage refers to the existence of fixed costs in a company's cost structure. Operating leverage can be measured through the following ratios: (1) fixed costs to total costs; (2) percentage change in operating income to the percentage change in sales volume; and (3) net income to fixed charges. An increase in (1) and (2) or decrease in (3) may indicate lower quality of earnings because higher fixed charges may result in greater earnings instability.

High leverage magnifies changes in earnings resulting from small changes in sales, and this leads to earnings instability. When high degrees of operating leverage are combined with highly elastic product demand conditions, variability of earnings will be at very high levels. Such conditions, though undesirable and leading to lower earnings quality, may be inherent in an entity's operations (airline and auto industries).

The effects of operating leverage diminish as revenue increases above the break-even point since the bases to which increases in earnings are compared get progressively larger. It may thus be fruitful to analyze the relationship between sales and the break-even point when evaluating a company's earnings stability.

A high break-even company is quite vulnerable to economic declines. A high percentage of variable costs to total costs indicates greater earnings stability. This is because variable costs can be adjusted more easily than fixed costs in meeting a decline in product demand.

Illustration ————————————————————————

Company I shows the following comparative income statement data:

	19X0	**19X1**
Net Income	$100,000	$102,000
Fixed costs	40,000	55,000
Variable costs	25,000	27,000
Total costs	65,000	82,000

Fixed costs are, of course, those that are constant irrespective of the production level (rental expense, insurance expense, property taxes, interest expense on long-term debt, interest expense on lease obligations).

Company I's operating leverage in 19X1 relative to 19X0 was higher as evidenced by the increase in the ratio of fixed costs to total costs and the decrease in the ratio of net income to fixed costs. Thus, greater earnings instability is indicated.

	19X0	**19X1**
Fixed costs to total costs	61.5%	67.1%
Net income to fixed costs	2.5%	1.86%

Illustration ————————————————————————

Company J wishes to evaluate its operating leverage. The following data are supplied:

Selling price per unit = $2.00
Fixed costs = $50,000
Variable cost per unit = $1.10

Year	Sales volume	Dollar sales	−	Fixed costs	−	Variable costs	=	Profit
19X0	100,000	$200,000	−	$50,000	−	$110,000	=	$40,000
19X1	130,000	260,000	−	50,000	−	143,000	=	67,000

The ratio of the percentage change in operating income to the percentage change in sales volume is:

$$\frac{\dfrac{\text{Change in profit}}{\text{Profit}}}{\dfrac{\text{Change in quantity}}{\text{Quantity}}} = \frac{\dfrac{\$67,000 - \$40,000}{\$40,000}}{\dfrac{130,000 - 100,000}{100,000}} = \frac{\dfrac{\$27,000}{\$40,000}}{\dfrac{30,000}{100,000}}$$

$$= \frac{67.5\%}{30.0\%} = 2.25$$

404.1 / Indicators of the Degree of Operating Leverage: A Checklist

☐ Fixed costs to total costs
☐ Operating income to sales
☐ Net income to fixed charges
☐ Break-even point relative to sales
☐ Fixed costs to variable costs

—— 405 / ORIGINAL SALE LEADS TO FURTHER REVENUE ——

A firm that derives further revenues from its original sales shows greater earnings stability than one that does not. An example is a company (Xerox, Otis Elevator) that provides maintenance services and replacement parts to its customers.

Analysts should determine the trend in a company's replacement and maintenance revenue as a percent of (1) new sales, (2) total revenue, and (3) net income. Rising trends are indicative of higher earnings quality.

———————— 406 / OPPORTUNIST MARKET ————————

An opportunist market (which is not a longevity market) is a low quality of earnings source because the saturation of a firm's market will lower its potential to generate continued earnings.

• The explosive growth in the electronic calculator market was short-term in nature and could not be sustained.

Short-term schemes that increase income temporarily are of lower quality, such as hula hoops and a single government contract. Thus, the analyst should determine the percent of such short-lived income to total revenue and to net income. Further, these sources of earnings should be eliminated when projecting the company's future earning power.

407 / SUDDEN DEVELOPMENTS

Earnings possess more stability if it is probable that business operations will not be affected by sudden and unexpected developments. An example is loss in the current year of a unique advantage, such as the exhaustion of mineral rights. In this case, currently reported net income is irrelevant in predicting future profits since in essence the analyst is dealing with a new and different enterprise.

408 / EVALUATING THE PRODUCT LINE

In evaluating the characteristics of a company's product line as it relates to earnings stability, consideration must be given to the effect of the business cycle, seasonality, type of products, diversification, price and cost variances, temporary bulge in product demand, products subject to rapid changes in taste, repeat business, product introduction, and product mix.

408.1 / The Business Cycle

Fundamental economic conditions are outside the control of any given company or industry. To the degree, however, that a firm is insulated from the impact of the broader economy, its earnings stability will be higher.

Companies with product lines having inelastic demand (e.g., health care products) are least affected by the business cycle. Companies with product lines that are closely correlated to changes in real gross national product show more variability in earnings. An example is the auto industry.

Companies should attempt to change their product lines to more stable demand items.

A company with a product line of low unit cost items offers promise of both continued success in times of economic health and resistance to demand decline during recession. If a company with low-priced goods also provides an adequate substitute for more expensive goods (as cereal for higher-priced protein foods), it has a built-in hedge in an inflationary and recessionary period.

408.2 / Effects of Seasonal Variations

Seasonal variations affect production and consumption. In order to stabilize its production and marketing operations, management should add products having different seasonal peaks. In so doing, earnings stability will be enhanced.

408.3 / Type of Product

Certain product lines tend to promote earnings stability. They are necessity items and retail trade (primarily low-priced items appealing to a wide market). These products usually perform well during recessionary periods as well as in times of economic growth. Contributing to fluctuating earnings are the following: (1) novelty and nonessential goods; (2) high prices, as with expensive jewelry, which add to variable demand during recessionary periods; and (3) production of heavy goods and raw materials. The demand for high-priced quality goods that serve a select market may remain stable during recessionary periods. An example is an expensive automobile like the Rolls Royce. This is because the affluent are not significantly affected by short-term changes in economic conditions. Companies engaged in the production of heavy goods and raw materials experience significant fluctuations in sales records because curtailment in buying is compounded as it proceeds from the consumer to the source of production. In the case of raw materials, this arises partly because of fluctuations in prices that are so prevalent in commodity markets and partly because of the instability in the demand for end-products. The variation in sales of capital goods stems to a large degree from the ability of industry to postpone purchases of durable equipment.

408.4 / Variances in the Product Line

A company's product line may have three types of variances: volume, price, and cost. The greater the extent to which each of these components is subject to variability, the more instability in the company's earnings stream. Examples of product lines showing variability are sugar, copper, and fertilizer. For instance, a copper company earning $4 a share is not as good as IBM earning $4 a share. This is because it is probable that IBM's earnings will be more repetitive in nature than the copper company's earnings. This arises since the demand and selling price for IBM's product line show greater stability than those of a copper company. It should be noted that earnings may still show stability, even though there is variability in these components. For example, the price variance may fully offset the cost variance.

    The analyst should examine the variability in quantity, selling price, and cost of each of the company's major product lines. Charting via graphs may highlight trends over time. The standard deviation may also be computed for one or more of the elements. Standard cost variance analysis[3] is recommended to highlight particular variances and then to analyze the reasons for such variances. Possible means of corrective action should be

---

[3] J. Shim and J. Siegel, *Variance Analysis for Cost Control and Profit Maximization* (New York: American Institute of CPAs, 1982).

identified. Sales mix, price, cost, and quantity variances should be computed if they have material effects.

Illustration ───

Western Corporation's budgeted sales for 19X1 were:

Product A 10,000 units at $6.00 per unit	$ 60,000
Product B 30,000 units at $8.00 per unit	240,000
Expected sales revenue	$300,000

Actual sales for the year were:

Product A 8,000 units at $6.20 per unit	$ 49,600
Product B 33,000 units at $7.70 per unit	$254,100
Actual sales revenue	$303,700

There is a favorable sales variance of $3,700 which consists of the sales price variance and the sales volume variance.

The sales price variance equals:

Actual selling price vs. budgeted selling price × actual units sold

Product A ($6.20 vs. $6.00 × 8,000)	$1,600	Favorable
Product B ($7.70 vs. $8.00 × 33,000)	9,900	Unfavorable
Sales price variance	$8,300	Unfavorable

The sales volume variance equals:

Actual quantity vs. budgeted quantity × budgeted selling price

Product A (8,000 vs. 10,000 × $6.00)	$12,000	Unfavorable
Product B (33,000 vs. 30,000 × $8.00)	24,000	Favorable
Sales volume variance	$12,000	Favorable
Proof:		
Sales price variance	$ 8,300	Unfavorable
Sales volume variance	12,000	Favorable
Sales variance	$ 3,700	Favorable

408.5 / Diversification in the Product Line

A single product company may have less earnings stability than a multiproduct company. The former is more susceptible to fluctuating net income and has a higher risk of product obsolescence. A *diversified* product line reduces the range of results that may stem from differing economic conditions.

A diversified product mix consisting of negatively correlated items results in greater earnings stability. This arises because revenue obtained from one product increases at the same time that revenue obtained from the other decreases. Examples of products that are negatively correlated are (1) winter clothing and summer clothing and (2) air conditioners and heaters. Of course, products may also have no correlation between them, such as typewriters and T.V. sets. However, a diversified product mix results in earnings instability when the products show positive correlations. Examples of such products are automobiles and tires.

In evaluating a company's product line, the analyst should determine (1) the *degree of correlation* that exists between products and (2) the *elasticity of product demand*. The correlation between products is revealed through a *correlation matrix* determined by a computer run. The elasticity of a product's demand is measured by the percentage change in quantity sold associated with a percentage change in price. The following ratio is used:

$$\frac{\text{Percentage change in quantity sold}}{\text{Percentage change in price}}$$

If the ratio is greater than 1, elastic demand is indicated. If it is exactly 1, demand is unitary. If the ratio is less than 1, inelastic demand exists.

Low earnings quality exists when products are positively correlated and have elastic demands.

Illustration

The correlation matrix of company I's product line follows:

Product	A	B	C	D	E	F
A	1.0	.13	−.02	−.01	−.07	.22
B	.13	1.0	−.02	−.07	.00	.00
C	−.02	−.02	1.0	.01	.48	.13
D	−.01	−.07	.01	1.0	.01	−.02
E	−.07	.00	.48	.01	1.0	.45
F	.22	.00	.13	−.02	.45	1.0

Of course, perfect correlation exists with the same product. For example, the correlation between product A and product A is 1.0.

High positive correlation exists between products E and C (.48) and products E and F (.45). Since these products are *closely* tied to each other, risk is indicated.

Low negative correlation exists between products A and D (−.01) and products A and C (− 02).

No correlation exists between products B and E (.00) and products B and F (.00).

It would be better for company I if it had some products that had significant negative correlations (i.e., −.6). Unfortunately, it does not.

Illustration

The two major products of company J are X and Y. Data relevant to them follow:

	X	Y
Selling price per unit	$ 10.00	$ 8.00
Current sales in units	10,000	13,000

It is determined that if the selling price of product X is increased to $11.00, the sales volume will decrease by 500 units. If the selling price of product Y is increased to $9.50, the sales volume will decrease by 4000 units.

The elasticity of demand is:

$$\frac{\text{Percentage change in quantity sold}}{\text{Percentage change in price}}$$

Product X has inelastic demand:

$$\frac{\dfrac{500}{10,000}}{\dfrac{\$1}{\$10}} = \frac{.05}{.10} = .5$$

Product Y has elastic demand:

$$\frac{\dfrac{4,000}{13,000}}{\dfrac{\$1.50}{\$8.00}} = \frac{.308}{.188} = 1.64$$

408.6 / Unusual Product Demand

A substantial increase in earnings is of low quality if it results from *extraordinary product demand coupled with skyrocketing prices* (e.g., copper, fertilizer). This is an unusual situation which is not expected to recur.

• Company K had an unusually large increase in earnings in 19X4, principally because of a temporary bulge in demand for sugar due to a shortage situation. In 19X4, the company reported earnings of $14.07 per share compared to $4.22 per share in 19X3. The company's product market returned to competitive conditions in 19X5.

408.7 / Rapid Changes in Consumer Taste

A company with a product line that is subject to rapid changes in consumer taste has lower earnings stability. A case in point is "gimmick" products (novelty goods) because they are susceptible to changing fads. The garment industry is highly sensitive to fashion trends. In addition, the loss of a top fashion designer will have a devastating effect on earnings.

408.8 / New Product Introduction

A company with a "piggy-back" product base (similar products associated with its base business) has greater earnings stability. An example is Kellogg's with its dozens of cereals. By extending its basic formula, the company attains efficiency through economy of scale as well as reducing advertising and distribution costs through increased volume.

A company that is able to introduce new products to replace existing ones that are losing their market appeal has greater earnings stability. Analysts should thus look at the number of *patented* products coming on stream.

408.9 / The Product Mix

S. Goodman[4] believes that in evaluating the quality of profit, the financial manager asks himself the following questions related to the company's product mix: How long will we receive this flow of profits? What is its weighting in the product mix? How much of a contribution is there from growth, mature, declining, and developmental products? What is the nature of the risk entailed in each life cycle category? Shouldn't profit be weighted for the degree of risk inherent in its formation?

With respect to product mix, a dollar of profit derived from growth products with a foreseeably longer stream of earning potential is worth more than that derived from mature products. Developmental products generate a lower quality dollar relative to mature products because of the higher risk of their not succeeding. Mature products already have a proven track record.

A move in sales mix to more stable demand products with higher profit margins improves a company's revenue stability. B. Graham, B. Dodd, and S. Cottle state that "it is almost a universal law of security

---

[4] S. Goodman, *Techniques of Profitability Analysis*, (New York: John Wiley & Sons, 1970), pp. 70, 106.

analysis that the units with better profit margins show smaller percentage declines in recession years."[5]

408.10 / Product Line Characteristics That Indicate Poor Quality of Earnings: A Checklist

☐ Novelty goods
☐ Heavy goods
☐ Variability in product cost
☐ Single product line
☐ Positively correlated products
☐ Elastic product demand
☐ Variability in demand over time
☐ Fad products
☐ Lack of new patented products
☐ High percentage of developmental products
☐ Low profit margin products

———— 409 / THE REVENUE BASE: IS IT STABLE? ————

When product demand is vulnerable to external factors, the stability in sales revenue is decreased. For example, if a major portion of demand is derived from a few very large industrial users, changes in the nature of their business may filter down to the supplier. Further, a loss of a major customer can have a devastating effect on earnings. Export sales to a major foreign market may suddenly disappear as that country seeks to develop a domestic capacity for making the goods in question.

A company with sales to diversified industries (industries that are affected in different ways by cyclical factors) has greater protection from cyclical turns in the economy. This is because there is a higher probability that the demand factors in these industries may counteract each other.

• Skil Corporation manufactures portable electric tools. Its product is well diversified, with sales being distributed among industrial and service trades and the home consumer. Due to this diversity, sales are partly insulated from business cycles. Shipments to industrial markets are closely tied to such cyclical elements as general industrial activity and housing

---

[5] B. Graham, B. Dodd, and S. Cottle, *Security Analysis: Principles and Techniques*, (New York: McGraw-Hill, 1962), p. 244.

starts and to such less cyclical factors as industrial repair and maintenance activity.

A company can reduce its exposure to the effects of the economic cycle by entering noncyclical or countercyclical lines of business.

• American Express has two primary revenue sources—insurance and travel. The tendency of property and casualty underwriting profits is to decline normally during a period of economic strength, and to strengthen during periods of economic stagnation. The opposite in each case applies to the behavior of travel (cards and checks) operations.

A company that *geographically diversifies* has less susceptibility to economic downturns.

• A department store chain that reduces its reliance on metropolitan stores as it has an increasing contribution from suburban stores has lessened its exposure to downturns in economic, regional, and retail cycles.

An analysis should be made of the sales backlog in order to monitor sales status and planning.

$$\text{Days of sales in backlog} = \frac{\text{Backlog balance}}{\text{Sales volume divided by sales in period}}$$

Is the backlog for long-range delivery (e.g., 5 years) or on a recurring basis to maintain stability?

409.1 / Poor Quality of Earnings Sources: A Checklist

☐ Few, large customers
☐ Cyclical customer base
☐ Foreign country developing its ability to manufacture product

——————— 410 / RAW MATERIAL EXPOSURE ———————

A company that has variability in its raw material costs (e.g., agricultural products) shows greater fluctuation in earnings. The analyst can ascertain price instability by reviewing trade publications.

A firm that does not have alternative raw material sources possesses higher risk and uncertainty with respect to its future earnings stream. The analyst should determine if a company is highly dependent on potentially unreliable sources of supply (e.g., petroleum).

Vertical integration that reduces a company's price and supply risk of raw materials improves its earnings stability.

- An example is an electronics company that has a joint venture with a mining company in order to guarantee a steady source of supply of an important raw material.

___ 411 / THE LAWSUIT'S EFFECTS ON EARNINGS STABILITY ___

Analysts should consider litigation in their evaluation of reported results. Litigation against a company that will have a harmful effect on operations (antitrust action) will lower its earnings stability. However, litigation of a routine nature or litigation that covers matters that will not affect future income (tax disputes) has no impact on earnings quality.

_____ 412 / EVALUATING RISK AND UNCERTAINTY _____

Earnings are affected by controllable factors (e.g., management decision) and uncontrollable factors (e.g., political interference). The greater the extent to which uncontrollable factors exist, the more uncertain is a company's earnings stream.

Risk and uncertainty are associated with the abnormal and the unexpected. The frequency of occurrence of abnormal or special items is an important measure of the element of risk in a company. The potential impact of uncertainties facing a firm may be of such magnitude that reported results have little predictive value. Therefore, a risky business (retail land sales) generally has lower earnings stability than a more secure business (manufacturing).

A trade-off exists between risk and return. A company manufacturing fad items, for example, should earn more of a return than a company producing staple products.

To evaluate a firm's risk exposure, the analyst should compare such exposure to that of other companies in the industry as well as to past trends of the firm.

412.1 / Risks Bearing Upon the Quality of Earnings: A Checklist

- ☐ Corporate
- ☐ Financial
- ☐ Economic
- ☐ Political
- ☐ Social
- ☐ Ethnic
- ☐ Environmental
- ☐ Industry

412.2 / Risk in Basic Operations

Risk in the basic operations of the firm are too numerous to mention. Only a few are cited here just to get a flavor. A firm that is highly dependent on a few key employees has lower earnings stability, as the loss of them will cause a significant adverse effect on operations. A company dependent upon a few unreliable suppliers, as indicated by past delivery problems, has inherent operating risk. One should also consider the dependency of one company upon another. For example, if the newspaper industry is consistently plagued by strikes, an advertising agency will lose profits from a lack of newspaper advertising.

412.3 / Political Uncertainties

Political risk applies to foreign operations and governmental regulation.

Multinational companies having material foreign operations face uncertainties regarding the repatriation of funds, currency fluctuations, and local customs and regulations. The inability of a U.S. company to fire employees in Japan, for instance, makes labor a fixed cost.

Operations in politically and economically unstable foreign regions indicate poor quality of earnings. The potential for change in government, with its concurrent negative effects, must be considered. The analyst should determine the earnings derived and assets in each questionable foreign country. Useful ratios here are:

1. Questionable foreign revenue to total revenue
2. Questionable foreign earnings to net income
3. Total export revenue to total revenue
4. Total export earnings to net income
5. Total assets in "questionable" foreign countries to total assets
6. Total assets in foreign countries to total assets

Illustration ━━━

An example of a useful disclosure with regard to foreign exposure is that made by G Company in its 19X9 annual report. The company disclosed that of total export sales of $316,336,000 through foreign military contracts with the U.S. government in 19X8, $301,198,000 was made to the Middle East. This is a significant percentage, 95.2%. In 19X9, such export sales to the Middle East dropped to $54,265,000, of total export sales of $73,186,000. This percentage is materially less, 74.1%. It is significant to note that the tremendous decline in total export sales from 19X8 to 19X9 of 76.9% ($243,150,000 divided by $316,336,000) was due to the decline in business to the Middle East.

Firms relying on government contracts and subsidies may have lower stability of earnings because government spending is vulnerable to changing political whims of legislators and war-threatening situations. Fortunes of companies in the defense industry shift in response to the shifting perceived requirements of the Department of Defense. Farmers were hurt by the embargo of grain to the Soviet Union. *Analysts should ascertain the percentage of earnings derived from government contract work and subsidies, and the degree to which such work and subsidies are of a recurring nature.*

Is governmental regulation over a company very strict? If it is, management's hands may be tied. For example, the real estate rental industry in New York is subject to strong rent control requirements regarding the passing along of higher costs to tenants. The analyst should ascertain the current and prospective effects of governmental interference on the firm by *reviewing current and proposed laws and regulations* of governmental bodies as indicated in legislative hearings, trade journals, and newspapers.

One should analyze whether the company might be affected by current and proposed tax legislation. The real or potential effects of such legislation may be revealing as to a firm's future tax liability position.

Tight environmental and safety regulations may exist. An example is safety and pollution control equipment for new cars, which may further depress the profitability of auto manufacturers.

• In 19X3, ABC Gas and Fuel Associates disclosed that "3.8 million was expended to meet changing health and safety regulations at two coal mines."

An unfriendly regulatory agency will lower corporate earning power. For example, it may take a long time to get a rate increase, and when such increase is approved it may be significantly less than what is needed. The analyst should be familiar with the regulatory environment in which the firm operates.

412.4 / Political Implications in Earnings Quality Evaluation: A Checklist

☐ Foreign operations in current and potential problem areas
☐ Unusual foreign country customs and laws
☐ Government contracts and subsidies
☐ Regulatory environment
☐ Environmental and safety legislation
☐ Prospective changes in the tax law
☐ Areas of Internal Revenue Service concentration (i.e., tax shelters)

412.5 / Social Factors: How Is the Company Viewed by Society?

According to J. Siegel and M. Lehman, the failure of a company to take into account social risks will have an adverse impact on corporate earning power.[6] Companies viewed negatively by society have lower potential due to their "bad will." For example, consumer boycotts and governmental intervention may take place. In prior years, certain companies have experienced adverse community relations (Adolph Coors Co.), legal suits emanating from prejudice cases (AT&T), and government-forced rebates due to the sale of defective merchandise (certain Firestone tires). Ethnic considerations must also be noted. For example, a company that has recently been acquired by Iraquis may find its sales drop.

412.6 / Environmental Risk

Companies have variability in earnings and greater operating risk when their product lines or services are susceptible to changes in the weather. For example, a recreation business will experience a sharp drop in income if weather is unusually bad during the summer months. Thus, the analyst should take into account whether the geographic location of a business causes it to be affected by the whims of nature (earthquakes, floods).

• Giant Portland Cement discloses: "The Company suffered an ice storm in January and an unprecedented 21-inch snowfall in February, which were extremely disruptive to production."

412.7 / Is the Company Adequately Insured?

Underinsured assets will not provide adequate income to compensate for losses. By underinsuring its productive assets, the company has made the sustenance of its earnings stream less certain.

A company with a high-risk product line (e.g., explosives) that involves potential product liability suits, in which insurance coverage is nonexistent, has greater uncertainty.

In some industries where exceptionally high risk exists, companies are either unable to get insurance or must pay exorbitant rates to do so. To minimize such risk, however, it is recommended that companies pool their risks via the establishment of mutual insurance companies in which they retain an equity interest and to which insurance premiums are paid.

A declining trend in insurance expense to fixed assets may signal inadequate insurance coverage. High turnover rate in insurance companies may

---

[6] J. Siegel and M. Lehman, "Own Up to Social Responsibility," *Financial Executive*, (March, 1976), pp. 44–48.

also signal a problem. Analysts may attempt to determine the difference between insurance recoveries and the cost basis of property destroyed. *Unusual losses may indicate inadequate coverage.*

Illustration

Relevant data with regard to company K's insurance coverage:

	19X1	19X2
Insurance expense	$ 300,000	$ 100,000
Fixed assets	10,000,000	11,000,000
Casualty losses	70,000	300,000

Insurance-related ratios follow:

	19X1	19X2
Insurance expense to fixed assets	3.0%	.9%
Casualty losses to fixed assets	.7%	2.7%

Company K's insurance protection deteriorated in 19X2 relative to 19X1. The ratio of insurance expense to fixed assets decreased from 3.0% to .9%. Also, casualty losses as a percentage of property, plant, and equipment went up over the same period from .7% to 2.7%. The rise in casualty losses is probably due to the inadequate insurance coverage.

412.8 / Evaluating Corporate Disclosures

According to Accounting Series Release No. 166, companies must disclose unusual risks and uncertainties in financial reporting. Examples cited by the release are instances where deferred fuel costs of utilities may not be fully recouped in new rates and where crude oil prices are subject to negotiation with foreign host governments.

FASB No. 14 requires financial reporting for segments of a business enterprise. If a company derives 10% or more of its revenue or earnings from an industry, product line, foreign geographic area, single customer, or domestic government contract, disclosure of the percent so derived must be made. This disclosure is extremely helpful in risk evaluation as well as in determining corporate earning power. For example, if a high percentage of earnings is derived from a customer who is on the verge of bankruptcy, there will be significant financial effects upon the company.

The *contingency and commitment footnote* should be examined. Litigation, renegotiation of contract disputes with other firms and/or the government, and tax disputes with the IRS are matters of concern. The analyst should look at the past uncertainties and appraise how well management resolved them. This serves as a benchmark to predict how present uncertainties may affect the future. If management repeatedly loses its arguments with the IRS, for instance, a similar expectation now exists.

———— 413 / IS MANAGEMENT OF GOOD QUALITY? ————

A lack of a qualified and stable leadership gives one less confidence in the company. Previous incidents of mismanagement of corporate affairs (introduction of the Edsel car, an airline buying too many 747s), the past occurrence of corporate bankruptcy, or consistent overexaggeration and inaccurate expectation given in the annual report, make one question management's ability and forthrightness.

If management is unable to adjust to changes in the nature of the business as well as to the current social, political, and economic environment, the company's earning potential is lessened. Past incidents of management's failure to meet these changes adequately and on a timely basis suggest that management will have such difficulty again.

• The auto industry was late in recognizing the shift in demand to small, economical automobiles. In fact, Chrysler almost went bankrupt, partly because its plant facilities were geared primarily to "big car" production.

Planning strategies must exist that enable the enterprise to quickly adapt to changes in the business environment.

———————— 414 / EMPLOYEES ————————

A company with good employee relations (Delta Airlines) has greater earnings stability. Labor tranquility can be evaluated by determining the number and duration of previous strikes, degree of union militancy, and employee turnover. These data are sometimes provided by companies in their "Management's Analysis of Results of Operations" sections.

Typically, a consistent relationship should exist between indirect labor and direct labor since both are needed to efficiently run the organization.

———————— 415 / THE INTEREST RATE ————————

Interest expense may be unstable because of changes in the prime rate, the level of borrowing, and changes in the type of financing. Interest expense on short-term obligations varies with changes in the prime interest rate, which in turn varies with the business cycle. Interest expense on long-term obligations shows greater stability. A firm with substantial interest expense on short-term debt will show fluctuation in this expense category.

Similarly, interest income on short-term investments has more volatility and is therefore of lower quality than interest income on long-term investments.

Illustration

Company J shows the following comparative balance sheet data:

	19X1	**19X2**
Short-term debt	$10,000,000	$25,000,000
Long-term debt	30,000,000	32,000,000

The percent of short-term debt to long-term debt increased from 19X1 to 19X2 from 33.3% to 78.1% signaling a deterioration in liquidity (ability to meet current liabilities out of current assets) and generating instability in the interest expense category.

416 / INDUSTRY CHARACTERISTICS

In evaluating earnings quality, the analyst should consider the pattern of expansion or decline in the industry of which the corporation is a part. The profit dollar is valued in one way if earned in a healthy, expanding industry, and in another if earned in an unhealthy, declining one. For instance, the expanding and mature industry, with a limited number of companies controlling a high percentage of the market and whose selling prices can be upwardly adjusted for rising costs, normally generates a good-grade earnings dollar.

A company in a rapidly changing technological industry (e.g., computers) has more uncertainty because of the obsolescence factor. The analyst must appraise the technological skill of the firm as evidenced by its prior ability to keep up-to-date, as in the case of IBM.

Labor-intensive companies generally have greater earnings stability than capital intensive ones, because the former have a high percentage of variable costs while the latter have a high percentage of fixed costs. As J. Paulos notes, "with the exception of some utilities, most capital intensive industries have a record of cyclical performance."[7]

---

[7] J. Paulos, "Inflation and Capital Intensive Industries," *Financial Executive*, (February, 1975), p. 56.

Companies in a staple industry have greater earnings stability because product demand is inelastic.

A company may have earnings variability due to an industry cycle. For example, the steel industry has a 5–10 year cycle in which steel furnaces must be disconnected and refurnished. In the year of rehabilitation, the company may suffer a nonrecurring decline in earnings since overhead must still be met while production volume is curtailed.

The reliance of the industry on energy sources is also relevant. A company highly dependent on oil is more vulnerable to possible energy shortages than one reliant upon coal.

Attention should also be focused on the past and projected stability of the industry by appraising competitive factors. Examples are the ease of entry, price wars, and cheaper imports in the foreign car market.

416.1 / Industry Characteristics and Earnings Quality: A Checklist

☐ Expanding or Declining

☐ Technological

☐ Labor or Capital Intensive

☐ Staple

☐ Degree of Competition

☐ Degree of Regulation

☐ Energy Dependence

☐ Length of Industry Cycle

—————————— 417 / INFLATION ——————————

As noted in the May 4, 1981 issue of *Business Week*,[8] reported earnings are not representative of reality:

> • Double-digit inflation has rendered the traditional yardstick of company performance illusory and suspect . . . Measured against the two new inflation-adjusted profits figures—in current costs and constant dollars—reported profits for 370 of the nation's largest industrial companies for fiscal 1980 shrink by more than half.

To the degree that net income includes inflationary profits, reported earnings are overstated in an economic sense, because such profits result from changes in the price level and/or replacement cost rather than from operational performance. The analyst should thus determine the impact

---

[8] "How 1980 Profits at 370 Companies Were Hit," *Business Week*, (May 4, 1981), p. 84.

of inflation on reported results by comparing CPI adjusted net income and current cost net income with the reported earnings. If the amount reported in the income statement is materially higher than the other net income measure(s), the quality of earnings is poor. The wider the difference, the lower the quality of net income. Furthermore, the following ratios may prove enlightening: (1) constant dollar earnings to net income and (2) current cost earnings to net income. The lower the ratios, the lower the quality of earnings.

Illustration

Company K's income statement for 19X1 shows a net income of $4,000,000. The footnote titled "Inflation" reveals that constant dollar net income is $3,500,000 and current cost net income is $3,200,000. Company L, a competitor, reports net income for 19X1 of $2,000,000. A related footnote discloses that constant dollar net income is $1,900,000 and current cost net income is $1,800,000.

Ratios showing inflationary effects for the companies follow:

	Co.K	Co.L
Constant dollar net income to net income	87.5%	95.0%
Current cost net income to net income	80.0%	90.0%

Company K's quality of earnings is lower than that of company L as evidenced by its lower ratios of (1) constant dollar net income to net income and (2) current cost net income to net income. In effect, company K's historically determined net income relative to inflation-adjusted profits is proportionately overstated compared with that of company L. The more that a company's net income exceeds the inflationary adjusted net income, the lower is its quality of earnings.

The absolute dollar amount of reported net income is irrelevant.

Inflation affects the reported earnings of companies differently. Companies that are more capital intensive will generally have greater inflationary profits than those that are less capital intensive. The former have a higher percent of fixed assets to total assets and therefore depreciation expense (which is based on the historical cost of assets) is understated to a greater degree during inflationary periods. Also, companies with very old fixed assets will show greater inflationary profits than companies with newer but identically efficient assets because depreciation charges of the former are understated. If, however, the newer assets are more efficient, which is likely, they will provide additional profitability because of greater productive capacity and certain cost savings (e.g., less repair expense).

417.1 / How Management Can Counteract Inflation

In an article in *The Financial Executive,* I enumerate the following avenues available to a company to counteract inflationary effects.[9]

1. Selling Price Considerations. Inflation risks should be passed on to customers by upwardly adjusting selling prices at short intervals (e.g., monthly), so that adequate profit margins are maintained. Further, the company should build in the ability to swiftly modify price catalogues and sales literature. Price quotations should be held only for short periods of time (e.g., two months). Before prices are increased, however, one should take into account the realities of the marketplace (product substitution, product demand elasticities).

The sales pricing policy should be determined on a Next-In, First-Out basis so that replacement costing is taken into account. The current cost of capital should be determined so that it is considered in the formulation of the selling price. Pricing ahead of inflation is a key weapon.

In sales agreements, there should be a provision that prices may be upwardly adjusted to the point of actual shipment when a long lead time exists between the time an order is received and the goods are shipped. Further, in such cases, progress collections should be asked for as the work is being performed.

Long-term contracts should contain a "cost plus" provision, possibly tied to the Consumer Price Index. Price escalation clauses are essential to incorporate in construction and engineering contracts because of the material time period between receiving an order and filling it.

2. Control over Costs. Is there a cheaper way of doing things? For example, product components that customarily experience excessive price increases should be avoided. The company should contract for long-term purchase agreements and encourage suppliers to quote firm prices. A change in suppliers may be justified if they grant more liberal credit or easier terms.

When inflation is expected to worsen, the company should enter into contracts in the futures market in order to lock itself in to buying raw materials at currently lower prices.

It is advantageous to constantly obtain competitive bids from insurance companies and periodically change carriers when cost beneficial.

Due to the high cost of energy and its possible unavailability, activities highly dependent upon oil should be avoided. Thus, processes should be designed that are minimally tied to energy sources.

The company should redesign its truck logistics system so that economies of petroleum products can arise.

---

[9] J. Siegel, "How to Combat the Effects of Inflation," *Financial Executive,* (March, 1982), pp. 16–24. Reprinted with permission from the Financial Executive Institute.

3. Marketing Aspects. The firm should de-emphasize products materially affected by inflation through less production and promotion. Inflation-resistant product substitutes should be emphasized.

Marketing proposals that require significant investments and have long payback periods should be avoided. Unprofitable products should not be introduced unless technological change or design improvement can make such products profitable in the future.

4. Labor Implications. Companies having automated facilities and a minimal labor force do better during inflation.

A labor-intensive firm experiences difficulty during inflation because of employee discontent resulting from the decline in real earnings. When salary increments are greater, they should be keyed to improvements in productivity. Also, during inflation, a problem may arise in satisfying pension obligations. The company should communicate in some way (weekly newsletter, management report) that increasing costs arising from inflation require productivity gains.

5. Financial Matters. During inflation, a company having a net monetary position (monetary assets less monetary liabilities) will experience a purchasing power loss. Hence, cash and receivables should be kept at minimum balances.

In inflation, debt is advantageous, as it results in a purchasing power gain due to the fact that we are paying creditors back in cheaper dollars. If a firm has already reached the limit of its borrowing ability, further debt is not recommended, since higher costs of financing will occur because of the financial risk associated with the firm. It is essential that a careful analysis be given to the company's present degree of financial leverage (debt to equity ratio).

A good hedge against inflation is real estate. Another is to borrow from insurance companies against the cash surrender value of life insurance. The rates provided for in the policies are most likely less than the going interest rate.

In inflation, dividends should be restricted to preserve earning power and retain needed cash flow. In no case should dividends be paid out exceeding the firm's inflation-adjusted earnings. When inflation is expected to worsen, the company should reduce its dividend-payout ratio so stockholders get used to receiving lower dividends.

6. Management of Assets. Proper asset management is designed to lower costs as well as risks. For example, cash management techniques will accelerate cash inflow and defer cash outflow. Cash flow may be improved by prebilling customers. Invoices should immediately be mailed when merchandise is shipped and should be sent to arrive before the customer's cutoff period for payment. Also, to assure prompt cash receipt, errors in shipping and billing should be corrected immediately. Customer payments should be sent to strategic regional areas. A lockbox should be used so that the remittance is immediately credited to the company's account.

With regard to accounts receivable management, in order to hasten collection from delinquent customers, interest should be charged on overdue accounts. Discounts should be offered to customers for the early payment of the accounts when the return earned on the higher cash inflow exceeds the cost of the discount. Credit should be extended to more marginal credit-worthy customers when the contribution margin earned (assumes idle capacity) exceeds the additional bad debts and the opportunity cost of tying up funds in accounts receivable.

Investments should be made in areas requiring minimal expenditures, such as obtaining licenses for new developments.

Projects should be segregated into self-contained economic units so that success does not depend on the completion of the entire project. This enables the control of rising costs.

The firm should avoid expenditures in projects having long lead times since here inflationary cost increases are difficult to control. Joint ventures sometimes help in minimizing risks.

7. Accounting Ramifications. Also to be taken into account are tax aspects. Companies that depend on investments in property, plant, and equipment are in a poorer tax position than those relying on R&D expenditures. For fixed assets, depreciation is charged constantly each period and hence the reduction in tax comes ratably. The present value of future tax savings should be determined here. Firms with significant R&D outlays benefit from tax savings because of the full deductibility of such costs. Immediate cash flow is thus obtained.

In inflationary times, the firm should adopt the LIFO inventory method; lower taxable income occurs as current costs are being charged against current revenue.

417.2 / Weapons Against Inflation: A Checklist

- ☐ Selling Price Strategy
- ☐ Controlling Expenses
- ☐ Implementing Efficiencies in Operations
- ☐ Proper Marketing Strategy
- ☐ Improved Managerial Planning
- ☐ Automation
- ☐ Employee Communication
- ☐ Financial Planning and Control
- ☐ Optimally Managing Assets
- ☐ Providing Inflation-Adjusted Data
- ☐ Obtaining Tax Benefits

———— 418 / SUMMARY CHECKLIST OF KEY POINTS ————

418.1. The quality of earnings depends on the stability and growth trend of earnings as well as the predictability of factors that affect their future levels. It also depends on a company's financial and operating characteristics that have a bearing on its future growth.

418.2. Stable earnings are of higher quality than unstable earnings.

418.3. Earnings generated from recurring transactions related to the basic business of the company are of higher quality than those emanating from isolated transactions.

418.4. Nonrecurring operating gains and losses should be considered as part of the results of operations of the period.

418.5. Nonrecurring nonoperating gains and losses should be omitted from the analyst's evaluation of net income for a single year.

418.6. When companies have vacillating nonrecurring items included in net income, analysts should emphasize the average earnings over a period of years.

418.7. / Low Quality of Earnings Indicators Follow

1. One-Time Gains and Losses

What to Watch Out For

- ☐ Abnormal and erratic income statement elements
- ☐ Sale of low-cost basis assets
- ☐ Changes in demand for the company's products or services

What to Do

- ☐ Reduce net income for one-time gains to arrive at normal earnings.
- ☐ Increase net income for one-time losses to obtain normal earnings.
- ☐ Look at the trend in typical earnings over time.
- ☐ Determine the ratio of one-time gains and losses to net income and to sales.

2. Stable Earnings have been Intentionally Portrayed by Management Via Income Smoothing.

What to Watch Out For

- ☐ The company is known as an "income smoother."

- Management's compensation is significantly keyed into profits.
- The company uses *liberal* accounting policies.
- The firm is closely regulated or is under the public eye.
- The company is a monopoly.

What to Do

- Restate net income, showing what it would have been if income smoothing had not been practiced.

3. An Unstable Earnings Trend

What to Do

- Measure earnings stability over a period of years (e.g., 10 years) by the following methods: average reported earnings, average pessimistic earnings, standard deviation, coefficient of variation, instability index, and beta.

4. A Poor Growth Rate

What to Do

- Determine the implied growth rate.
- Determine the growth rates in EPS, dividends, sales, and total assets.

5. A Low Gross Profit Percentage

What to Watch Out For

- The company is not in control of its manufacturing costs.

6. High Operating Leverage Exists

What to Watch Out For

- High operating leverage coupled with highly elastic product demand
- A very capital-intensive industry (e.g., autos)
- A high break-even company

What to Do

- Determine the trend in fixed costs to total costs.
- Determine the trend in net income to fixed costs.

☐ Ascertain the percentage change in operating profit to the percentage change in sales volume.

☐ Determine the relationship between sales and the break-even point.

7. Earnings Arising from an Opportunist Market

What to Watch Out For

☐ The *saturation* of a company's market (e.g., calculators)

☐ Short-term schemes that bolster earnings temporarily (e.g., single government contract)

What to Do

☐ Determine the trend in the percentage of "short-lived" profit to total revenue and to net income.

☐ Eliminate one-shot boosts in earnings arising from short-term schemes.

8. Corporate Operations Are Susceptible to Sudden and Unexpected Developments.

What to Watch Out For

☐ The entity losing a special advantage—the exhaustion of oil deposits

9. Earnings are Affected by the Business Cycle

What to Watch Out For

☐ Cyclical and/or seasonal business

☐ Elastic product demand

☐ A *high unit cost* product line

☐ Nonexistence of adequate substitutes for more expensive goods

☐ A luxury product line of novelty and nonessential goods

☐ High-priced merchandise that does not appeal to a select market (Rolls Royce)

☐ Production of heavy goods and raw materials

10. Variances in the Components of the Product Line—Namely Volume, Price, and Cost

What to Watch Out For

☐ Unstably priced products (sugar)

What to Do

☐ Determine variances in selling price, cost, quantity, and sales mix by each major product line.

☐ Determine the standard deviation in selling price, cost, and volume.

☐ Chart movements by a graph of product line elements.

11. A Single Product Company

What to Watch Out For

☐ Obsolescence risk

☐ Product and/or customer concentration

12. Positively Correlated Products, or even no Correlation Products

What to Watch Out For

☐ Lack of diversification in the product line

What to Do

☐ Determine the degree of correlation between products by a computer-determined correlation matrix.

☐ Determine the elasticity of product demand by looking at the percentage change in quantity to the percentage change in price for each product.

13. A Significant Boost in Profits Arising from Extraordinary Product Demand Coupled with Skyrocketing Prices (Copper)

14. A Product Line Subject to Rapid Changes in Consumer Taste

What to Watch Out For

☐ "Gimmick" products (novelties)

15. A High Percentage of Developmental or Declining Products

16. Product Demand Is Vulnerable to External Factors

What to Watch Out For

☐ Major demand is derived from a few large industrial users.

☐ Export sales to a country that is developing its own capacity to manufacture the goods in question.

17. Variability in Raw Material Costs

What to Do

☐ Ascertain cost instability by reviewing trade publications.

18. Lack of Availability in Raw Materials

What to Watch Out For

☐ Manufacturing operations are directly tied into raw material sources.

☐ Substitute raw materials are very expensive.

19. Foreign Currency Gains and Losses Arising from Erratic Foreign Exchange Rates

What to Do

☐ Determine the variability in the exchange rates associated with the countries the firm is operating in.

☐ Determine the trend in the ratio of foreign exchange gains and losses to net income and to total revenue.

20. Litigation Against the Company that will have a Harmful Impact on Operations

What to Do

☐ Review estimated liability provisions and footnote disclosures.

21. Excessive Business Risk

What to Watch Out For

☐ The company is susceptible to numerous uncontrollable factors.

☐ Nature of corporate operations is risky, as in a retail land sale business.

☐ Dependency on a few "key" employees

☐ Dependency on a few unreliable suppliers as evidenced by previous delivery problems

☐ More than 10% of the company's revenue and/or earnings is derived from an industry, product line, foreign geographic area, single customer, and domestic government contract.

What to Do

☐ Examine the contingency, commitment, and business segment footnotes.

☐ Compare a company's risk exposure to other companies in the industry and to past trends of the company.

22. Political Risk

What to Watch Out For

☐ Foreign operations in politically and economically unstable foreign regions

☐ Stringent foreign customs and regulations

☐ Overreliance on government contracts and subsidies

☐ Excessive governmental regulation

☐ Current and proposed adverse tax legislation

What to Do

☐ Compute the following ratios: questionable foreign revenue to total revenue, questionable foreign earnings to net income, total export revenue to total revenue, total export earnings to net income, total assets in questionable foreign countries to total assets, and total assets in foreign countries to total assets.

☐ Appraise the current political attitude of legislators and the world situation.

☐ Determine the percentage of revenue and earnings derived from government contracts and subsidies as well as the extent to which such sources are recurring.

☐ Review present and proposed laws and regulations of governmental agencies by examining legislative hearings, trade journals, and newspapers.

☐ Determine if there are stringent environmental and safety regulations.

☐ Determine if the regulatory agency gives the company a hard time: does it take an excessively long time to obtain a rate increase and when obtained, is the increase substandard?

23. Social Risk

What to Watch Out For

☐ The company has a bad name.

☐ Prejudice cases against the firm

☐ Governmental forced rebates

☐ Corporate ownership is by controversial foreign parties.

What to Do

☐ Determine if there have been consumer boycotts and governmental intervention.

☐ Determine the potential liability emanating from a lawsuit against the company (prejudice suit).

24. Environmental Risk

What to Watch Out For

☐ Product lines and services are susceptible to changes in the weather, as in a recreation-oriented business.

☐ A geographic location that is effected by the whims of nature (floods)

25. Inadequate Insurance

What to Watch Out For

☐ High-risk product line in which product liability insurance coverage is nonexistent or exists at exorbitant rates

What to Do

☐ Determine the trend in the ratio of insurance expense to fixed assets.

☐ Determine the trend in the ratio of casualty losses to fixed assets.

☐ Determine if the company has been dropped by an insurance company.

☐ Determine if there have been unusual losses arising from damages because of inadequate insurance protection.

26. Poor Quality Management

What to Watch Out For

☐ Previous incidents of mismanagement of corporate affairs

☐ Overexaggerated and inaccurate expectations given in the annual report

☐ Management's inability to adjust to change

27. Discontented Work Force

What to Watch Out For

☐ Union militancy
☐ High employee turnover

What to Do

☐ Determine the number and duration of prior strikes.
☐ Check the expiration date of union contracts.

28. The Company is Part of an Unhealthy or Risky Industry.

What to Watch Out For

☐ Declining industry
☐ Highly technological industry
☐ Highly capital-intensive industry
☐ Industry that is highly dependent upon energy sources
☐ Highly competitive industry

29. Inflationary Profits Exist as Evidenced by the Fact that Reported Earnings Exceed Constant Dollar Net Income and/or Replacement Cost Net Income.

What to Watch Out For

☐ Capital-intensive company with old fixed assets
☐ Inventory profits

What to Do

☐ Compare the difference between (1) net income and constant dollar net income and (2) net income and current cost net income.
☐ Compute the following ratios: (1) constant dollar earnings to net income and (2) current cost earnings to net income.

30. Inability of the Company to Cope with Inflation

What to Watch Out For

☐ Inability to quickly adjust selling prices for increasing costs
☐ Fixed-fee contracts

☐ Inability to control costs

☐ A product line materially affected by inflation

☐ A high amount of net monetary assets (basically, cash and receivables less liabilities)

☐ A high percentage of monetary assets to monetary liabilities

☐ Dividends paid out that exceed inflation-adjusted earnings

☐ Poor management of assets

☐ Projects with long payback periods

☐ FIFO inventory method

How to Do It

☐ Determine the ratio of monetary assets to monetary liabilities.

☐ Determine the difference between dividend payments and constant dollar net income or replacement cost net income.

31. Complexity of Operations—the Increased Difficulty of Analysis (e.g., Conglomerate)

418.8 / High Quality of Earnings Indicators

1. Nonoperating Income that Shows Stability

What to Do

☐ Determine if nonoperating income shows more stability than sales over a long time period (e.g., five years).

☐ Determine the recurrence associated with other income sources such as royalty income, franchise income, rental income, interest income, and dividend income.

2. Original Sale Leads to Subsequent Revenue.

What to Watch Out For

☐ A company that furnishes maintenance services and replacement parts to customers

What to Do

☐ Determine the trend in a firm's replacement and maintenance revenue as a percent of (a) new sales, (b) total revenue, and (c) net income.

3. A "Piggy-Back" Product Line

What to Watch Out For

☐ New, similar products can be produced easily from the company's basic manufacturing operation.

☐ High rate of patented products being developed.

☐ New products that generate supplementary demand rather than eating into existing product lines.

4. Sales Made to Diversified Industries—Industries Affected in Different Ways by Cyclical Factors

5. Geographic Diversification

6. Vertical Integration that Reduces the Price and Supply Risk of Raw Materials

CHAPTER FIVE

How to Determine if a Business Is Going Bankrupt

The ability of a company to meet its impending obligations has important effects upon the availability of further financing as well as on the costs associated with incremental financing. A key consideration in liquidity analysis is the funds flow status of the entity, which may be evaluated through the use of various ratios. Also to be considered is the nature of the firm's assets and liabilities.

The entity's financial ability to meet its long-term commitments is essential to consider because the long-run viability of the entity is dependent upon this. Various measures can be utilized in evaluating the solvency of a business. Further, besides looking at the reported figures in the financial statements, it is of utmost importance that attention be paid to off-balance sheet assets and liabilities.

The Statement of Cash Flows is revealing in terms of the entity's investing, financing, and operating activities.

Any warning signs that it is not a going concern must be recognized so that appropriate corrective action may be taken.

501 / SHORT-TERM DEBT-PAYING ABILITY

The short-term debt-paying ability of a firm involves its capability to convert noncash assets into cash or to obtain cash to satisfy impending obligations. Involved in such analysis are the stock and flow of liquid resources. The stock is the amount of the liquid asset base. The flow is the difference between expected cash inflows and outflows. Also important to consider is the timing of such future cash flows.

Liquidity is impacted by numerous financial attributes, including the ability to continually obtain financing from prior sources and the ability to postpone cash payments. The mixture of current assets and current liabilities is also relevant. A further consideration is the "nearness to cash" of assets and liabilities.

501.1 / Seasonality

When analyzing a seasonal business, analysts may find that year-end financial data are not representative. Hence, averages based upon quarterly or monthly information should be used to level out seasonality effects.

With regard to a company's seasonal financing needs, short-term credit should be used to satisfy short-term cash deficiencies. Seasonal businesses must also have readily available lines of credit.

501.2 / Cash

In evaluating cash adequacy, we must determine the following "hard" cash amounts:

1. Cash flow generated from operations. This is equal to net income plus expenses and charges that did not involve the payment of cash (depreciation, amortization expense, loss on sale of fixed assets) less revenues and reductions of expenses that did not involve the receipt of cash (amortization of deferred revenue, amortization of bond premium, gain on sale of fixed assets).
2. Cash flow generated from operations before interest expense
3. Cash flow generated from operations less cash payments required to pay debt principal, dividends, and capital expenditures
4. The amount of internally generated cash having restrictions against it that might limit the company's ability to meet its impending obligations

Illustration _____

Company A provides the following data for the year ended December 31, 19X1:

Net income	$800,000
Depreciation expense	25,000

Amortization expense	10,000
Interest expense (paid in cash)	130,000
Amortization of bond premium	8,000
Gain on sale of land	12,000
Payments on debt principal	320,000
Dividends	85,000
Capital expenditures	400,000

The cash flow provided from operations is:

Net income	$800,000
Adjustments:	
Depreciation expense	25,000
Amortization expense	10,000
Amortization of bond premium	(8,000)
Gain on sale of land	(12,000)
Cash flow provided from operations	$815,000

The cash flow provided from operations before interest expense is $945,000 ($815,000 + $130,000). This indicates that adequate cash flow from operations is available to meet interest costs.

Cash flow provided from operations less cash payments required for debt principal, dividends, and capital expenditures is:

Cash flow provided from operations		$815,000
Less:		
Debt principal payments	$320,000	
Dividends	85,000	
Capital expenditures	400,000	805,000
Residual cash provided from operations available for other purposes		$ 10,000

As can be seen, not much cash is left over from operations after taking the above cash requirements into account.

The analyst should examine the trend in the ratio of sales to cash. A high turnover rate points to cash inadequacy and may lead to financial problems if further financing is not available at reasonable rates. On the other hand, a low turnover rate implies "excess" cash, which of course has associated with it an opportunity cost. Reaching the optimum trade-off between return and liquidity risk should be the company's goal.

Illustration ——

Company B reports the following data:

	19X1	19X2
Cash	$ 500,000	$ 400,000
Sales	8,000,000	9,000,000
Industry norm for cash turnover rate	15.8	16.2

The turnover of cash is 16 ($8,000,000/$500,000) in 19X1 and 22.5 ($9,000,000/$400,000) in 19X2. It is clear that company B has a cash deficiency in 19X2, which implies a possible liquidity problem.

——

The analyst should distinguish between two types of cash—that required for operating purposes and that needed for capital expenditures. While the former must be paid, the latter is postponable.

501.3 / Indicators of Cash Adequacy: A Checklist

☐ Current balance of cash

☐ Amount and timing of expected cash inflows and cash outflows

☐ Ability to postpone cash payments

☐ Ability to obtain financing

☐ "Nearness to cash" of assets and liabilities

☐ Cash flow generated from operations

☐ Cash flow generated from operations before interest charges

☐ Cash flow generated from operations less cash payments for debt principal, dividends, and capital expenditures

☐ Trend in the ratio of sales to cash

☐ Restrictions placed upon cash

501.4 / Short-Term Liabilities

The analyst should look at the trends in current liabilities to (1) total liabilities, (2) stockholders' equity, and (3) sales. Significantly increasing trends may be indicative of a liquidity problem. Creditors look unfavorably upon a company's credit standing if it must resort to material stretching of short-term payables.

In evaluating current liabilities, a determination should be made whether they are "patient" or "pressing." A supplier having a long relationship with, or dependence upon, the company will be "patient." In times of corporate financial difficulty, the supplier may postpone or even modify the amount of the debt. "Pressing" obligations are taxes and loans payable. These must be paid without excuse. In fact, a loan agreement may stipulate that the principal of the loan shall be forthcoming if an installment payment is not made. The analyst should determine the trend in the relationship of "pressing" liabilities to "patient" liabilities. An increasing trend reflects greater liquidity risk.

Also, a differentiation should be made between spontaneous and negotiated financing sources. Spontaneous sources emanate from typical operating activities. They are essentially interest-free funds and in consequence should be used to their maximum. Included here are accounts payable and accrued expenses. Obligations when due are in essence replaced with new ones. Hence, spontaneous debt should not be taken into account in predicting future cash requirements unless there exists a decline in sales or a change in the entity's usual activities. Negotiated sources emanate from periodic agreements with creditors such as bankers and finance companies. They also include money market securities like commercial paper. Such sources must be considered in forecasting future cash flows. Refinancing does not occur automatically but rather requires new credit evaluation. In consequence, financing risk exists.

Illustration _____

Company C reports the following data:

	19X1	19X2
Current Liabilities		
Accounts payable	$ 30,000	$ 26,000
Short-term loans payable	50,000	80,000
Commercial paper	40,000	60,000
Total current liabilities	$ 120,000	$ 166,000
Total noncurrent liabilities	300,000	302,000
Total liabilities	$ 420,000	$ 468,000
Sales	$1,000,000	$1,030,000
Relevant ratios follow:		
Current liabilities to total liabilities	28.6%	35.5%
Current liabilities to sales	12.0%	16.1%
"Pressing" current liabilities to "patient" current liabilities (short-term loans payable plus commercial paper/accounts payable)	3.0	5.4

Company C has greater liquidity risk in 19X2 as indicated by the higher ratios of current liabilities to total liabilities, current liabilities to sales, and "pressing" current liabilities to "patient" current liabilities.

A low ratio of sales to accounts payable indicates a company's ability to obtain short-term credit in the form of cost-free funds to finance sales growth.

A company may attempt to hide a short-term liability under long-term liabilities. For example, instead of taking out a 12 month loan a company may take out a 13 month loan under a line of credit agreement.

A seasonal business that is a net borrower should use more long-term financing as a precautionary measure. Also, a company with financial troubles should have debts mature during its peak season rather than in the trough.

501.5 / Increasing Trends in Ratios That Point to Greater Liquidity Risk: A Checklist

☐ Current liabilities to total liabilities

☐ Current liabilities to stockholders' equity

☐ Current liabilities to sales

☐ "Pressing" liabilities to "patient" liabilities

☐ Negotiated financing sources to spontaneous financing sources

501.6 / Ability to Modify Financial Policies

The ability to alter financial policies relates to actions that an entity may take to change the amount and timing of future cash flows in order to adjust to sudden problems or attractive opportunities. Cash flow may be improved through financing, selling assets, and altering operations.

In evaluating a firm's financial flexibility, the analyst should consider the nearness to cash of assets, the ability to obtain further financing, the degree of nonoperating assets, and the ability to alter operating and investing activities.

Financial flexibility is enhanced when projects have short payback periods, as a higher return can be earned on improved cash flow. Also, since time intervals are short, the entity is more equipped to adjust to changes in the environment.

A company should incur debt when the return earned on borrowed funds exceeds the after-tax cost of that debt. This assumes that the incurrence of such obligations does not severely impair corporate liquidity.

It should be noted, however, that too much financial flexibility may lower a company's rate of return. For example, holding cash improves liquidity but lowers return. Having open lines of credit assures that funds will be available when needed but involves a cost. Ascertaining the optimum level of financial flexibility involves a trade-off between risk and return.

501.7 / Considerations in Evaluating an Entity's Financial Flexibility: A Checklist

☐ Closeness to cash of assets

☐ Disposability of assets

☐ Open lines of credit

☐ Payback period on projects

☐ Ability to adjust quickly to changes in business conditions

501.8 / Analysis of Funds Flow

Numerous measures exist to evaluate a company's funds flow position, including the following ratios:

1. The commonly known current ratio (current assets/current liabilities) and quick ratio (cash plus marketable securities plus accounts receivable/current liabilities). High ratios are needed when a company has difficulty borrowing on short notice. A limitation of these ratios is that they may rise just prior to financial distress because of a company's desire to improve its cash position by, for example, selling fixed assets. Such dispositions have a detrimental effect upon productive capacity. A limitation peculiar to the current ratio is that it will be excessively high when inventory is carried on a LIFO basis. NOTE: Current assets that are pledged to secure long-term liabilities are not available to meet current debt. If these current assets are included in the calculation of the current and quick ratios, a distortion results.

2. The commonly known age and turnover rates for receivables and inventory. (These were discussed in Chapter 2.)

3. Working capital. The analysis of working capital is important to creditors since working capital is the liquid reserve available to satisfy contingencies and uncertainties. A high working capital balance is mandated if the entity is unable to borrow on short notice.

Working capital must be related to other financial statement elements, such as sales and total assets. Working capital to sales, for example, tells whether the entity is optimally using its liquid balance.

To spot changes in the composition of working capital, the analyst should determine the trend in the percentage of each current asset to total current assets. A shift from cash to inventory, for instance, implies less liquidity.

4. Sales to current assets. A high turnover rate may point to deficient working capital. Perhaps current liabilities will become due before inventories and receivables turn to cash. A low turnover implies excessive current assets

5. Sales to working capital. A high ratio indicates the ability to generate revenue from liquid funds.

6. Working capital provided from operations to net income. Liquidity is deemed better when earnings are backed up by liquid funds.

7. Working capital provided from operations to total liabilities. This indicates the degree to which internally generated working capital flow is available to satisfy obligations.

8. Cash plus marketable securities to current liabilities. This indicates the immediate amount of cash available to satisfy short-term debt.

9. Cost of sales, operating expenses, and taxes to average total current assets. The analyst should look at the trend in this ratio in analyzing the adequacy of current assets to satisfy ongoing business-related expenses.

10. Quick assets to year's cash expenses. This reveals the days of expenses that highly liquid assets could support.

11. Sales to short-term trade liabilities. This tells whether the entity can partially finance via cost-free funds. If trade credit declines, that means that creditors have less faith in the entity's financial strength.

12. Net profit to sales (profit margin). This indicates the profitability generated from revenue and hence is an important measure of operating performance. It also provides clues to a company's pricing, cost structure, and production efficiency. If the ratio drops, loan repayment difficulty may be indicated because declining profitability spells financial distress.

13. The ratios of fixed assets to short-term debt and short-term debt to long-term debt can indicate dangerous financial policies. If an entity finances long-term assets with short-term obligations, it may have a problem meeting the debt when due because the return and proceeds from the fixed assets will not be realized prior to the maturity dates of the current obligations. The company will be particularly vulnerable in a money-market squeeze. A recent example of this was New York City when it was unable to satisfy its short-term obligations.

14. Accounts payable to average daily purchases. This reveals the number of days it takes for the entity to pay creditors.

15. Accounts payable payment period (in days). This equals 365 divided by the accounts payable turnover. (The accounts payable turnover equals the purchases divided by accounts payable.) A decline in the payment period may indicate the company is taking advantage of prompt payment discounts, or has used the shorter purchase terms as leverage in negotiating with suppliers in order to lower the purchase price. However, an extension of the payment terms may infer the company is having financial problems. Perhaps that is why the firm is stretching its payables. Alternatively, the lengthening of the payment terms may mean the business is properly managing its payables. By delaying payments to creditors, it is taking greater advantage of interest-free financing

16. Current liabilities to total liabilities. A high ratio means less corporate liquidity since there is a greater proportion of current debt.

17. The difference between accounts receivable plus inventory and accounts payable plus accrued expenses payable. Some banks look at this figure as a major indicator of a company's liquid position since it deals with major current accounts.

18. Liquidity index. This indicates the number of days during which current assets are removed from cash. It is computed in the following manner:

	Amount	×	Days Away from Cash	=	Total
Cash	$20,000	×	—		—
Accounts receivable	50,000	×	30		$1,500,000
Inventory	80,000	×	50		4,000,000
	$150,000				$5,500,000

$$\text{Index} = \frac{\$5,500,000}{\$\ 150,000}$$
$$= \ 36.7 \text{ days}$$

Illustration

Company D provides the following financial data:

Current assets	$ 400,000
Fixed assets	800,000
Current liabilities	500,000
Noncurrent liabilities	600,000
Sales	5,000,000
Working capital provided from operations	100,000

Assume the following industry norms:

Fixed assets to current liabilities	4.0×
Current liabilities to noncurrent liabilities	45.0%
Sales to current assets	8.3×
Working capital provided from operations to total liabilities	30.5%

Company D's ratios are:

Fixed assets to current liabilities	1.6×
Current liabilities to noncurrent liabilities	83.3%
Sales to current assets	12.5×
Working capital provided from operations to total liabilities	9 1%

Company D's liquidity ratios are all unfavorable relative to industry norms. There is a high level of current debt as well as deficiency in current assets. Further, working capital generated from operations to meet total debt is insufficient.

The failure to take cash discounts raises a question as to management's financial astuteness since this involves a very high opportunity cost.

Illustration

Company E purchased merchandise for $100,000 on terms of 3/10, net/40. It failed to take the discount by waiting till the 40th day to pay. The opportunity cost involved is:

$$\frac{\text{Discount foregone}}{\text{Proceeds use of}} \times \frac{360}{\text{Days delayed}}$$

$$\frac{\$3,000}{\$97,000} \times \frac{360}{30} = \frac{37.1\%}{}$$

The company would have been better off financially paying within the discount period by taking out a loan (the interest rate would be much less than 37.1%).

501.9 / Characteristics of Assets

A company that can sell given assets without negatively impacting the profitability of other assets has a financial advantage. This is particularly true when a company's assets are not excessively interdependent. For example, the disposition of a marketable security will not adversely affect the value of other securities. Also, a diversified company may be able to dispose of a group of assets (even a whole segment) without adversely impacting the business. On the other hand, certain assets may be so interrelated that the sale of one of them will materially effect others, as in the disposition of a machine on the assembly line. It should also be mentioned that a significant sale of assets without replacement may point to a distress situation.

Also of interest are the price characteristics of assets that largely depend upon their marketability. For example, sharp variability in price (e.g., book value exceeding market value) may inhibit management from selling assets at a time of financial difficulty because of the ensuing loss. Further, greater risk exists with long-term assets (equipment) than short-term assets (inventory) because the former are more difficult to dispose of.

The analyst should be assured that none of the current assets are used to secure any of the long-term debt or contingent liabilities as pledges or guarantees.

Even though current assets are about the same or slightly above current liabilities, the company may still experience liquidity difficulties if the maturity schedule of the liabilities is ahead of the expected cash realization of the assets. For example, the payment schedule of the debts may be concentrated towards the beginning of the year but the cash realization of the assets may be evenly disbursed throughout the year. If this occurs, the company may be forced to discount its receivables or quickly liquidate inventory at lower prices. Although this will generate immediate cash, it dilutes the realizable value of the current assets. In effect, the actual value of the assets becomes less than the fair value of the liabilities.

501.10 / Consolidated Financial Statements

As we all know, a consolidated statement shows the parent and subsidiaries as a single unit. However, individual entities within the group may have to be considered in liquidity evaluation. For instance, creditor rights apply to each entity, not the consolidated group.

It is conceivable that a particular subsidiary may have more cash than is needed while another has sizable liabilities and legal restrictions (restrictive covenants in debt agreements, currency restrictions). The restrictions may be with regard to the transfer of funds between subsidiaries.

Consolidated statements may lead to erroneous conclusions since the urgent liabilities may be the parent's, but the liquid assets may be the subsidiary's, and such assets may be unavailable for the parent's use.

501.11 / Availability and Cost of Financing

A company's availability and cost of financing is affected by external constraints (monetary policy) and internal constraints (relationship with bankers). Availability of funds is needed for a firm to grow. Analysts should ascertain any restrictions on the company's borrowing ability such as breaches in loan provisions, and should assess the company's ability to obtain financing at reasonable interest rates. Further, anticipated money-market trends should be looked into.

The analyst should take into account the mixture of commercial paper and short-term bank debt. These sources are of lower cost than others and can generally be issued only by creditworthy companies.

The analyst should closely evaluate the debt footnote. An increase in compensating balances and the effective interest rate relative to competition means that banks are looking more unfavorably upon the company. The firm may now be more susceptible to tight money-market conditions. It may also have to look to higher-cost financing means (finance companies rather than banks). Also disclosed is the weighted average debt outstanding for the year. A company may clean up its debt posture at year-end in order to improve the debt/equity ratio. However, such maneuvers are revealed if the weighted average debt for the year materially exceeds the year-end balance.

Attention should be given to loan acceleration clauses. Failure to meet a current installment may cause the loan principal to become immediately due. Hence, the analyst should note the existing terms of debt vs. the firm's actual financial status to ascertain the degree to which the current position exceeds the compliance requirement.

The analyst should consider any disclosure regarding the collateral pledged for loans. Usually, the book and market values are indicated. When the value of the property falls below the principal of the loan, additional security will probably have to be given.

501.12 / Considerations in Evaluating the Entity's Financing Position: A Checklist

☐ Effect of external and internal constraints upon the company
☐ Unused lines of credit
☐ Commercial paper issued
☐ Amount of compensating balances
☐ Change in the effective interest rate
☐ Weighted average debt during the year
☐ Restrictions in loan agreements
☐ Loan acceleration provisions
☐ Compliance requirements of loans to company's current position
☐ Collateral pledged for the loan relative to the loan's principal

———— 502 / LONG-TERM DEBT-PAYING ABILITY ————

The long-term debt-paying ability of the firm looks at whether the entity can satisfy long-term principal and interest payments. Solvency analysis moves from cash flow to long-term funds flow evaluation. It highlights the long-term funds that are forthcoming to satisfy noncurrent debt. Also considered is the long-term financial and operating structure of the entity. Concern is with the magnitude of noncurrent liabilities in the capital structure as well as the realization risk in noncurrent assets. When debt is excessive, additional financing perhaps should be obtained from equity sources. Further, solvency depends upon corporate earning power because a company will not be able to meet its obligations unless it is making money.

Auditors are much concerned with solvency because it relates to an entity's ability to operate effectively and profitably. The going-concern assumption relies on the premise of a solvent business. Creditors are also concerned with the concept because they want to get paid back. Investors look to solvency since it affects share price.

502.1 / Measures of Long-Term Debt-Paying Ability

When practical, it is better to use the market value of assets rather than book value in ratio computations because it is more representative of true worth. Also, consideration should be given to undisclosed asset values, such as those applicable to timberlands and natural resource deposits.

Ratios of long-term debt-paying ability should of course be looked at over time and compared to industry norms. Some useful ratios follow:

1. Long-term debt to stockholder's equity (commonly called financial leverage). High leverage has a riskiness implication because it may be difficult for the firm to satisfy interest and principal payments as well as obtain further reasonable financing. The problem is especially acute in the case of companies with cash problems, particularly when adverse business conditions exist. Also, excessive debt will result in less financial flexibility since the company will have greater difficulty obtaining funds during a tight money market. Also, high fixed interest charges cause earnings instability.

The usefulness of the ratio is enhanced if securities are valued at their year-end market value rather than book value. When year-end values are unrepresentative, average market prices can be used.

It should be noted that a favorable leverage situation occurs when the return on borrowed funds exceeds the interest cost, provided that the firm is not in debt over its head. A desirable debt/equity ratio depends on many variables including the rates of other companies in the industry, the access for further debt financing, and the stability of earnings.

2. Cash flow to long-term debt. This appraises the adequacy of available funds to meet noncurrent obligations.

3. Net income before taxes and interest to interest. This reflects the number of times interest expense is covered. It reveals the magnitude of the decline in income that a firm can tolerate.

An even better ratio is the cash flow generated from operations plus interest to interest since it indicates the cash actually there to meet interest charges. It is cash and not net income that is used to pay interest.

4. Net income before taxes and fixed charges to fixed charges. This ratio is useful in gauging a company's ability to satisfy its fixed costs. A low ratio indicates risk because when business activity falls, the firm may be unable to satisfy its fixed charges.

A better measure is the ratio of cash flow provided from operations plus fixed charges to fixed charges since cash is what is used to meet fixed charges.

In looking at these ratios for a given company it should be determined whether that entity has stability in both operations and funds flow. Such stability affords more confidence in the firm's ability to meet its fixed charges.

5. Noncurrent assets to noncurrent liabilities. Long-term debt will eventually be paid out of long-term assets and hence a high ratio indicates protection for long-term creditors.

6. Retained earnings to total assets. By looking at the trend in this ratio one can see the entity's profitability over the years.

7. J. Wilcox's gambler's ruin prediction formula.[1] This is used to obtain a company's liquidation value and is thus useful in solvency evaluation. The liquidation value equals cash and marketable securities at market value plus inventory, accounts receivable, and prepaid expenses at 70% of the reported amount plus other assets at 50% of the carrying amount less current liabilities and long-term debt.

Illustration _____

Partial balance sheet and income statement data for company F follows:

Long-term assets	$700,000
Long-term liabilities	500,000
Stockholder's equity	300,000
Net income before tax	80,000
Cash flow provided from operations	100,000
Interest expense	20,000

Average norms taken from competitors:

Long-term assets to long-term liabilities	2.0
Long-term debt to stockholders' equity	.8
Cash flow to long-term liabilities	.3
Net income before tax plus interest to interest	7.0

Company F's ratios are:

Long-term assets to long-term liabilities	1.4
Long-term debt to stockholders' equity	1.67
Cash flow to long-term liabilities	.2
Net income before tax plus interest to interest	5.0

_____

[1] "How to Figure Who's Going Bankrupt," *Dun's Review*, (New York: Dun and Bradstreet, October 1975) and J. Wilcox, "A Gambler's Ruin Prediction of Business Failure Using Accounting Data," *Sloan Management Review*, (Spring 1971).

After comparing Company F's ratios with the industry norms, it is clear that the firm's solvency is worse than its competitors' because of the greater extent of long-term liabilities in the capital structure and lower interest coverage ratio.

502.2 / Off-Balance Sheet Assets

Important in solvency analysis is recognizing the existence of unrecorded assets. These are items that either represent resources of the entity or are expected to have future economic benefit. They are positive attributes of financial position even though they are not shown on the balance sheet. Of course, a going concern is assumed here, as in a distress situation unrecorded assets would generally not be realizable. Unrecorded assets include:

1. Tax loss carryforward benefit
2. Purchase commitment where the firm has a contract to purchase an item at a price significantly less than the going rate
3. Anticipated rebates
4. A contingent asset, as when the entity may receive a payment if a certain event occurs

  • An example is a lessor who will receive incremental rental payments if the lessee's sales go above a specified amount.

  • P Company discloses: "The corporation may receive an additional payment not to exceed $321,574, contingent upon the sum of the net income of M Corporation for the years 19X5 and 19X6. No recognition has been given to this contingent payment."

5. Research and development
6. Internally developed goodwill
7. Fully depreciated fixed asset

502.3 / Evaluating Noncurrent Liabilities

The deferred tax credit account requires careful analysis. The analyst should determine the expected time period for the tax postponement by looking at planned capital expenditures. Deferred taxes relating to depreciation may never become due in the case where fixed assets are continually acquired. In this case, the account is in essence a source of long-term funds. However, in the case where the deferred credit will reverse, it is a legitimate long-term liability. The analyst may wish to formulate an earnings forecast to estimate possible higher future tax payments.

  When evaluating estimated liability accounts, one should consider the nature of their source as well as the adequacy of their amounts. For example, estimated liabilities for lawsuits can eventually require significant payments.

Preferred stock having a maturity date or subject to sinking fund requirements is more in the nature of debt than equity.

Some reported liabilities may not really be so like convertible bonds that possess attractive conversion features.

Unearned revenue is reported as a liability but will not require future payment in dollars. It is payable in future services.

502.4 / Off-Balance Sheet Liabilities

Off-balance sheet liabilities are those not reported in the body of the financial statements but possibly necessitating future payments or services. They include:

1. Excess of projected benefit obligation over the accumulated benefit obligation
2. Noncapitalized lease commitments
3. Litigation
4. Postretirement benefits including those for health care
5. A sales commitment where the locked-in sales price is significantly less than the current price
6. Renegotiation of claims under a government contract
7. Guarantees of future performance
8. Cosigning of a loan
9. Debt of an unconsolidated finance subsidiary

• Assume a finance subsidiary borrows money from a bank and the loan is guaranteed by the parent. The finance subsidiary then buys receivables from the parent. The parent now has the newly borrowed cash and the receivables have been shifted between the companies, but the debt will not be shown on the consolidated balance sheet.

10. Sale of receivables without recourse

• Receivables may be sold to a bank with or without recourse. If the arrangement is without recourse and the receivables become uncollectible, the bank will not be able to get reimbursed from the seller. Such sales are not reflected on the balance sheet as potential liabilities. But sales with recourse are shown as such. Hence, if it is desired not to report the potential liability, the company will most likely pay the bank a premium to design the arrangement as one without recourse.

11. Debt arising from a joint venture

• When a company has an interest between 20% and 50% in a joint venture, it reports its proportionate share of the earnings but no debt.
• If $500,000 is paid for a 50% interest in a plant and another $10,000,000 is borrowed for the plant, which is guaranteed by the joint venture, under the equity method the company reports only the $500,000 as an investment. The debt is not consolidated.

Useful disclosure of long-term obligations is provided by FASB 47. The analyst should review commitments relating to unconditional purchase obligations and future payments on long-term debt and redeemable stock.

FASB Interpretation 34 requires disclosure of indirect guarantees of indebtedness. Included therein are contracts in which a firm promises to advance funds to another if financial difficulties arise, as when sales fall below a stipulated level.

According to FASB 105, a company must disclose the extent, nature, and terms of financial instruments with off-balance sheet risk (credit or market risk) of accounting loss. Examples of financial instruments include loan commitments, futures or forward contracts, put and call options written, letters of credit written, interest rate and foreign currency swaps, and financial guarantees written. The analyst must view negatively those situations in which the financial instrument has unrecorded risk of accounting loss when the actual loss may exceed the amount recognized as an asset, or when the ultimate obligation may exceed the amount recognized as a liability in the balance sheet.

___ 503 / APPRAISING THE STATEMENT OF CASH FLOWS ___

An analysis of the Statement of Cash Flows will provide analysts with vital information regarding the company's cash receipts and cash payments for a period as they relate to operating, investing, and financing activities. The Statement assists in the evaluation of the impact on the firm's financial position of cash and noncash investing and financing transactions.[2]

Comparative Statements of Cash Flows must be thoroughly appraised because they hold clues to a company's earnings quality, risk, and liquidity. They show the degree of repeatability of the company's sources of funds, their costs, and whether such sources may be relied upon in the future. Uses of funds for growth as well as for maintaining competitive

---

[2] J. Siegel, "A Financial Analysis and Evaluation of the Statement of Cash Flows," *Practical Accountant*, (June 1989), pp. 71–73.

share are revealed. An analysis of Comparative Statements of Cash Flows holds the key to a complete and reliable analysis of corporate financial health in the present and future. It aids in planning future ventures and financing needs. Comparative data help financial analysts identify abnormal or cyclical factors as well as changes in the relationship among each flow component.

The Statement serves as a basis to forecast earnings based on plant, property, and equipment posture. It assists in evaluating growth potential and incorporates cash flow requirements, highlighting specific fund sources and future means of payment. Will the company be able to meet its obligations and pay cash dividends?

The Statement reveals the type and degree of financing required to expand long-term assets and to bolster operations.

The financial person should calculate for analytical purposes cash flow per share equal to net cash flow divided by the number of shares. A high ratio is desirable because it indicates the company is in a very liquid position.

We now discuss the analysis of the operating, investing, and financing sections of the Statement of Cash Flows.

503.1 / Operating Section

An analysis of the operating section of the Statement of Cash Flows enables the analyst to determine the adequacy of cash flow from operating activities to satisfy company requirements. Can the firm obtain positive future net cash flows? The reconciliation tracing net income to net cash flow from operating activities should be examined to see the effect of noncash revenue and noncash expense items.

An award under a lawsuit is a cash inflow from operating activities that results in a nonrecurring source of revenue.

An operating cash outlay for refunds given to customers for deficient goods indicates a quality problem with the firm's merchandise.

Payments of penalties, fines, and lawsuit damages are operating cash outflows, which show poor management in that a problem arose which required a nonbeneficial expenditure to the organization.

503.2 / Investing Section

An analysis of the Investing Section of the Statement of Cash Flows enables identification of an investment in another company that may point to an attempt at eventual control for diversification purposes. It may also indicate a change in future direction or change in business philosophy.

An increase in fixed assets indicates capital expansion and future growth. An analysis should be made as to which assets have been purchased. Are they assets for risky (specialized) ventures or are they stable (multipurpose) ones? An indication exists as to risk potential and expected returns. The nature of the assets provides signs as to future direction and earning potential with regard to the introduction or reinforcement of product lines, business segments, etc. Are these directions sound and viable?

The analyst should ascertain whether there is a contraction in the business arising from the sale of fixed assets without adequate replacement. Is the problem corporate (e.g., product line is weakening) or industry-wide (e.g., industry is on the downturn)? If corporate, management is not optimistic regarding the future. Nonrecurring gains may occur because of the sale of low-cost basis fixed assets (e.g., land). Such gains cause temporary increases in profits above normal levels and represent low quality of earnings sources. They should be discounted by the analyst.

503.3 / Financing Section

An evaluation of the Financing Section will provide the analyst with an opinion regarding the company's capability to obtain financing in the money and capital markets as well as its ability to meet its obligations. The financial mixture comprising bonds, long-term loans from banks, and equity instruments affect the cost of financing. One major advantage of debt is the tax deductibility of interest while dividends are not deductible. Further, during inflation, paying back debt will result in purchasing power gains since the payback is made in cheaper dollars. However, there is greater risk associated with debt financing in that the company must have adequate funds to pay interest and retire the obligation at maturity. If funds are insufficient higher interest sources may have to be used (e.g., factors). The stability of the fund source must be appraised to determine if it may be relied upon continuously, even during tight money markets. Otherwise, potential difficulties in maintaining corporate operations during recessionary periods exist. The question is: Where can the company go for funds during times of cash squeezes?

By evaluating the financing sources, the financing preferences of management are revealed. Is there an inclination toward risk or safety? Creditors would prefer to see equity issuances as protection of their loans. Excessive debt may be a problem during economic downturn.

The ability of a company to finance with the issuance of common stock on attractive terms (high stock price) indicates that the investing public is optimistic about the financial well-being of the entity.

The issuance of preferred stock may be a negative sign since it may mean the company has difficulty issuing common stock.

An appraisal should be made of the company's ability to satisfy debt. If debt is excessive, it points to greater corporate risk. The problem is acute if earnings are unstable or declining. On the other hand, the reduction in long-term debt is favorable because it points to less risk associated with the firm.

A financing cash outflow for the early extinguishment of debt will result in an extraordinary gain or loss resulting in a one-time effect upon earnings.

The analyst should evaluate the firm's dividend paying ability. Stockholders favor a company that has a high dividend payout.

Is there a purchase of treasury stock resulting in an artificial increase in earnings per share?

503.4 / Schedule of Noncash Financing and Investing Activities

A bond conversion is a positive sign about the entity's financial health since it indicates that bondholders are optimistic about the company's financial health or that the market price of the common stock has risen. A conversion of preferred stock to common stock is also favorable because it shows preferred stockholders are positive on the company's future and are willing to have a lower priority in the event of corporate liquidation.

Note that bond and preferred stock conversions affect the existing position of long-term creditors and stockholders. For example, a reduction in debt by conversion to stock protects to a greater degree the loans of the remaining bondholders and banks.

503.5 / Conclusion

Current profitability is only one important factor for corporate success. Also essential are the current and future cash flows. In fact, a profitable company may have a cash crisis.

Management is responsible for planning how and when cash will be used and obtained. When planned expenditures necessitate more cash than planned activities are likely to produce, managers must decide what to do. They may decide to obtain debt or equity financing or to dispose of some fixed assets or a whole business segment. Alternatively, they may decide to cut back on planned activities by modifying operational plans, such as ending a special advertising campaign or delaying new acquisitions. Or, they may decide to revise planned payments to financing sources, such as delaying bond repayment or reducing dividends. Whatever is decided, the managers' goal is to balance, over both the short and the long term, the cash available and the needs for cash.

Managerial planning is aided when evaluating the Statement of Cash Flows in terms of coordinating dividend policy with other corporate activities, financial planning for new products and types of assets needed, strengthening a weak cash posture and credit availability, and ascertaining the feasibility and implementation of existing top management plans.

The analysis and evaluation of the Statement of Cash Flows is essential if the analyst is to properly appraise an entity's cash flows from operating, investing, and financing activities. The company's liquidity and sol-vency positions as well as future directions are revealed. Inadequacy in cash flow has possible serious implications since it may lead to declining profitability, greater financial risk, and even bankruptcy.

Illustration ———————————————————————

X Company provides the following financial statements:

X Company
Comparative Balance Sheets
December 31
(In Millions)

	19X8	19X9
ASSETS		
Cash	$ 47	$ 40
Accounts receivable	35	30
Prepaid expenses	2	4
Land	35	50
Building	80	100
Accumulated depreciation	(6)	(9)
Equipment	42	50
Accumulated depreciation	(7)	(11)
Total assets	$228	$254
LIABILITIES AND STOCKHOLDERS' EQUITY		
Accounts payable	$ 16	$ 20
Long-term notes payable	20	30
Common stock	100	100
Retained earnings	92	104
Total liabilities and stockholders' equity	$228	$254

X Company
Income Statement
For the Year Ended December 31, 19X9
(In Millions)

Revenue		$300
Operating expenses (excluding depreciation)	$200	
Depreciation	7	207
Income from operations		$ 93
Income tax expense		32
Net income		$ 61

Additional information:

1. Cash dividends paid: $49.
2. The company issued long-term notes payable for cash.
3. Land, building, and equipment were acquired for cash.

We can now prepare the Statement of Cash Flows under the *indirect method* as follows:

X Company
Statement of Cash Flows
For the Year Ended December 31, 19X9
(In Millions)

Cash flow from operating activities		
Net income		$ 61
Add (deduct) items not effecting cash		
Depreciation expense	$ 7	
Decrease in accounts receivable	5	
Increase in prepaid expenses	(2)	
Increase in accounts payable	4	14
Net cash flow from operating activities		$ 75
Cash flow from investing activities		
Purchase of land	($ 15)	
Purchase of building	(20)	
Purchase of equipment	(8)	(43)
Cash flow from financing activities		
Issuance of long-term notes payable	$ 10	
Payment of cash dividends	(49)	(39)
Net decrease in cash		$ 7

A financial analysis of the Statement of Cash Flows reveals that the profitability and operating cash flow of X Company improved. This indicates good earnings performance as well as the fact that earnings are backed up by cash. The decrease in accounts receivable may reveal better collection efforts. The increase in accounts payable is a sign that suppliers are confident in the company and willing to give interest-free financing. The acquisition of land, building, and equipment points to a growing business undertaking capital expansion. The issuance of long-term notes payable indicates that part of the financing of assets is through debt. Stockholders will be happy with the significant dividend payout of 80.3% (dividends divided by net income, or $49/$61). Overall, there was a decrease in cash of $7 but this should *not* cause alarm because of the company's profitability and the fact that cash was used for capital expansion and dividend payments. We recommend that the dividend payout be re-duced from its high level and the funds be reinvested in the profitable business. Also, the curtailment of dividends by more than $7 would result in a positive net cash flow for the year. Cash flow is needed for immediate liquidity needs.

Illustration

Y Company presents the following statement of cash flows.

Y Company
Statement of Cash Flows
For the Year Ended December 31, 19X8

Cash flows from operating activities		
Net income		$134,000
Add (deduct) items not effecting cash		
Depreciation expense	$ 21,000	
Decrease in accounts receivable	10,000	
Increase in prepaid expenses	(6,000)	
Increase in accounts payable	35,000	60,000
Net cash flow from operating activities		$194,000
Cash flows from investing activities		
Purchase of land	($70,000)	
Purchase of building	(200,000)	
Purchase of equipment	(68,000)	
Cash used by investing activities		(338,000)
Cash flows from financing activities		
Issuance of bonds	150,000	
Payment of cash dividends	(18,000)	
Cash provided by financing activities		132,000
Net decrease in cash		$ 12,000

An analysis of the Statement of Cash Flows reveals that the company is profitable. Also, cash flow from operating activities exceeds net income, which indicates good internal cash generation. The ratio of cash flow from operating activities to net income is a solid 1.45 ($194,000/$134,000). A high ratio is desirable because it shows that earnings are backed up by cash. The decline in accounts receivable could indicate better collection efforts. The increase in accounts payable shows the company can obtain interest-free financing. The company is definitely in the process of expand-ing for future growth as evidenced by the purchase of land, building, and equipment. The debt position of the company has increased indicating greater risk. The dividend payout was 13.4% ($18,000/$134,000). Stockholders look positively on a firm which pays dividends. The decrease in cash flow for the year of $12,000 is a negative sign.

———— 504 / INDICATORS THAT A FIRM IS NOT A GOING CONCERN ————

The analyst should note any warning signs that a firm may not be a going concern.

In a study done by W. Beaver,[3] it was found that bankruptcy could be predicted at least five years prior to such occurrence by looking at certain key ratios—the most important being cash flow to total debt, net income to total assets, and total debt to total assets. W. Beaver's cash flow ratio (net income plus depreciation divided by total debt) predicts bankruptcy within the next two years if the ratio is less than 1. In a later study,[4] he found that stock price changes forecast failure better than financial ratios.

E. Altman[5] formulated a mathematical model, termed the "Z-score," that is useful in predicting bankruptcy within the short run (one or two years). The "Z-score" equals:

$$\frac{\text{Working capital}}{\text{Total assets}} \times 1.2 + \frac{\text{Retained earnings}}{\text{Total assets}} \times 1.4$$

$$+ \frac{\text{Operating income}}{\text{Total assets}} \times 3.3$$

$$+ \frac{\text{Market value of common stock and preferred stock}}{\text{Total debt}} \times .6$$

$$+ \frac{\text{Sales}}{\text{Total assets}} \times 1.$$

His scoring chart follows:

Score	Probability of short-term illiquidity
1.80 or less	Very high
1.81 to 2.7	High
2.8 to 2.9	Possible
3.0 or higher	Not Likely

---

[3] W. Beaver, "Financial Ratios as Predictors of Failure," *Empirical Research in Accounting: Selected Studies, (1966)*, Supplement to Volume 4, *Journal of Accounting Research*, pp. 77–111.

[4] W. Beaver, "Market Prices, Financial Ratios, and the Prediction of Failure," *Journal of Accounting Research*, (Autumn 1968), pp. 179–92.

[5] E. Altman, "Financial Ratios, Discriminant Analysis and the Prediction of Corporate Bankruptcy," *The Journal of Finance*, (September 1978), pp. 589–609.

Analysts and creditors will of course find the score useful in predicting failure. The score is also important to management in indicating whether capital expansion and dividends should be curtailed to keep needed funds within the business.

Illustration ———————————————————————————————

Company H provides the following relevant data:

Working capital	$ 250,000
Total assets	900,000
Total liabilities	300,000
Retained earnings	200,000
Sales	1,000,000
Operating income	150,000
Common stock	
Book value	210,000
Market value	300,000
Preferred stock	
Book value	100,000
Market value	160,000

The "Z-score" is:

$$\frac{\$250,000}{\$900,000} \times 1.2 + \frac{\$200,000}{\$900,000} \times 1.4 + \frac{\$150,000}{\$900,000} \times 3.3 + \frac{\$460,000}{\$300,000} \times .6$$

$$+ \frac{\$1,000,000}{\$\ 900,000} \times 1 = .333 + .311 + .550 + .920 + 1.111 = \underline{3.225}$$

The score indicates that the probability of failure is unlikley.

H. Kennedy found the equity to debt and quick ratios meaningful indicators of future bankruptcy.[6]

Dun and Bradstreet came up with some important conclusions in a study undertaken in 1976.[7] Small companies had much higher rates of failure than large companies. Size can be measured by total assets and sales. Age is also a key factor. For example, 46.4% of the failures taking place in 1975 were from companies in existence four years or less. Further, it was found that failure rates were highest among furniture and apparel manufacturers as well as retailers.

---

[6] H. Kennedy, "A Behavioral Study of the Usefulness of Four Financial Ratios," *Journal of Accounting Research*, (Spring 1975), pp. 97–116.

[7] *The Business Failure Record*–1975, (New York: Dun and Bradstreet, 1976).

E. Altman, R. Haldeman, and P. Narayanan[8] uncovered the following measures as best for forecasting bankruptcy: operating income to total assets, earnings stability, times-interest-earned, retained earnings to total assets, current ratio, common equity to total capital, and total assets.

For a fee, ZETA Services will determine the possibility of business failure within 5 years through the use of their "secret" ZETA model.

504.1 / Measures to Be Used in Predicting Business Failure: A Checklist

☐ "Z-score"
☐ Cash flow to total debt
☐ Common stockholders' equity to total debt
☐ Net income to total assets
☐ Operating income to total assets
☐ Total debt to total assets
☐ Retained earnings to total assets
☐ Interest coverage
☐ Current ratio
☐ Quick ratio
☐ Stability in earnings
☐ Size
☐ Age
☐ Industry

———— 505 / HOW MANAGEMENT CAN AVOID BUSINESS FAILURE ————

There are many things management can do to protect itself against business failure including:

- Avoid excessive debt, staggering debt payments, and lengthening the maturity dates of debt.
- Note those loan restrictions that the company may end up violating. A comparison should be made between the current status and the compliance requirement to determine what "safety buffer" exists.
- Divest of unprofitable business segments as well as low return assets.

---

[8] E. Altman, R. Haldeman, and P. Narayanan, "ZETA Analysis: A New Model to Identify Bankruptcy Risk of Corporations," *Journal of Banking and Finance*, (1977), pp. 29–54.

- Anticipate future trends in the marketplace.
- Assure the adequacy of insurance coverage.
- Be careful about moving from a labor-intensive to capital-intensive business when the economic picture looks dismal.
- Make necessary expenditures for future growth, such as research and development and advertising.
- Avoid operations in risky foreign countries and where foreign currency rates widely fluctuate.
- Use the hedging approach to finance by matching the maturity dates of debt to the maturity dates of assets. In this way, the return on and proceeds from the asset will be adequate to meet the debt at maturity. In addition, negotiate futures contracts so that an item is contracted for at the current price regardless of what the price will be at the delivery date.
- Keep up-to-date with changes in technology.
- Restrict capital expansion during economic downturns.
- Diversify horizontally and vertically.
- Avoid moving into industries with past history of failure.
- Avoid long-term, fixed-fee contracts (if possible).
- Avoid poor management, such as overdependence on a "few" key executives, lack of communication, or a power hungry executive.
- Avoid markets on the downturn or those that are highly competitive.
- Lower prices on slow-moving items and raise them on heavy-demand items.
- Do not overextend financially or operationally. It is always dangerous to "go over one's head."
- Properly manage assets such as cash, receivables, and inventory for attractive returns while controlling risk.

———— 506 / SUMMARY CHECKLIST OF KEY POINTS ————

506.1 / Indicators of Poor Liquidity

1. Inability to Obtain Recurring Financing at Reasonable Interest Rates

What to Watch Out For

☐ No open lines of credit with banks

☐ High effective interest rate

What to Do

☐ Examine the debt footnote.

2. Inadequate Cash Available

What to Watch Out For

☐ Restrictions placed against corporate cash, such as compensating balances

What to Do

☐ Determine and analyze the following:
   a. Cash flow generated from operations.
   b. Cash flow generated from operations before interest expense.
   c. Cash flow generated from operations less cash payments needed to pay debt principal, dividends, and capital expenditures.
   d. Sales to cash.

3. Excessive Current Liabilities

What to Watch Out For

☐ Stretching short-term payables
☐ A high proportion of "pressing" liabilities compared to "patient" liabilities
☐ A high proportion of "negotiated" liabilities compared to "spontaneous" liabilities
☐ The weighted-average of debt for the year significantly exceeds the year-end debt balance

What to Do

☐ Compute and analyze the following ratios:
   a. Current liabilities to total liabilities
   b. Current liabilities to stockholders' equity
   c. Current liabilities to sales
☐ Identify and determine the trend in "pressing" liabilities to current liabilities.
☐ Compare the weighted-average of short-term debt for the year to the year-end balance. This disclosure is required under Accounting Series Release No. 148.

4. Inability to Adjust Financial Policies

What to Watch Out For

☐ Assets that are not "near" cash

☐ Inability to change operating and investing activities in times of financial stress

☐ Projects having long payback periods

5. Inadequate Funds Flow Position

What to Watch Out For

☐ Failure to take advantage of cash discounts

☐ Deficiency in internally generated funds

What to Do

☐ Compute and analyze the following ratios:

    a. Current ratio

    b. Quick ratio

    c. Age and turnover rates for receivables and inventory

    d. Working capital

    e. Working capital to sales and working capital to total assets

    f. Individual current asset to total current assets

    g. Sales to current assets

    h. Working capital provided from operations to net income

    i. Working capital provided from operations to total liabilities

    j. Cash plus marketable securities to current liabilities

    k. Cost of sales, operating expenses, and taxes to average total current assets

    l. Quick assets to year's cash expenses

    m. Sales to accounts payable

    n. Net income to sales

    o. Fixed assets to short-term liabilities

    p. Short-term liabilities to long-term liabilities

    q. Accounts payable to average daily purchases

    r. Liquidity index

6. Poor Profile of Assets

What to Watch Out For

☐ Interdependency of assets
☐ Sharp variability in price of assets
☐ Difficulty in disposing of assets

7. Unavailability and High Cost of Financing

What to Watch Out For

☐ Restrictions on firm's borrowing ability
☐ Breaches in loan agreements
☐ Loan acceleration clauses
☐ Collateral pledged for loans has values lower than the principal balances of the loans.

What to Do

☐ Review the debt footnote.
☐ Determine the degree of low-cost financing (commercial paper and bank debt) to high-cost financing (finance company loans).

506.2 / Indicators of Deficient Long-Term Debt-Paying Ability

1. The Market Values of Assets Are Less Than Their Book Values.

What to Do

☐ Use market values rather than book values for assets in ratio determination.

2. Poor Solvency

What to Do

☐ Compute and analyze the following ratios:
   a. Long-term liabilities to stockholders' equity
   b. Cash flow to long-term liabilities
   c. Net income before taxes and interest to interest
   d. Cash flow provided from operations plus interest to interest
   e. Net income before taxes and fixed charges to fixed charges

    f. Cash flow provided from operations plus fixed charges to fixed charges

    g. Noncurrent assets to noncurrent liabilities

    h. Retained earnings to total assets

    ☐ Use J. Wilcox's gambler's ruin prediction formula.

3. A Stockholders' Equity Account That Is More In the Nature of Debt

What to Watch Out For

☐ Preferred stock having a maturity date or subject to sinking fund requirements

4. Unrecorded Liabilities

What to Watch Out For

☐ Unfunded pension cost

☐ Noncapitalized leases

☐ Litigation

☐ A sales commitment with a contract price materially less than the current price

☐ Renegotiating a claim under a government contract

☐ Future guarantees

☐ Cosigning a loan

☐ Obligations of an unconsolidated finance subsidiary

☐ Selling receivables without recourse

☐ Debt emanating from a joint venture.

What to Do

☐ Review the pension, lease, contingency, debt, receivable, and merger footnotes.

506.3 / Indicators of Good Long-Term Debt-Paying Ability

1. Off-Balance Sheet Assets

What to Watch Out For

☐ Tax loss carryforward benefit

☐ Purchase commitment where the contract price is less than the current price

☐ Expected rebates

☐ Contingent assets

☐ Research and development

2. Noncurrent Liabilities That Do Not Require Future Cash Payment

What to Watch Out For

☐ Deferred tax credit account applying to an item that may never reverse (e.g., temporary difference due to depreciation when fixed assets will be continually acquired)

☐ Unearned revenue

☐ Convertible bonds having a lucrative conversion feature

What to Do

☐ Review the tax footnote.

506.4 / Warning Signs Revealed in the Statement of Cash Flows

1. Low Quality of Earnings Elements

What to Watch Out For

☐ Nonrecurring gain on the sale of a low-cost basis fixed asset

☐ Extraordinary gain on the early extinguishment of debt

☐ Sizable increase in deferred charges

☐ Low ratio of cash provided from operations to net income

2. Sharp Increase in Long-Term Debt

3. Significant Sale of Property, Plant, and Equipment Without Concurrent Replacement

4. Acquisition of Risky Assets

5. Investments in Other Companies that are Considered to be Potential Problems

506.5 / Indicators That a Firm Is Not a Going Concern

1. Signs of Financial Distress

What to Watch Out For

☐ Instability in earnings
☐ Small company
☐ New company
☐ Problem industry

What to Do

☐ Compute the "Z-score."
☐ Compute and analyze the following ratios:
  a. Cash flow to total liabilities
  b. Common stockholders' equity to total liabilities
  c. Net income to total assets
  d. Operating income to total assets
  e. Total liabilities to total assets
  f. Retained earnings to total assets
  g. Times-interest-earned
  h. Current ratio
  i. Quick ratio
☐ Determine the standard deviation in earnings.

CHAPTER SIX

Specialized Topics in Earnings Quality Evaluation

This chapter addresses the analytical implications of various specialized areas in accounting that cover the integrated analysis of the balance sheet and income statement and hence are best looked at in their entirety rather than in a specialized manner. Topics discussed herein are business combinations, intercorporate investments, construction contracts, pensions, leases, and foreign operations.

601 BUSINESS COMBINATIONS

As we know, there are two methods of accounting for business combinations—pooling of interests and purchase.

Acquisitions must be thoroughly analyzed, particularly by looking at footnote disclosures, because acquisitions can create an appearance of earnings and growth when they are not really present.

The pooling of interests method requires a company to pick up earnings of the acquired firm for the entire year even though the acquisition is made during the period. This can result in illusory earnings growth through merely acquiring businesses.

• A manufacturer of electrical components discloses: "Acquisitions of other companies in the electronics and computer-based services category accounted for $60 million or 18% of the Company's total increase in net sales of $321 million."

• A steel company discloses: "Earnings benefited partially from the effects of the inclusion of the Standard Steel Division for a full year—acquired July 19X2."

In a pooling, the assets of the acquired company are stated at book value rather than market value. Of course, because of inflation, book value is most often lower than market value. The understatement of assets (inventory, fixed assets, and intangible assets) results in the understatement of expenses (cost of sales, depreciation, amortization) with the concurrent overstatement in net income. The analyst should adjust the net assets of the acquired company from book value to fair market value. In this way, the omitted value arising from the pooling will be reflected. He should then depreciate and amortize this difference against net income to arrive at a more realistic profit figure that is comparable to what net income would be if the purchase method (which employs fair market value) were used to account for the business combination.

The suppression of asset values also leads to the overstatement of gains on the later sale of the assets. In effect, by bringing forth the net assets of the acquired company at unrealistically low amounts, the company may easily boost its earnings by disposing of them. What we have here is a cost recovery rather than a profit. The analyst should examine corporate disclosures to determine whether such low-basis assets were sold and what was the resulting gain. Net income should be downwardly adjusted for the difference between the reported gain and what the gain would have been if the assets were valued at fair market value.

The analyst must recognize that pooling can result in meaningless ratios, as in the overstatement of ROI due to the overstatement of net income and understatement of total assets.

Illustration

Company A reports that it acquired company X on December 1, 19X1 in a business combination accounted for under the pooling method.

The following data are available in the annual report:

	19X1	19X2
Company A's net income without including the acquired company's earnings	$ 800,000	$ 810,000
Inclusion of company X's net income for the entire year	200,000	210,000
Reported earnings	$1,000,000	$1,020,000

The net income for company X from December 1, 19X1 to December 31, 19X1 is disclosed as $15,000.

Also disclosed is that in 19X2, company A had sold assets, picked up from acquiring company X, for $65,000 which were originally recorded at $40,000 book value (market value is approximated at $60,000).

The restatement of earnings for 19X1 and 19X2 follows:

		19X1	19X2
Reported earnings:		$1,000,000	$1,020,000
Less:			
Company X's net income prior to the acquisition date (Jan. 1–Nov. 30) $200,000–$15,000		(185,000)	
Low quality gain from the sale of company X's undervalued assets:			
Reported gain	$25,000		
Gain if assets were recorded at fair market value	5,000		
Overstated gain–to 19X2	$20,000		(20,000)
Restated earnings		$ 815,000	$1,000,000

The purchase method is more realistic than the pooling method because it uses fair market value to reflect the net assets acquired rather than the outdated original cost.

The analyst must carefully scrutinize footnote disclosures relating to deriving fair market values of the assets and liabilities of the acquired company. He must ascertain the reasonableness of such valuations.

If equity securities are involved in the purchase transaction, the analyst should determine whether the market prices of the securities were unusually high at the transaction date. If so, net assets will be inflated due to the temporary ceiling market prices. In this case, the analyst may wish to use the average market price of the securities for his own valuation of the acquired assets.

The analyst must be alert to the possible overstatement of estimated liabilities for future costs and losses that may increase post-acquisition earnings. A case in point is the disclosure made by ABC Investing Company in its 19X1 prospectus:

Illustration ——

Certain Accounting Adjustments made in connection with the Acquisition of The H Insurance Company. ABC accounted for its acquisition of The H Insurance Company on August 31, 19X8 as a "purchase of assets." As a result, ABC was required to establish a new cost basis of H's net assets at the date of acquisition based upon the fair values of H's assets and liabilities in the light of conditions then prevailing. In arriving at such fair values, it was determined that the reserves for underwriting losses and loss expenses on H's books at the date of acquisition did not adequately reflect the amounts that could reasonably be expected to be paid in respect of casualty losses which actually occurred prior to the acquisition. Accordingly, such reserves were increased by $43,181,000 through a charge to the income of H for the eight-month period ended August 31, 19X8, the period prior to the acquisition of H by ABC. As a result of this adjustment, payments by H in respect of casualty losses which occurred prior to the acquisition will not be deducted from ABC's income unless they exceed by $43,181,000 the reserves on H's books for such losses prior to such adjustment. In addition, in determining the estimated realizable value of H's investment portfolio as of the date of acquisition, it was considered appropriate, in the opinion of L Brokerage Firm, to recognize a discount from quoted market of 15%, or $65,709,000, in the case of equity securities and 5%, or $14,074,000 in the case of debt instruments so as to reflect liquidation factors such as block transaction discounts and trading volume. As a result of this adjustment, the aggregate amount of gains ultimately recognized in ABC's income from the sale of all portfolio securities held by H at the date of acquisition will exceed by $79,783,000 the amount that would have been recognized if such adjustments had not been made. Net pre-tax gains on the sale of investments include approximately $13,000,000 and $25,000,000 during the years ended April 30, 19X9 and 19Y0, respectively, and $1,356,000 and $15,661,000 during the eight months and year ended December 31, 19Y0, respectively, attributable to such portfolio adjustment.

———

The analyst should adjust reported earnings for the effect of unrealistic accruals and reversals of estimated liability accounts by increasing net income for an overstated expense provision.

Under the purchase method, companies can still portray favorable results by acquiring very profitable companies. Thus, the trend and dollar impact upon profitability of purchase transactions should be noted.

601.1 Questions to Be Asked: A Checklist

☐ Is there "phantom" earnings growth arising from acquisitions?

☐ As a result of using the pooling method, is the book value of the net assets acquired significantly less than their fair market value?

☐ For the pooling method, were there material gains on the subsequent sale of low-cost-basis assets?

☐ For the purchase method, were the valuations of fair market value used by the acquiring company realistic?

☐ Did the purchase transaction involve the issuance of equity securities at abnormally high market prices?

☐ Have any unrealistic estimated liability provisions been established?

—————— 602 INTERCORPORATE INVESTMENTS ——————

According to APB 18, intercorporate investments are accounted for by using one of the following methods:

1. Cost. The investor owns less than 20 percent of the voting common stock of the investee.

2. Equity. The investor owns between 20 percent and 50 percent of the voting common stock of the investee. It is also appropriate for joint ventures or in cases where consolidation is negated. The equity method can be used even when less than 20 percent is owned as long as the investor has significant influence.

3. Consolidation. The parent owns more than 50 percent of the voting common stock of the subsidiary. Even though more than 50 percent is owned, consolidation is prohibited in cases where the parent is not in actual control of the subsidiary (subsidiary is in receivership), parent and subsidiary are unrelated (parent is a manufacturer and the subsidiary is a transportation company), or the parent has sold or contracted to sell the subsidiary shortly after year-end.

602.1 Cost Method

Under the cost method, income is reported on the basis of dividends paid to the investor. The investee's reported net income is ignored. It is conceivable that dividends included in the investor's income may be unrelated to the investee's earnings, and losses may not be recognized for a number of years. The trend in profit can therefore be distorted under the method.

• A petroleum refiner discloses: "10.7% ownership in B Industries was not large enough for equity accounting, and only the $250,000 received in dividends was taken into income for 19X4. However, B Industries had total earnings of $46.3 million, of which the Company's share was $4.8 million."

• In 19X8 and 19X9, B Company and L Company paid out more dividends than their reported incomes.

If the investor can exert control over the investee, it can manage income by deciding whether to have it declare dividends. For example, the managers of the investor could wait to year-end, determine its income, and then ask the investee to declare dividends of an appropriate amount. Further, since dividend income has advantageous tax treatment, it has a better effect on moderating after-tax income than other revenue or expense items.

FASB 12 does not require the write-down of a particular long-term investment from cost to market value when the decline in value is considered temporary. But what is or is not temporary is nebulous, thus affording management some flexibility in reporting its financial position. If a company does not make a write-down, the analyst must make his own determination as to whether the decline is temporary and will be reversed. If he concludes that the decline is more permanent, he should downwardly adjust the company's security portfolio.

Illustration _____

Company B owns 18% of company X. Company X paid dividends to company B of $80,000. Company X's net income for the year was $1,000.

The cost of company X stock was $100,000 but its current market value is $70,000. Company B's management considers the decline to be temporary and thus has not made a write-down.

Although company B recognizes dividend income of $80,000, the analyst should note that if the equity method were appropriate, company B would have shown investment income of only $180 (18% × $1,000). The analyst may thus conclude that company B's earnings for analytical purposes are overstated.

Further, the analyst may question an investee's financial astuteness in paying out dividends that substantially exceed its earnings.

If the analyst believes that there has been a permanent impairment in value of company X's stock, he should, for analytical purposes, value the security at $70,000 and reduce reported earnings by $30,000 for the loss.

602.2 Equity Method

When the equity method is used, equity securities do not have to be adjusted to market value except for permanent declines; they are reflected at their equity value. Equity value basically represents the initial cost for the investment plus a proportionate share of investee profit less a proportionate share of investee dividends. The investor's investment revenue account only picks up the investee's net income. It is possible that the equity value at year-end may be significantly higher or lower than market value. The analyst should attempt to compare the equity value with the market value and adjust such securities to market value when a material variance exists. APB 18 requires that the market value of investments in common stock of investees be disclosed, when available.

Earnings picked up under the equity method do not represent income from the basic business operations of the investee and hence may distort its earning power. Further, if equity earnings exceed the cash dividends received from the investee, there is lower quality of earnings since equity earnings are not supported by cash flow. Note that undistributed earnings increase book earnings but are not available funds for stockholders.

Long-term investments other than equity securities such as regular and convertible bonds are carried at book value. The analyst may wish to use their year-end market values for ratio computations. When market value is used it should be that expected after taxes and the cost of selling.

Illustration

Company C owns 30% of company Y. The investment in investee account shows a year-end balance of $400,000. The market value of company Y's stock is $250,000. Company Y has been operating at losses.

The analyst may conclude that the equity value of $400,000 is unrealistic in light of the significant decline in market value and the continued net losses. For analytical purposes, he may downwardly adjust company C's net income by $150,000 to reflect the unrealized loss and use the $250,000 market value as the valuation basis of the investment account for ratio purposes.

602.3 Consolidation

According to B. Cushing, "consolidation prevents a parent company from income manipulation and is generally favored by financial analysts."[1]

Although consolidated financial statements are the best measure of the financial position and results of operations of a group, there are some limitations that the analyst must take into account, including:

1. A financially deficient subsidiary may be combined with a financially healthy one, producing a satisfactory net position in consolidation. Analysis of the consolidated financial statements may thus not reveal financial problems of a component entity.

2. The financial statements of individual subsidiaries may not be on a comparable basis due to the use of different accounting methods, estimates, and year-ends. This may inhibit the meaningfulness of trends and relationships.

[1] B. Cushing, "The Effects of Accounting Policy Decisions on Trends in Reported Corporate Earnings Per Share," Unpublished Ph.D. dissertation, Michigan State University, (1969).

Consolidation is based upon the assumption that a dollar of subsidiary earnings is equal to a dollar of the parent's earnings. Even ignoring taxes, this assumption may not always be correct. The subsidiary may be forced to restrict its dividends because of either provisions in loan agreements, governmental regulatory restrictions (e.g., utility commission), or restrictions in a foreign country that the subsidiary is operating in relating to the remittance of earnings. *The analyst must therefore decide whether a subsidiary's earnings is the equivalent of the parent's earnings.*

Liabilities reported on the consolidated balance sheet do not have a lien upon total assets. A creditor of a specific subsidiary can be paid *only* from the assets of that subsidiary unless the parent has guaranteed the debts of the subsidiary. Thus, creditors and bank loan officers, when looking at the consolidated statements of an entity, must concentrate on the financial soundness of the particular subsidiary that is asking for credit; individual financial statements of the subsidiary must be analyzed. If such subsidiary's financial health is weak, a guarantee of the loan by the parent must be received.

B. Graham, B. Dodd, and S. Cottle write:[2]

> Subsidiaries' profits and losses should be taken fully into account in stating the parent's earnings. However, if a continually unprofitable subsidiary exists, that could be eliminated without an adverse effect upon the rest of the business, it would be logical to view such subsidiary losses as temporary—since good sense would dictate that in a short time the subsidiary must either become profitable or be disposed of. In this case, the loss is considered the equivalent of a nonrecurring item. This is not the case when important business relations exist between the parent and the subsidiary.

The Week in Review reports:[3]

> Wholly owned unconsolidated finance subsidiaries should be consolidated with the parent before any financial statement analysis is performed. The potential bias in the data from not consolidating can be significant, especially when a material portion of the parent's sales are funneled through the subsidiary—as occurs frequently in the automobile, farm equipment and industrial equipment manufacturing industries.

APB 23 requires a parent to provide for taxes on the undistributed earnings of a subsidiary except in cases where supportive evidence exists that the subsidiary will hold on to the undistributed earnings permanently or

---

[2] From *Security Analysis: Principles and Techniques* by B. Graham, B. Dodd, and S. Cottle, pp. 191–92. Copyright 1962 McGraw-Hill Book Company. Used with the permission of McGraw-Hill Book Company.

[3] "Accounting and Reporting," *The Week in Review*, (New York: Deloitte, Haskins & Sells, February 6, 1981), p. 2.

where such income will be distributed in a tax-free liquidation. Management has leeway in this matter. Since companies must disclose the amount of undistributed earnings on which taxes were not provided, the analyst should determine what the tax expense would be if he or she believes that future remission is likely.

It is interesting to note that taxes must always be provided for when the equity method is used.

Illustration

Company D discloses in its tax footnote that taxes have not been provided on foreign subsidiary X's earnings because of management's belief that income will not be remitted in the foreseeable future. The amount of unremitted earnings is $1,700,000. Company D's effective tax rate is 45%.

The subsidiary is operating in a foreign country that may be politically troublesome in the near future.

In light of the potential political instability of the foreign country, the analyst may conclude that the future remission of earnings is likely. Hence, for analytical purposes, he may wish to make his own tax provision for the unremitted earnings of $765,000 (45% × $1,700,000), with its concurrent reduction in company D's reported earnings.

602.4 Areas of Analysis: A Checklist

- Financial soundness of the subsidiaries making up the consolidated figures
- Restrictions on the remission of earnings by the subsidiary to the parent
- Determining whether a tax provision should be made on undistributed foreign subsidiary earnings
- Change in the subsidiary's fiscal year-end
- Considering a wholly owned unconsolidated finance subsidiary when evaluating the consolidated entity
- Parent guarantee of subsidiary loans

—— 603 LONG-TERM CONSTRUCTION CONTRACTS ——

The two methods of accounting for long-term construction contracts are percentage-of-completion and completed contract. In the former, profit is recognized gradually as work is being performed based upon costs incurred to date to total costs or upon time spent. In the latter, profit is recognized when the project has been completed.

Since management has discretion in determining which costs are to be considered construction costs vs. period costs, the analyst must appraise whether the firm's classification policy is realistic.

The analyst must watch out for *cost overruns* that are not being recognized. For example, Lockheed continued to ignore the cost overruns on its C-5A project until massive write-offs were required.

A company's earnings quality deteriorates when it unjustifiably shortens its performance schedules to complete long-term construction projects where the percentage-of-completion method is used. This is nothing more than an accounting gimmick.

The analyst must watch for cases where income is being recognized even though the earnings process has not been completed.

• S Company recognized earnings when housing modules were "manufactured and assigned to specific contracts." The method was in essence an earning-by-producing process and the questionable sales were reversed in 19X2. This resulted in loan defaults and corporate bankruptcy eventually ensued.

The completed contract method is justifiable only in cases where one *cannot* make reliable estimates of future costs as well as the extent of project completion. Difficulties with the method include determining the completion point of the project and the nature of the deferred expenses. A company that defers all costs (including general and administrative overhead) up to the contract's completion date has lower earnings quality than a company that takes a more conservative approach and expenses such costs as incurred. Further, the method can result in erratic earnings since profit is only recognized when the project is completed.

Illustration ─────────────────────────────────

Company E uses the percentage-of-completion method to account for its construction contracts. A given project has a contract price of $3,000,000. The estimated total costs of the contract is $1,600,000. In the first year of the contract, company E estimates that 30% of the work was performed. The company therefore recognized profit of $420,000 (30% × $1,400,000) on the contract.

If the analyst believes that only 20% of the work was actually performed, he should downwardly adjust reported earnings by $140,000 ($420,000 − $280,000).

603.1 Warning Signs: A Checklist

☐ Period costs being deferred as construction costs

☐ Costs overruns being ignored

- ☐ Accelerating profit recognition under the percentage-of-completion method by unjustifiably shortening production schedules
- ☐ Recognizing profit before the earnings process has been completed

604 PENSION PLANS

FASB 87 deals with the employer's accounting for pension plans. The components of pension expense are:

Service Cost. Pension expense assigned for services rendered in the current year.

Amortization of Prior Service Cost. Prior service cost is the cost attributable for years before plan adoption or amendment. The cost is amortized over current and future years.

Return on Plan Assets. The return equals the return rate times the moving average asset value over the time period.

Interest on Projected Benefit Obligation. This equals the interest rate times the projected benefit obligation at the beginning of the year. Projected benefit obligation is the pension plan obligation at a point in time based on future salaries.

Actuarial Gains and Losses. These are the effects on actuarially calculated pension cost of (1) deviations between actual prior experience and the actuarial assumptions used or (2) changes in actuarial assumptions about future events. Actuarial gains and losses are deferred and amortized to pension expense of future periods.

The difference between pension expense and the related funding results in a deferred pension charge or a deferred pension credit.

Immediate recognition must be made of a minimum pension liability when the accumulated benefit obligation (year-end pension obligation based on current salaries) is greater than the fair value of plan assets. But no recognition is given in the opposite case.

When a deferred pension liability exists, only an additional liability equal to the minimum liability can be recorded. When an additional liability is recorded, it is offset by recognizing a new intangible asset not exceeding the amount of unamortized prior service cost. If it does, the excess is shown as a reduction of stockholders' equity.

Footnote disclosure follows:

1. Description of plan including type of benefit formula and funding policy

2. Components of pension cost
3. Assumptions including the discount rate and the return rate on plan assets
4. Reconciliation of the fund status of plans with employer amounts recognized in the balance sheet including:
   a. Fair value of plan assets
   b. Projected benefit obligation
   c. Amount of unrecognized prior service cost

The disclosed projected benefit obligation is a better measure than the accumulated benefit obligation in reflecting the pension plan's obligations because it is based on anticipated future salary levels rather than current salaries. Thus, the analyst should use the projected benefit obligation rather than the accumulated benefit obligation in evaluating potential liability exposure. The real unfunded obligation is the difference between the projected benefit obligation and the fair value of plan assets. For example, assume the accumulated benefit obligation is $5,000,000, the projected benefit obligation is $6,000,000, and the fair value of assets is $3,500,000. The *booked* liability is $1,500,000 ($5,000,000–$3,500,000). However, the real obligation for analytical purposes is $2,500,000 ($6,000,000 − $3,500,000). Hence, the analyst must consider the difference between the projected benefit obligation and accumulated benefit obligation of $1,000,000 as an *unbooked* (off-balance sheet) liability.

The analyst should note the amount of unrecognized prior service cost because it represents future charges against net income when amortized.

The analyst must be on guard against the possible manipulation of net income. For example, a company may settle a portion of its pension obligations (not terminating the plan) by purchasing annuities to cover selected employees. Since the company is no longer responsible for paying benefits to those employees, it can recognize a portion of its excess pension fund assets as income.

In examining the pension footnote, the analyst should watch out for changes in pension plan assumptions (mortality, interest rate) and their consequent effect upon reported earnings. The analyst should downwardly adjust net income if it has been artificially boosted by an unwarranted change in estimate, as when the firm increases its assumed interest rate above what can realistically be expected in the money market.

604.1 / Areas to Note: A Checklist

☐ Changes in actuarial assumptions and their effect upon net income
☐ Amount of unrecognized prior service cost
☐ The quality of the assets comprising the pension fund

☐ The difference between the projected benefit obligation and the accumulated benefit obligation

☐ Fair value of plan assets vs. projected benefit obligation

————— 605 / LEASES —————

FASB 13 deals with the accounting for leases by lessees and lessors.

With regard to the lessee, a lease may be either an operating lease (regular rental) or a capital lease (leased property is treated as an asset).

Many long-term leases are in essence debt from an analytical point of view. The failure to meet lease payments on important leased property of the organization and its resulting loss will have pronounced adverse effects upon future corporate profitability. Further, the company is contractually obligated for future noncancellable payments. In an extreme case, inability to meet such payments may result in insolvency.

The analyst should note the magnitude of the *capital* lease obligation reported in the balance sheet. He or she should also examine the lease footnote for the off-balance sheet liability representing the future rental payments on *operating* leases. Finally, the analyst should ascertain the significance of the firm's lease commitment in terms of the future payments required and time period involved as well as the significance of the leased property to the company's basic operations.

With regard to the lessor, there are three methods of accounting: (1) sales method (manufacturer or dealer), (2) direct financing method (nonmanufacturer/nondealer), and (3) operating method (regular rental).

The net receivable under lease is recorded at the present value of the future minimum rental payments. In evaluating the quality of the receivable we should ascertain the probability of collection from lessees and the salability of the leased property if reverted to the lessor.

Analysis should also be undertaken of the stability of lease income to the overall earnings of the firm.

————— 606 / FOREIGN OPERATIONS —————

A summary of the major requirements of FASB 52 (Foreign Currency Translation) follows:

1. In foreign currency translation, we put the foreign subsidiary's financial statements in conformity with U.S. GAAP. Then we translate from the foreign currency to U.S. dollars. Assets and liabilities are translated using the current exchange rate at the balance sheet date. Income statement accounts are translated at the weighted-average exchange rate

for the period. Translation gains and losses are shown as a separate component of stockholders' equity. They shall not be included in net income until there is a sale or liquidation of the entire investment in a foreign entity.

2. Transaction gains and losses arise from redeeming receivables/payables that are fixed in terms of amounts of foreign currency received/paid. Transaction gains and losses are included in the income statement for the period in which the exchange rate changes.

3. Significant rate changes after the balance sheet date require subsequent event disclosure.

Numerous analytical implications ensue from foreign currency accounting and reporting. When there is a devaluation of the dollar, foreign assets and income in strong currency countries are worth more dollars as long as foreign liabilities do not offset this beneficial effect.

An entity that properly balances its foreign assets and liabilities protects the parent from exchange rates and its resulting variability effect upon consolidated profit. In evaluating a company, the analyst should consider the exposed position of the firm by each foreign country in which there exists a major operation.

Illustration

A subsidiary located in England experiences unchanged operations in 19X5 and 19X6. However, the English exchange rate has decreased by 10% on average against the dollar. A simplified, partial income statement is shown below.

	19X5	19X6	Percentage Change
Sales	$100,000	$90,000	− 10%
Operating expenses (exclusive of depreciation	$ 60,000	$54,000	− 10%
Depreciation	20,000	20,000	
Total expenses	$ 80,000	$74,000	
Net income	$ 20,000	$16,000	− 20%

The computation of income statement effects can be quite complex and as such FASB 52 requires disclosure of the methods and *assumptions* used. The analyst should carefully scrutinize these disclosures to determine if they are realistic in the circumstances. Otherwise, she should make her own adjustments by computing the differential effect upon profitability of her relevant assumptions compared to management's assumptions.

The analyst must consider the following in her evaluation of the impact that foreign operations have on the entity's financial health:

1. The extent of intercountry transactions
2. Different year-ends of foreign subsidiaries
3. Foreign restrictions on the transfer of funds
4. Tax structure of the foreign country
5. The economic and political stability of the foreign country

Foreign currency gains and losses represent low quality of earnings elements *if* the foreign exchange rate is erratic. *The degree of vacillation of the foreign exchange rate may be measured by its percentage change over time and/or its standard deviation.*

• International Telephone and Telegraph's 19Y0 annual report discloses that net foreign exchange gains and losses on a per share basis from 19X8 to 19Y0 were ($.98), ($.59), and $1.00, respectively.

• Company A's 19X4 annual report discloses: "The translation of foreign currencies into U.S. dollar equivalents resulted in an unrealized loss for 19X4 of $7.4 million. Comparable translation adjustment for 19X3 resulted in a gain of $14.9 million."

On the other hand, if the exchange rate is stable, there will be no exchange problem. Since the exchange rates of some countries are more unstable than that of others, analysts should determine in which countries the company is operating. They should also determine for those countries that have erratic exchange rates whether such instability is long-term or short-term. Long-run instability means that there is a greater likelihood of continued vacillation in earnings arising from foreign currency translation.

Analysts should evaluate the extent to which foreign currency gains and losses contribute to variability in the earnings stream. Rapid exchange shifts detract from earnings stability. *The trend in the ratio of foreign exchange gains and losses to net income and to total revenue should be examined.*

Illustration ————————————————————————

Company K's comparative income statements reveal:

	19X1	19X2	19X3
Foreign currency gains and losses	$1,000,000	$2,000,000	$ 400,000
Net income	4,000,000	4,300,000	3,900,000
Revenue	7,000,000	7,200,000	6,800,000

Relevant ratios follow:

	19X1	19X2	19X3
Foreign currency gains and losses to net income	25.0%	46.5%	10.3%
Foreign currency gains and losses to revenue	14.3%	27.8%	5.9%

The trend in foreign currency gains and losses is erratic in terms of absolute dollars and as a ratio of net income and revenue. Further, earnings quality in 19X2 was poor because of the high percentage of foreign currency gain to net income (46.5%). Such gain lacks repeatability as evidenced by the significantly lower percentage of foreign currency gain to net income (10.3%) in 19X3.

A forward exchange contract is an agreement to purchase or sell identifiable foreign currency where the actual delivery of the foreign currency is at a later date. It is used to protect or hedge against exchange risks emanating from foreign currency transactions. The analyst should look upon such a contract favorably since the company is minimizing its potential foreign currency exposure.

A forward exchange contract can also be used to speculate in the foreign exchange market. The analyst should be wary of a company that does this since it implies that management is risk-prone.

606.1 / Low Quality of Earnings Indicators: A Checklist

- ☐ Foreign operations in countries that experience rapid changes in their exchange rates
- ☐ High tax structures in the foreign countries
- ☐ Foreign restrictions upon the remission of earnings from the subsidiaries to the parent
- ☐ Foreign subsidiaries located in countries subject to economic and political risk
- ☐ A business with a high proportion of fixed assets and intangible assets to total assets
- ☐ Speculative forward exchange contracts

——— 607 / SUMMARY CHECKLIST OF KEY POINTS ———

607.1 / Business Combinations

1. Pooling-of-interests Method

What to Watch Out For

☐ "Illusory" earnings growth through acquisitions

☐ Significant gains on the sale of the acquired company's suppressed value assets

What to Do

☐ Adjust the net assets of the acquired company from book value to fair market value.

☐ Adjust net income to what it would have been if the purchase method were used rather than the pooling method.

☐ Reduce net income by the difference between the reported gain on the sale of low-cost-basis assets and what the gain would have been if the assets were initially valued at fair market value at the time of the business combination.

☐ For ratio computations, use the fair market value rather than the reported value for the acquired company's net assets.

☐ Eliminate the portion of the acquiring company's net income that includes the earnings of the acquired company prior to the acquisition date.

2. Purchase Method

What to Watch Out For

☐ When the market prices of issued equity securities are unrealistically high, average market prices of the securities should be used in deriving the analytical valuation of the acquired company's net assets.

☐ Adjust net income for the effect of unwarranted accruals and reversals of estimated liability accounts.

    a. Increase net income for an overstated loss or expense provision.

    b. Reduce net income for an understated loss or expense provision.

607.2 / Intercorporate Investments

1. Cost Method

What to Watch Out For

☐ Dividends included in the investor's revenue account are unrelated to the investee's net income.

☐ The investee has been incurring net losses over the years but has been paying out dividends.

☐ The investor considers temporary the decline in value of a particular long-term investment that is really permanent.

What to Do

☐ Downwardly adjust net income for the decline in market value of a given long-term investment that is considered permanent.

2. Equity Method

What to Watch Out For

☐ The equity value of the investment in investee account is materially greater than its market value.

What to Do

☐ Adjust the investment in investee account to market value and reduce net income for the unrealized loss.

3. Consolidation

What to Watch Out For

☐ A financially poor subsidiary is being combined with a financially strong one, resulting in a satisfactory *net* position in consolidation.

☐ Individual subsidiary financial statements are not on a comparable basis because different accounting methods and estimates are being used.

☐ Cases where a dollar of the subsidiary's earnings is not equivalent to a dollar of the parent's earnings.

☐ The subsidiary is being forced to hold back on dividends because of:

    a. Restrictions in loan agreements.

    b. Govermental regulatory restrictions.

    c. Restrictions in the foreign country where the subsidiary is located relating to the remission of earnings.

- ☐ A boost in earnings arising from changing the fiscal year-ends of foreign subsidiaries.

- ☐ A subsidiary that continually operates at losses but cannot be disposed of because it has a significant interrelationship with the parent.

- ☐ The parent is not providing for taxes on the undistributed earnings of a foreign subsidiary because it considers that the subsidiary will retain such earnings permanently or will remit them in a tax-free liquidation.

What to Do

- ☐ In evaluating a loan application by a subsidiary, the financial soundness of that subsidiary is the basis for repayment, as the parent is not obligated to meet the subsidiary's loan unless the parent has guaranteed the subsidiary's debt. Hence, the individual financial statements of the subsidiary must be analyzed and *not* the consolidated financial statement.

- ☐ Prior to engaging in financial statement analysis, wholly owned unconsolidated finance subsidiaries should be consolidated with the parent.

- ☐ If a parent is not providing for taxes on the undistibuted earnings of a foreign subsidiary, and if the analyst does not agree with such reasoning, he should compute what the tax expense would be and reduce reported earnings by that amount.

  a. Management's assumption that the foreign subsidiary will permanently hold on to the earnings would appear unreasonable if the foreign country is politically unstable or if a substantial increase in the foreign tax rate is likely, thus effecting the unremitted earnings.

  b. The tax expense is equal to the effective tax rate times the unremitted earnings.

607.3 / Long-term Construction Contracts

1. Construction Costs

What to Watch Out For

- ☐ The company is classifying period costs as construction costs in order not to burden current reported earnings.

- ☐ There are cost overruns on contracts that are not being recognized.

2. Percentage-of-completion Method

What to Watch Out For

☐ A company unjustifiably shortening its performance schedules in order to accelerate earnings recognition

What to Do

☐ Reduce net income for the incremental earnings arising from unwarranted shortening in production schedules.

3. Completed Contract Method

What to Watch Out For

☐ Excessive deferral of costs such as general and administrative overhead before the contract's completion date

What to Do

☐ Reduce net income and the related asset for costs that were improperly deferred.

607.4 / Pension Plans

1. Pension Plan Assumptions

What to Watch Out For

☐ Unwarranted change in assumptions that lower pension expense

What to Do

☐ Downwardly adjust net income for the incremental earnings due to improper changes in pension assumptions.

2. Off-Balance Sheet Pension Liabilities

What to Watch Out For

☐ A significant amount of unfunded prior service cost
☐ Projected benefit obligation exceeding accumulated benefit obligation
☐ Accumulated benefit obligation exceeding the fair value of plan assets
☐ Significant present value of vested and nonvested benefits
☐ A "financially deficient" company with a substantial amount of guaranteed unfunded pension benefits, since in liquidation up to

30% of a company's net worth may be used to meet pension plan deficiencies

☐ High realization risk assets that comprise more than 5% of the net assets available for benefits

☐ Unusual or infrequent events that take place after the benefit information date but prior to the issuance of the financial statements

What to Do

☐ Determine the existence, nature, and amount of off-balance sheet pension liabilities.

    a. Ascertain whether such liabilities are material by comparing them to total liabilities and/or total assets.

    b. Evaluate the company's financial ability to meet the unrecorded pension obligations.

☐ If a material event relating to the pension plan's valuation occurs after the financial statements are issued, adjust the pension fund for it.

    a. An example is a sharp drop in the market value of the pension fund portfolio.

607.5 / Leases

1. Nature of Leased Property

What to Watch Out For

☐ The lease is for property that is vital to the organization; the loss of it will have a significant adverse effect upon future corporate profitability.

What to Do

☐ Determine the company's financial ability to make future lease payments.

☐ Determine the present value of future lease payments by adding the *capital* lease obligation in the balance sheet with the footnoted present value of future rental payments on *operating* leases.

607.6 / Foreign Operations

1. In times of devaluation of the dollar, foreign assets and income in strong currency countries are worth more dollars.

2. **An entity that properly balances its foreign assets and liabilities insulates itself from the variability in exchange rates and its resulting effect upon profitability.**

   What to Do

   □ Determine the exposed position of the entity by each foreign country in which there exists a major operation.

   □ Examine the variability in the foreign currency gain or loss reported in the income statement.

3. **Capital Intensiveness**

4. **The Translation Process**

   What to Do

   □ Scrutinize corporate disclosures of the methods and assumptions used in the translation process to ascertain whether they are realistic.

5. **Impact of Foreign Operations on the Entity's Financial Health**

   What to Watch Out For

   □ Rapid changes in the exchange rate
   □ A high degree of intercountry transactions
   □ Foreign subsidiaries having different year-ends
   □ Adverse tax structure in the foreign country

   What to Do

   □ Determine the percentage over time and the standard deviation in the exchange rate.

6. **A forward exchange contract designed to hedge in the foreign currency is a favorable sign since it minimizes foreign currency risk.**

   What to Do

   □ Examine footnote disclosures regarding the particulars of forward exchange contracts.

CHAPTER SEVEN

The Financial
Valuation of
a Business

A business may need to be valued for many financial reasons including a purchase, sale, merger, buy-back agreement, litigation between the parties, attempt to expand the credit line, or tax matter. The valuation depends on the purpose at hand. The valuation process is an art and *not* a science since everyone's perception is slightly different. In fact, the financial analyst may be asked to serve as an expert witness in a lawsuit to support his/her business valuation. In litigation matters, the valuation method used should be logically consistent, reasonable, cost-effective, and simply explained. This chapter provides the financial analyst with several sound ways to determine what a business is worth. The valuation methods may apply to any situation in which the value of a business must be made. Further, various IRS Revenue Rulings have been issued recommending specific valuation measures in the case of income taxes.

In valuing the business, the following factors should be considered: history of the business, nature of the company and its major activities, maturity of the business, economic and political conditions, health of the industry, financial status of the company, degree of risk, growth potential, trend and stability of earnings, competition, marketing factors, customer base, quality of management, and ease of transferability of ownership.

As an initial step in valuation, the key financial information must be accumulated and analyzed including historical financial statements, forecasted financial statements, and tax returns. There must be a full familiarity with the business. Further, the major assumptions of the valuation must be clearly spelled out.

The valuation methods are based on the assumption that an entity is a "going concern." The valuation approaches may be profit- or asset-oriented. Adjusted earnings may be capitalized at an appropriate multiple. Future adjusted cash earnings may be discounted by the projected rate of return. Assets may be valued at fair market value, such as through appraisal. Comparative values of similar companies may serve as excellent benchmarks.

701 / COMPARISON WITH INDUSTRY AVERAGES

Valid comparisons can be made between the entity being valued and others in the same industry. Industry norms should be noted. General sources of comparative industry data include:

• *Almanac of Business and Industrial Financial Ratios*—based on corporate tax returns to the Internal Revenue Service, written by Leo Troy and published by Prentice-Hall.

• *RMA Annual Statement Studies*—published by Robert Morris Associates, a national association of bank loan and credit officers.

• *Financial Studies of the Small Business*—published annually by Financial Research Associates (Washington, D.C.: Financial Research Associates, 1984).

702 / VALUATION METHODS

We now look at the various approaches to business valuation. A combination of these approaches may be used to obtain a representative value.

702.1 / Capitalization of Earnings

Primary consideration should be given to earnings when valuing a company. Analysis of historical earnings is typically the starting point in applying a capitalization method to most business valuations. In general, historical earnings are a reliable predictor of future earnings.

The value of the business may be based on its adjusted earnings times a multiplier indicating what the business would sell for in the industry.

Net income should be adjusted for unusual and nonrecurring revenue and expense items. In adjusting net income, we should add back the portions of the following items that are personal rather than business-related to determine the proper net income: auto expense, travel expense, and promotion and entertainment expense. Also we should add back expenses taken solely for the fringe benefits, health plan, pension plan, and life insurance. In addition, we should add back excessive salary representing the difference between the owner's salary and what a reasonable salary would be if we hired someone to do the job. All compensation should be considered including perks. Thus, if the owner gets a salary of $300,000 and a competent worker would get $80,000, we should add back $220,000 to net income. Interest expense should also be added back to net income because it is the cost to borrow funds to buy assets or obtain working capital, and as such is not relevant in determining the operating profit of the business.

In the event lease payments arise from a *low-cost* lease, earnings should be adjusted to arrive at a fair rental charge. Extraordinary items (e.g., gain on the sale of land) should be removed from earnings to obtain typical earnings. In addition, the financial analyst should consider the arms-length nature of business transactions and consider the guidance provided by AICPA Statement on Auditing Standard No. 6 when considering related-party transactions.

If business assets are being depreciated at an accelerated rate, you should adjust net income upward. Therefore, the difference between the straight-line method and an accelerated depreciation method should be added back.

A tax provision should be made in arriving at the adjusted net income. The tax provision should be based on the tax rates that were in effect for each year being analyzed.

If the company has a significant amount of investment income (e.g., dividend income, interest income, rental income from nonoperating property), net income should be reduced for the investment income and taxes adjusted accordingly since we are concerned only with the income from operations.

The adjusted (restated) earnings results in a quality of earnings figure. An illustration of the adjustment of historical net income follows.

Illustration

Reported net income	$325,000
Adjustments:	
Personal expenses	50,000
Extraordinary or nonrecurring gain	(60,000)
Owner's fringe benefits	40,000
Excessive owner's salary relative to a reasonable salary	30,000
Interest expense	20,000
Dividend revenue	(10,000)
Low cost rental payments relative to a fair rental charge	(5,000)
Excess depreciation from using an accelerated method	10,000
Restated net income	$400,000

The restated earnings is then multiplied by a multiplier to determine the value of a business. The multiplier should be higher for a low-risk business but generally not more than 10. The multiplier should be lower for a high-risk business, often only 1 or 2. Of course, an average multiplier would be used when average risk exists, such as 5. The P/E ratio for a comparable company would be a good benchmark. Typically, a five-year average adjusted historical earnings figure is used. The five years' earnings up to the valuation date demonstrates past earning power. The computation is:

Average Adjusted Earnings over 5 years
× Multiplier (Capitalization Factor, P/E Ratio) of 5 (based on industry standard)
= Value of Business

Instead of a simple average, a weighted-average adjusted historical earnings figure is recommended. This gives more weight to the most recent years, which reflects higher current prices and recent business performance. If a five-year weighted-average is used, the current year is given a weight of 5 while the first year is assigned a weight of 1. The multiplier is then applied to the weighted-average five-year adjusted earnings to determine the value of the business. An illustration follows:

Year	Net Income	× Weight	=	Total
19X9	$120,000	× 5	=	$600,000
19X8	100,000	× 4	=	400,000
19X7	110,000	× 3	=	330,000
19X6	90,000	× 2	=	180,000
19X5	115,000	× 1	=	115,000
		15		$1,625,000

Weighted-Average 5 year earnings:
    $1,625,000/15 = $108,333

Weighted-Average 5 year earnings	$108,333
× Capitalization Factor	× 5*
Capitalization-of-Earnings Valuation	$541,665

---

* The multiplier may be based on the price-earnings ratio for a comparable publicly traded company or may be based on such factors as risk, stability of earnings, expected future earnings, liquidity, etc.

If the company's financial statements are not audited, you should insist on an audit to assure accurate reporting.

Has the business failed to record cash sales to hide income? One way of determining this is to take purchases and add a typical profit markup in the industry. To verify reported profit, the financial analyst can mutiply the sales by the profit margin in the industry. If reported earnings is significantly below what the earnings should be based on the industry standard, there may be some hidden income.

702.2 / Capitalization of Excess Earnings

The best method is to capitalize excess earnings. The normal rate of return on the weighted-average net tangible assets is subtracted from the weighted-average adjusted earnings to determine excess earnings. It is suggested that the weighting be based on a five-year period. The excess earnings figure is then capitalized to determine the value of the intangibles (primarily goodwill). The addition of the value of the intangibles and the fair market value of the net tangible assets equals the total valuation. As per IRS Revenue Ruling 68—609 (to be discussed in detail later), the IRS recommends this method to value a business for tax purposes. An illustration follows.

Weighted-average net tangible assets is computed below:

Year	Amount	×	Weight	=	Total
19X1	$950,000	×	1		$ 950,000
19X2	1,000,000	×	2		2,000,000
19X3	1,200,000	×	3		3,600,000
19X4	1,400,000	×	4		5,600,000
19X5	1,500,000	×	$\underline{5}$		$\underline{7,500,000}$
			15		$19,650,000

Weighted-Average Net Tangible Assets:

$19,650,000/15 = $1,310,000

Weighted-Average Adjusted Net Income (5 years)-assumed	$ 200,000
Minus Reasonable Rate of Return on Weighted-Average	
Tangible Net Assets ($1,310,000 × 10%)	$\underline{131,000}$
Excess Earnings	$ 69,000
× Capitalization factor (20%)	$\underline{\times\ 5}$
Value of Intangibles	345,000
Plus Fair Market Value of Net Tangible Assets	$\underline{3,000,000}$
Capitalization-of-Excess-Earnings Valuation	$ 3,345,000

702.3 / Capitalization of Cash Flow

The adjusted cash earnings may be capitalized in arriving at a value for the firm. An example follows:

Adjusted Cash Earnings	$100,000
× Capitalization Factor (25%)	x 4
Capitalization of Cash Flow	$400,000
Less Liabilities Assumed	50,000
Capitalization-of-Cash-Flow Earnings	$350,000

702.4 / Present Value (Discounting) of Future Cash Flows

A business is worth the discounted value of future cash earnings plus the discounted value of the expected selling price. Cash flow may be a more valid criterion of value than book profits because cash flow can be used for reinvestment. This approach is suggested in a third-party sale situation.

Step 1: Present Value of Cash Earnings. The earnings should be estimated over future years using an estimated growth rate taking into account inflation. Once the future earnings are determined, they should be discounted. Future earnings may be based on the prior years' earnings and the current profit margin applied to sales. Cash earnings equals net income plus noncash expense adjustments such as depreciation.

Step 2: Present Value of Sales Price. The present value of the expected selling price of the business at the date of sale should be determined.

The financial analyst should use as the discount rate the rate of return earned by the business. The discount rate should take into account the usual return rate for money, a risk premium, and maybe a premium for the illiquidity of the investment. If the risk-free interest rate is 7% (on government bonds), the risk premium is 8%, and the illiquidity premium is 7%, the capitalization (discount) rate will be 22%. The risk premium may range from 5% to 10% while the illiquidity premium may range from 5% to 15%.

Illustration _____

In 19X1, the net income is $200,000. Earnings are expected to grow at 8% per year. The discount rate is 10%. The financial analyst estimates that the business is worth the discounted value of future earnings. The valuation equals:

Year	Net Income	PV of $1 Factor	Present Value
	(based on an 8% growth rate)	(at 10% interest)	

19X1	$200,000	×	.909	$ 181,800
19X2	216,000	×	.826	178,416
19X3	233,280	×	.751	175,193
19X4	251,942	×	.683	172,076
19X5	272,098	×	.621	168,973

Present Value of Future Earnings	$876,458

If the expected selling price at the end of year 19X5 is $600,000, the valuation of the business equals:

Present value of earnings	876,458
Present value of selling price $600,000 × .621	372,600
Valuation	1,249,058

702.5 / Book Value (Net Worth)

The business may be valued based on the book value of the net assets at the most *recent* balance sheet date. However, this method is unrealistic because it does not take into account current values. It may only be appropriate when it is impossible to determine fair value of net assets and/or goodwill.

702.6 / Tangible Net Worth

The valuation of the company is its tangible net worth for the current year equal to stockholders' equity, less intangible assets.

702.7 / Economic Net Worth (Adjusted Book Value)

Economic net worth equals: Fair market value of net assets, plus: Goodwill (as per agreement).

702.8 / Fair Market Value of Net Assets

The fair market value of the net tangible assets of the business may be determined through independent appraisal. Expert appraisers for different types of tangible assets may be used, such as specialized appraisers for real estate, equipment, and trucks. Further, reference may be made to published values for particular assets, such as the "blue book" for business automobiles. Typically, the fair value of the net tangible assets (assets less liabilities) is higher than book value. To this, we add the value of the goodwill (if any). Note that goodwill applies to such aspects as reputation of the company, customer base, and high quality merchandise.

A business broker may be retained to do the appraisal of property, plant, and equipment for a small business. A business broker is experienced because he or she puts together the purchase of many small businesses. According to Equitable Business Brokers, about 25% of businesses that change hands are sold through business brokers.

The general practice is to value inventory at a maximum value of cost.

Unrecognized and unrecorded liabilities should be considered when determining the fair market value of net assets since such off-balance sheet liabilities represent future commitments and contingencies. For example, one company the author consulted had both an unrecorded liability for liquidated damages for non-union contracts of $3,100,000 and an unrecorded liability for $4,900,000 related to the estimated employer final withdrawal liability. Obviously, as a result of unrecorded liabilities, the value of a business will be reduced further.

Off-balance sheet assets, such as tax loss carryforward benefits, represent unrecorded assets that will increase the value of the business.

A tax liability may also exist that has not been recognized in the accounts. For example, the company's tax position may be adjusted by the IRS which is currently auditing the tax return. This *contingent* liability should be considered in valuing the business.

702.9 / Gross Revenue Multiplier

The value of the business may be determined by multiplying the revenue by the gross revenue multiplier common to that industry. The industry standard gross revenue multiplier is based on the average ratio of market price to sales prevalent in the industry. Thus, if revenue is $14,000,000 and the multiplier is .2, the valuation is: $14,000,000 × .2 = $2,800,000. This approach may be used when earnings are questionable.

702.10 / Profit Margin/Capitalization Rate

The profit margin divided by the capitalization rate provides a multiplier which is then applied to revenue. A multiplier of revenue that a company would sell at is the company's profit margin. The profit margin may be based on the industry average. The formula is:

$$\frac{\text{Profit Margin}}{\text{Capitalization Rate}} = \frac{\text{Net Income/Sales}}{\text{Capitalization Rate}} = \text{Multiplier}$$

The capitalization rate in earnings is the return demanded by investors. In arriving at a capitalization rate, the prime interest rate may be taken into account.

The resulting multiplier when multiplied by revenue is the amount the buyer is willing to pay. Assume sales of $14,000,000, a profit margin of 5%, and a capitalization rate of 20%. The multiplier is 25% (5%/20%). The valuation is:

Sales × 25%
$14,000,000 × 25% = $3,500,000

The IRS and the courts have considered recent sales as an important factor.

702.11 / Price-Earnings Factor

The value of a business may be based on the price-earnings factor applied to earnings per share (EPS). An example follows:

Net Income	$800,000
Outstanding Number of Shares	100,000
EPS	$8
P/E Multiple	× 10
Estimated Market Price per Share	$80
× Number of Shares Outstanding	×100,000
Price-Earnings Valuation	$8,000,000

_____ 703 / COMPARATIVE VALUES OF SIMILAR GOING CONCERNS _____

Under this approach, the financial analyst obtains the market price of a company in the industry similar in nature to the one being examined. Recent sales prices of similar businesses may be used. What would another company pay for this business? Reference may be made to the market price of similar publicly traded companies. While a perfect match is not needed, the companies should be reasonably similar (e.g., size, product, structure, diversity). Several sources of industry information are Moody's, Standard & Poor's, Value Line, Dun and Bradstreet, Dow Jones-Irwin, on-line data bases, and trade association reports. Assume a competing company has just been sold for $60,000,000. If you believe the company is worth 90% of the competing company, the valuation is $54,000,000.

_____ 704 / RECENT SALES OF STOCK _____

If recent sales of stock have taken place, then the value of the business may be based on the outstanding shares times the market price of the stock. However, the market price of the stock should be based on a discounted amount from the current market price since selling all the shares at once may cause the market price per share to drop somewhat based on the demand/supply relationship.

705 / COMBINATION OF METHODS

The value of the business may be approximated by determining the average value of two or more methods. For example, assume that the fair market value of net assets approach gives a value of $2,100,000, while the capitalization of excess earnings method provides a value of $2,500,000. The value of the business would then be the average of these two methods, or $2,300,000 ($2,100,000 + $2,500,000/2). This is a sound approach because it looks at several methods in deriving a valuation.

Some courts have found a combination of methods supportable as long as greater weight is given to the earnings methods relative to the asset approaches. Using the above illustration, if a weight of 2 was assigned to the earnings approach and a weight of 1 was assigned to the fair market value of net assets method, the valuation would be:

Method	Amount	× Weight =	Total
Fair Market Value of Net Assets	$2,100,000 ×	1	$2,100,000
Capitalization-of-Excess Earnings	2,500,000 ×	2	5,000,000
		3	$7,100,000
			/3
Valuation			$12,366,667

706 / IRS REVENUE RULINGS

IRS Revenue Ruling 65–193 approves only those approaches where valuations can be determined separately for tangible and intangible assets.

IRS Revenue Ruling 66–49 discusses how the IRS arrives at valuations, citing what to include in a valuation report.

IRS Revenue Ruling 68–609, 1968–2 C.B. 327 provides a formula for valuation for income tax purposes. It may serve as an appropriate model or as a check on other methods.

The formula may be used to compute the fair market value of intangible assets of the business *only* when a better basis of valuation does not exist. The formula is based on the capitalization-of-excess-earnings method as follows:

Weighted-Average Adjusted Historical Earnings (5 years)
Less Normal Return on Average Net Tangible Assets (5 years)
Equals Excess Earnings

× Capitalization Rate
Equals Intangible Assets
Plus Fair Market Value of Tangible Net Assets
Equals Total Valuation

The past earnings on which the valuation is based should properly reflect potential future earnings. Abnormal and unusual income statement components should be excluded.

Preferably, no less than five years of data should be used to value the business.

The return on average net tangible assets should be the percentage prevailing in the industry. If an industry percentage is not available, an 8% to 10% rate may be used. An 8% return rate is used for a business with a small risk factor and stable earnings while a 10% rate of return is used for a business having a high risk factor and unstable earnings. The capitalization rate for excess earnings should be 15% (a multiplier of 6.67) for a business with a small risk factor and stable earnings and 20% (a multiplier of 5) for a business having a high risk factor and unstable earnings. To recap: the suggested return rate range is 8% to 10%, while the range for the capitalization rate may be 15% to 20%.

Appeals and Review Memorandums (ARM) 34 and 38 present formula methods to value goodwill.

707 / CONCLUSION

When valuing a company, more weight should be placed on the earnings approaches and less on the asset approaches. Valuation may be based on a combined approach of methods including earnings and asset valuation. In deriving a value, industry standards may be quite helpful. Consideration should be given to adjusted cash earnings, gross revenue, fair value of net assets, and recent sales of similar businesses. A proper valuation is needed so as to set a realistic price that is fair to all concerned parties.

REFERENCES

American Institute of CPAs, "Valuation of a Closely-Held Business," Small Business Consulting Practice Aid No. 8, Management Advisory Services Practice Aids, (New York, 1987).

Blackman, Irving, *The Valuation of Privately-Held Businesses* (Illinois: Probus Publishing, 1986).

Burke, Frank, *Valuation and Valuation Planning for Closely-Held Businesses* (New Jersey: Prentice-Hall, 1981).

Desmond, Glenn and Kelley, Richard, *Business Valuation Handbook* (California: Valuation Press, 1977).

Douglas, Gordon, *How to Profitably Sell or Buy a Company or Business* (New York: Van Nostrand Reinhold, 1981).

Hays, Charles and Finley, Lawrence, "Valuation of the Closely-Held Businesses," *National Public Accountant*, (March 1989), pp. 31–33, 38.

Lipper, Arthur, *Venture's Guide to Investing in Private Companies* (Illinois: Richard Irwin, 1984).

Martin, Thomas and Gustafson, Mark, *Valuing Your Business* (New York: Holt Rinehart and Winston, 1980).

McCarthy, George and Healy, Robert, *Valuing a Company* (New York: Ronald Press, 1971).

Miles, Raymond, *Basic Business Appraisal* (New York: John Wiley, 1984).

Pratt, Shannon, *Valuing Small Businesses and Professional Practices* (Illinois: Dow-Jones Irwin, 1986).

Schnepper, Jeff, *The Professional Handbook of Business Valuation* (Mass.: Addison-Wesley, 1982).

Woolery, Arlo, *The Art of Valuation* (New York: Lexington Books, 1978).

——— 708 / SUMMARY CHECKLIST OF KEY POINTS ———

708.1. Business valuation considers the type of company and its activities, industry trends, degree of competition, trend in earnings, and balance sheet posture.

708.2. The company's financial figures should be compared to industry averages and to the financial figures of competing companies.

708.3. Adjust net income for unusual and nonrecurring revenue and expense components.

What to Do

☐ Increase net income by personal expenses and fringe benefits.

☐ Increase net income by the express amount of an unrealistically high officer salary.

☐ Add back interest expense to net income.

☐ Add back to net income the difference between normal and unusually low rental payments.

☐ Eliminate extraordinary items from net income.

☐ Reduce net income by investment income.

What to Watch Out For

☐ Related party transactions

708.4 / Capitalization of Earnings

1. The value of a business equals the restated earnings times a multiplier.

What to Do

☐ A five-year average restated earnings figure should be determined.

☐ A weighted-average earnings figure is better than a simple average earnings figure.

☐ In computing a weighted-average figure, the first year is given a weight of 1 while the fifth year is given a weight of 5.

☐ The multiplier is higher for a low risk business and lower for a high-risk business.

☐ The multiplier should be based on such factors as expected growth rate, potential earnings, stability, and liquidity.

708.5. / Capitalization of Excess Earnings

What to Do

☐ Excess earnings equals weighted-average adjusted earnings less normal rate of return on weighted-average net tangible assets. The weighting should be based on a five-year period.

☐ Capitalize the excess earnings to determine the value of the intangibles.

☐ The total valuation equals the value of the intangibles plus the fair market value of the net tangible assets.

708.6. / Capitalization of Cash Flow

What to Do

☐ Adjusted cash earnings are multiplied by a capitalization factor to arrive at capitalized cash flow.

☐ Valuation equals capitalized cash value less liabilities.

708.7. / Present Value of Future Cash Flows

1. A business is worth the discounted value of future cash earnings plus the discounted value of the expected selling price.

What to Do

☐ Use the rate of return earned by the business as the discount rate.

☐ The discount rate should take into account the riskiness of the business.

☐ Use the present value of $1 table to discount future cash earnings.

☐ Use the present value of $1 table to discount the expected selling price.

☐ The valuation equals the sum of the present values.

708.8. / Book Value

1. **Use the book value of the net assets only if fair market value is not available.**

708.9. / Tangible Net Worth

1. **Tangible net worth equals stockholders' equity less intangible assets.**

708.10. / Economic Net Worth

1. **Economic net worth equals fair market value of net assets less goodwill.**

708.11. / Fair Market Value of Net Assets

1. **Determine the fair market value of assets.**

What to Do

☐ Obtain independent appraisals of tangible assets from experts.

☐ Estimate goodwill.

☐ Add the value of the tangible and intangible assets.

What to Watch Out For

☐ Off-balance sheet liabilities

☐ Off-balance sheet assets

☐ Potential tax liabilities

708.12. / Gross Revenue Multiplier

1. **Valuation equals revenue times gross revenue multiplier.**

What to Do

☐ Use the multiplier common in the industry.

708.13. / Profit Margin/Capitalization Rate

1. Valuation is based on the company's profit margin.

What to Do

☐ Multiplier equals profit margin divided by the capitalization rate.

☐ Valuation equals multiplier times sales.

What to Consider

☐ Recent sales

708.14. / Price-Earnings Factor

1. Valuation equals the estimated market price per share times outstanding shares.

What to Do

☐ Use a realistic price-earnings ratio given the nature of the company and industry.

☐ Multiply earnings per share times the price-earnings ratio to determine expected market price per share.

☐ Multiply expected market price per share times outstanding shares.

708.15. / Comparative Value of Similar Businesses

1. Valuation may be based on the going rates for similar companies in the industry

What to Watch Out For

☐ Recent sales of similar businesses

What to Do

☐ Obtain industry source information.

☐ Modify the selling price of a similar business to reflect the characteristics of the business being valued.

708.16. / Recent Sales of Stock

A. Value the business at the current market price of stock times the outstanding shares.

What to Watch Out For

☐ The current market price of stock will be higher than what the shares could be sold for with a significant issuance of securities.

What to Do

☐ Discount the current market price to take into account demand/supply market conditions.

708.17. / Combination of Methods

A. The valuation of the business may be based on an integration of methods.

What to Do

☐ Determine a weighted-average value of two or more appropriate methods based on the situation.

☐ Give greater weight to the earnings-based method than the assets-based method.

708.18. / Internal Revenue Service Guidelines

A. If an asset valuation method is used, valuations must be separately determined for tangible and intangible assets.

B. The IRS favors the capitalization of excess earnings method (see 708.5).

C. The return rate on average net tangible assets should be the one prevailing in the industry.

☐ If an industry percentage is not available, use 8% to 10% as the return rate depending on risk and earnings stability.

☐ Use 15% to 20% as the capitalization rate depending on risk.

CHAPTER EIGHT

Industry Characteristics as They Affect Earnings Quality*

The earnings quality of companies in an industry depends upon the accounting policies employed. We must be especially careful in our analysis of industries that are under public scrutiny or governmental regulation, such as the oil industry. Companies in such industries have more of an incentive to manage earnings so that there is a minimization of public and regulatory attention. The quality of earnings also depends upon the impact of qualitative factors on the firm. Included herein are economic, financial, and political considerations. For example, recently poor economic conditions have had pronounced effects upon the automobile and home-building industries.

The following industries are evaluated: Airline, Automobile, Banking, Broadcasting, Consumer Finance, Electric and Gas, Franchising, Home Building, Insurance, Land Development, Motion Picture, Petroleum Refining, Pharmaceutical, Real Estate Investment Trust, and Savings and Loan.

* This chapter is partially based on the author's article on the subject appearing in:

  J. Siegel and L. Savage, "Industry Characteristics and the Quality of Earnings," *The National Public Accountant*, (July 1979), pp. 11–15. It is printed with permission from the *National Public Accountant*, the official publication of the National Society of Public Accountants.

801 / AIRLINE

Airline earnings tend to be volatile because of the combined impact of high operating and financial leverage. Airlines invest significantly in expensive fixed assets and finance those assets typically with debt.

Airlines receive advance payments for future transportation services. Thus, current liabilities contain expected revenues to be derived from advance ticket sales, counterbalanced by a comparable current asset. The current liability "Unearned Transportation Revenue" should be thoroughly evaluated because part of the liability may involve a cash outlay related to airline tickets for interline trips on several carriers. In other words, the issuing airline must pay other carriers for travel on their flights. Managerial discretion is exercised in estimating the unused or partially used tickets for the accounting period. Adjustments to the "Unearned Transportation Revenue" account may result in out-of-phase changes in passenger revenues. Such adjustments provide airlines latitude in reporting earnings. The analyst must therefore appraise whether adjustments made are realistic. If not, net income should be adjusted for the earnings effect due to the improper adjustments.

• T Airline made a favorable adjustment to passenger revenues of $11.6 million in 19X1.

An airline that intentionally underaccrues for expected labor contract settlements has lower earnings quality than an airline that has a realistic provision for this purpose.

The analyst should determine the *percentage of nonoperating aircraft to total aircraft*. A high percentage indicates a nonproductive fleet and casts doubt upon the continuity in earnings.

• W Airlines ABC fleet of 27 aircraft was classified as nonoperating equipment in 19X1.

Airlines having long-term contracts that restrict fuel price increases are less impacted by energy shortages than airlines paying "open market" prices.

• N Airline paid "open market" prices in 19X4. Consequently, its average price significantly exceeded the industry's domestic average price.

801.1 / Low Quality of Earnings Indicators: A Checklist

☐ High degree of operating leverage
☐ High degree of financial leverage
☐ Improper adjustments to the "Unearned Transportation Revenue" account

☐ Underaccrual for expected labor contract settlements

☐ A high ratio of nonoperating aircraft to total aircraft

☐ Paying "open market" prices for energy sources

802 / AUTOMOBILE

Accounting for special tools by auto manufacturers is a key analytical area. Higher earnings quality is indicated when tools are amortized more quickly because it indicates a conservative policy. Further, since design changes often occur, it is more realistic to expect that the special tools will have limited future benefit. Another favorable sign is the commencing of the amortization of special tools when they are acquired rather than when they are used, as there is an obsolescence factor.

• General Motors has a conservative amortization policy by amortizing tools more quickly, which reflects favorably upon its earnings quality.

803 / BANKING

In an article appearing in *Forbes*, a number of criticisms are directed at banks. They are that banks misstate their loan loss reserves, overstate assets, overstate earnings, and have inadequate disclosures.[1]

Although most banks do not disclose the following data in their annual reports, it is important that the analyst determine: (1) the unrealized (and unreported) loss on the loan portfolio and (2) the extent to which the bank is mismatched on the maturities of the components of the loan portfolio and the sources of money.

The analyst must be on guard against earnings increments arising from hidden reserves and should eliminate such increments from reported earnings. In this regard, J. Bogen writes:[2]

• Many bank managements like to accumulate "hidden" reserves, usually by carrying certain assets far below their true worth, for emergencies. An example is marketable securities carried at cost when market value is higher.

A bank can manage earnings through the timing of its mortgage closings. If it wishes to increase earnings, it can accelerate these closings in order to recognize more closing fees. The bank can also accelerate or defer foreign loans in order to manage its commission fees. The analyst must *restate earn-*

---

[1] "The Numbers Game: The Awful Truth," *Forbes*, (February 15, 1975), pp. 53–54.

[2] J. Bogen, *Financial Handbook* (New York: Ronald Press Co., 1948), p. 295

ings as they would have been if such income management had not taken place. For example, net income should be reduced for the incremental effect of accelerated commission fees.

803.1 / High Risk Loans

Banks should not take credit for above average interest rates earned on higher risk loans without providing for higher anticipated loan losses. In general, the higher the ratio of loan loss provisions to actual loss charge-offs, the more conservative the accounting being used by the bank, and the higher the quality of the bank's earnings. Banks must update their loan loss provision percentages in light of current casualties rather than blindly using historical averages. If the analyst determines that the loan loss provision is understated, he or she should downwardly adjust net income for the difference between the reported provision and what the provision should have been.

Some banks have sharply cut their interest rates on delinquent loans [e.g., loans to Real Estate Investment Trusts (REITs)] and accrued the interest at the lower rates. When there is a possibility of default it is better to recognize interest income only when cash is *received.* The analyst should therefore eliminate from net income the accrued interest income on delinquent loans. He may even wish to go further and for analytical purposes write off the delinquent loans by charging reported earnings.

• REITs had a devastating effect on the banking industry. In 19X4, charge-offs by banks on REIT loans reached $2 billion, or 166% of 19X3 REIT loan losses.

The analyst should determine the point at which banks place questionable loans on nonaccruing interest basis. The longer the period, the lower the bank's quality of earnings.

First Bank System disclosed the following in its Management Analysis of Results of Operations section:

> Loan portfolios are reviewed regularly by senior management to determine whether specific loans should be placed on a nonaccrual basis. When in the opinion of management the collection of interest is unlikely, the loan is placed in a nonaccrual category. When a loan is placed on nonaccrual, all previously accrued and unpaid interest is charged against current earnings. Thereafter, no interest is taken into income unless received in cash or until such time as the borrower demonstrates the ability to pay interest and principal.

The bank has a conservative policy regarding its accounting for the interest income on these high risk loans. Perhaps as a *next step,* a write-off of the questionable loans should be made.

Illustration ——————————————————————————————————

Bank A reports the following information:

Total revenue	$4,000,000
Closing fees	200,000
Interest income	1,000,000
Loan loss provision	150,000
Net income	2,000,000
Total loans receivable	3,000,000

The analyst determines that closing fees have traditionally been 3% of total revenue. He or she believes the bank may have accelerated its closing fee recognition to boost earnings.

Loan loss charge-offs have been increasing in the industry. Almost all banks provide a loan loss provision as a percentage of total loans receivable of 7%.

The bank has extended loans to a number of companies that are having very severe financial problems. For the year, it has modified its interest rate on such loans from 13% to 4%. The aggregate amount of the loans is $250,000.

Based upon past experience, closing fee income should have been $120,000 (3% × $4,000,000). Since the analyst is of the opinion that the account has been managed to improve earnings, he or she should reduce net income by $80,000 ($200,000 − $120,000).

The bank's loan loss provision should be 7% rather than 5% ($150,000/$ 3,000,000). It should therefore be increased by $60,000 (2% × $3,000,000) and net income should accordingly be reduced by this amount.

Net income should be downwardly adjusted for the accrued interest on the delinquent loans amounting to $10,000 (4% × $250,000).

As a result of the foregoing, the restated net income is:

Reported net income		$2,000,000
Less:		
Overstatement in closing fee income	$80,000	
Additional loan loss provision required	60,000	
Accrued interest income on delinquent loans	10,000	
		150,000
Restated net income		$1,850,000

A high percentage of noninterest-paying loans in a portfolio indicates realization risk in assets and casts doubt upon the stability of the earnings stream. The question also arises: How many other loans are marginally poor?

• Chase Manhattan Mortgage and Realty Trust reported a number of years ago that 94 projects totaling $463 million in loans (representing 47% of its portfolio) were not collecting income.

The analyst should determine the existence of *bank commitments to lend further money to financially poor borrowers*. This represents an unrecorded liability of the bank since future collection of the prospective loans are subject to high risk. Also, earnings quality is poor in the case where interest income consists of a high percentage of interest received from low quality loans since such source of earnings may not be relied upon in the future. Commerce disclosed the following in its Management Analysis of Results of Operations section:

> As of June 30, 19X5, loans outstanding to REITs totaled $42 million. Unused commitments of $4.3 million were also outstanding at that date. Some REIT loans have been or are in the process of being renegotiated, and one loan in the amount of $4.2 million is currently not accruing interest. For the six months ended June 30, 19X5, all REIT loans contributed to interest revenue at an annual average rate of 7.8%.

In evaluating the realization risk of a bank's loan portfolio, the analyst should look at the balance of the loan relative to the collateral value of the property.

• For example, banks with sizable loan portfolios to owners of shipping vessels had difficulties. The value of the collateral standing behind the loans had fallen well short of the credit extended, ship values declining 50% or more. Banks were reluctant to repossess vessels because any attempts to sell them would further depress ship prices.

In looking at domestic loan portfolios, the analyst should ascertain the degree of *diversification*. For example, loans to countercyclical industries reduce portfolio risk. In appraising the quality of international loans, the analyst should classify them by country to facilitate an analysis of their riskiness.

A bank that has a high percentage of long-term loans, such as mortgages, at unrealistically low fixed interest rates (CAP loans) has lower quality of earnings because it is unable to adjust revenue to meet its increasing costs. The analyst should determine the proportion of a bank's loan portfolio that consists of outdated interest CAP loans.

Illustration ———————————————————————————————

Bank B reports the following data:

Loans receivable	$10,000,000
Noninterest-paying loans	1,000,000

A footnote discloses:

"The loan portfolio consists of about 30% of loans made to the shipping industry, which at the current time are paying interest. The collateral values have dropped to about 60% of the carrying balances of the loans."

"Bank B has outstanding commitments to lend $400,000 to certain companies currently experiencing severe financial difficulties."

"Home mortgages averaging an interest rate of 9% are about 13% of the loan portfolio."

The realization risk of Bank B's loan portfolio is quite high. Noninterest-paying loans comprise 10% of its loan portfolio ($1,000,000/$10,000,000). Another 30% of the portfolio consists of loans to a *concentrated* industry having financial problems. Huge loan losses may arise since the collateral values are significantly less than the loan principals.

There exists an unrecorded liability of $400,000 since the bank is committed to lend additional funds to "problem" companies.

The bank is earning a low fixed-interest rate relative to current rates on its mortgages that will have a significant drain upon future profitability.

803.2 / Growth in Earnings

A bank's earnings growth may be of low quality if it cannot be sustained. Such a situation may be indicated when liquidity has been sharply reduced and/or the growth in loan volume has been excessive relative to deposit growth.

In an interview, F. Garcia (author of *How to Analyze a Bank Statement*) stated:

> A bank with a lower growth in average deposits relative to its competitors has lower earnings quality, because revenue from investments on deposits will decline to a greater extent than the decline in the costs of deposits (interest expense). This has a negative effect on earnings.

803.3 / Indicators of Poor Earnings Quality: A Checklist

- ☐ The existence of "hidden" reserves
- ☐ Managing closing and commission fees.
- ☐ A decline in the ratio of loan loss provisions to actual loss charge-offs
- ☐ Accruing interest income on delinquent loans.
- ☐ Waiting an excessively long time to place questionable loans on a nonaccruing interest basis
- ☐ A high ratio of noninterest-paying loans to total loans receivable
- ☐ A high percentage of interest income on questionable loans to total interest income

- ☐ Commitments to lend additional money to high risk borrowers
- ☐ The collateral value of loans is substantially less than the principal balances of the loans.
- ☐ Lack of diversification in the loan portfolio
- ☐ Loans to problem industries
- ☐ Loans to unstable foreign countries
- ☐ There is a high percentage of long-term loans having unrealistically low fixed-interest rates.

804 / BROADCASTING

Broadcasters have discretion in allocating costs for television programs. An illustration of the result of such discretion follows. Assume the cost of a television program is $100,000 for the first showing, and an estimated $20,000 for the rerun in the following year. Assume also that the revenue from the first showing is $80,000 while the rerun brings in an estimated revenue of $60,000. If the allocation is based on revenue derived from each showing, the following will result:

	19X4		19X5	
Revenue		$80,000		$60,000
Cost Allocation (approximate)	$120,000 \times \dfrac{80}{140}$	68,600	$120,000 \times \dfrac{60}{140}$	51,400
Profit		$11,400		$ 8,600

On the other hand, the company may elect to charge its actual costs to each showing in the year incurred. In this case, the first showing results in a loss of $20,000 (Revenue of $80,000 less costs of $100,000) while the second showing results in a profit of $40,000 (Revenue of $60,000 less costs of $20,000).

Broadcasters might allocate costs on other bases. Because different allocation methods can be employed for each type of television program, broadcasters can very easily manage their income.

The analyst must assure himself or herself that the broadcaster's policy of allocating costs for television programs is consistent. Further, if income has been managed, the analyst should restate the broadcaster's earnings as they *should* have been.

Networks often acquire film packages at lump-sum prices. For example, a network paid $6 million for six James Bond films, and established a sliding scale of costs for each film. The network was therefore able to smooth earnings by deciding which film would be shown in a given period. If earnings were too low, the network would flow out a low-cost film. The analyst should be on guard against such an artificial earnings boost.

804.1 / Deferral of Costs

If earnings are low, networks can continue to defer the costs of outdated and low-quality films. The decision to write down these films is subjective and is based on the company's estimated future revenue to be derived from them. A broadcaster's failure to make an adequate write-down results in overstated earnings. For analytical purposes, the analyst should eliminate the deferred costs of obsolete and unsuccessful films and downwardly adjust reported earnings accordingly.

804.2 / Statement of Position

The AICPA Accounting Standards Division has prepared a Statement of Position on the *Accounting Practices in the Broadcasting Industry* (dated December 29, 1975). The Statement provides:

> The Division believes that film rights should now be amortized based on the number of future showings estimated by management . . .
>
> The Division has concluded that an accelerated method of amortization which takes into consideration the station's programming pattern is now required when the first showing, as is usually the case, is more valuable to a station than reruns. Accordingly, the straight-line method of amortization is only acceptable in those instances where each telecast is expected to generate similar revenues.

804.3 / Expense Recognition

Programming expenses are capitalized and amortized over the first run of a series. However, they are expensed when the decision is made that the program being developed will not be aired. The timing of the reporting of such expense is largely discretionary in nature and as such the analyst should employ the analytical techniques discussed previously relating to discretionary costs.

Some broadcasters allocate all interest expense on borrowed funds to new systems thereby deferring all interest charges. Interest expense should be allocated to both new and existing projects because borrowed funds are used for both purposes. The deferral of the entire interest expense results in overstated earnings. The analyst should eliminate from the deferred account the portion of interest charges applicable to existing projects. She should also reduce net income by the charges.

An intentional overaccrual for possible record returns and discounts results in lower earnings quality because it understates net income. The analyst should increase reported earnings for the portion of the expense provision that has been overaccrued.

• In 19X4, a network added substantially to its allowance for doubtful accounts and for record returns and discounts. The amount charged to costs and expenses significantly exceeded the amounts actually written off, and reserves were boosted by $24 million to $61 million, although gross receivables rose only slightly. The amount charged off was excessive and probably represented an accounting cushion.

Illustration

A broadcaster provides the following financial data:

Revenue	$2,900,000
Net income	550,000
Deferred costs of films	800,000
Expense provision for record returns and discounts	200,000

The deferred cost account includes $70,000 applicable to unsuccessful films.

For the industry, the expense provision for record returns and discounts relative to total revenue is about 9.0%, which is considered the norm.

The broadcaster's expense provision should be $261,000 (9.0% × $2,900,000) rather than $200,000.

The reported earnings should be downwardly adjusted as follows:

Reported net income		$550,000
Less:		
Write down of the film inventory account	$70,000	
Understatement in the expense provision for record returns and discounts	61,000	131,000
Restated net income		$419,000

804.4 / Signs of Low Quality Earnings: A Checklist

- ☐ The discretionary allocation of costs for television programs
- ☐ Improperly accelerating or deferring the recognition of programming expenses
- ☐ Intentionally showing a low-cost film to boost earnings
- ☐ Overaccruing or underaccruing the provision for record returns and discounts
- ☐ Deferring costs of outdated and unsuccessful films
- ☐ Deferring interest expense applicable to existing projects

——————— 805 / CONSUMER FINANCE ———————

Deferred income relates to the precomputed interest and discount charges that borrowers must pay over the loan period. Some finance companies recognize in income a portion of deferred income as an "acquisition" charge when the loan is made. An unrealistically high rate assigned to deferred income for acquisition charges results in the overstatement of earnings. The analyst should reduce earnings reported for the effect of using a higher rate than is justified.

The balance of deferred income may be recognized in a number of ways. Under the sum-of-the-years'-digits method, higher amounts of income are recognized in the earlier years than in the later years. (For example, in a twelve-month loan, 12/78 of the finance charge is recognized in the initial month while 1/78 will be recognized in the final month). The method results in greater earnings variability over the life of the loan, and in front-end loading of profits. Quality of earnings is thereby lowered.

With regard to insurance subsidiaries, T. O'Glove writes:[3]

> Consumer finance companies include in operating earnings capital gains derived from insurance subsidiaries. These gains should be eliminated in arriving at real operating performance because they are not representative of business generated income. In the event that this portion of income is material, earnings may be accelerated either upward or downward depending on how fast new business is being placed on the books.

In general, income should be recognized based on business placed since that is the crucial event to the earnings process.

——————— 806 / ELECTRIC AND GAS ———————

Allowance for funds during construction (AFC) represents capitalized interest charges on funds borrowed to finance plant expansion. In most cases, charging the interest on these funds to net income would seriously penalize earnings. Therefore, regulatory commissions allow utilities to capitalize these costs during plant construction, spreading the cost over the life of the plant similar to other construction costs. This results in an AFC credit, an addition to current earnings. However, AFC does not represent cash earnings and cannot be used to pay dividends and interest.

AFC accounts for a very high percentage of net income of some utilities. It accounted for 67 percent of V's 19X2 reported earnings after preferred dividends. AFC is a constructive fiction. The more a company spends

———————

[3] T. O'Glove, "Finance Company Accounting," *Financial Analysts Journal*, (January/February 1968), p. 41.

on construction, the higher its net income. A utility that accrues AFC at an unrealistic rate has lower earnings quality. An unrealistic rate may be either a rate that is in excess of what is likely to be granted by the regulatory agency or a rate that exceeds the utility's cost of capital.

AFC can create problems when a utility experiences a regulatory lag after "plant under construction" is incorporated in the rate base. A utility may not always obtain approval for the entire rate of return upon which it was predicting AFC. Also, new plants may encounter delays or there may be excessive start-up costs.

It is recommended that the analyst determine the percentage of a utility's earnings that is comprised of AFC. Further, the analyst should downwardly adjust net income for the earnings increment arising from the overaccrual of AFC.

A utility that has a policy of expensing fuel costs as incurred has higher earnings quality than a utility that defers such costs since the former policy is conservative. The analyst must always be on guard against the capitalization of increased fuel costs by a utility when it is highly unlikely that the regulatory body will allow all or part of such costs to be passed on to consumers.

The analyst must always watch for the appropriateness and earnings effect of accounting changes.

• For the ten months ended October 31, 19X3, Electric and Gas announced a $40 million increase in income over the comparable period in 19X2. $18.5 million of that increment was due to an accounting change. The utility initiated the recording of revenue and fuel costs on "services rendered" rather than on "services billed."[4]

B. Graham, B. Dodd, and S. Cottle write:[5]

> In the typical balance sheet, utility plant is usually shown as a single figure; or, in the case of a combination company—i.e., one rendering more than one type of service, such as electricity and gas, water, heating, etc.—the plant account may be further segregated to show the investment in facilities used to provide each service. This segregation is important to the analyst since, from a regulatory viewpoint, departmental earnings are commonly related to the investment made to furnish the particular service, and if the latter is not revealed a correct evaluation of reported earnings is difficult if not impossible.

---

[4] "The Numbers Game: A Switch in Time," *Forbes*, (January 15, 1974), p. 49.

[5] From *Security Analysis: Principles and Techniques* by B. Graham, B. Dodd and S. Cottle, p. 270. Copyright 1962 McGraw-Hill Book Company. Used with the permission of McGraw-Hill Book Company.

J. Bogen and S. Shipman write:[6]

Analysis of the earning power of a public utility must take into account both regulatory and economic factors. If earnings are substantially above the fair return rate of the rate base, they are vulnerable. Conversely, if earnings fall below a fair return level, rate increases may be obtainable if they are economically feasible.

Illustration

A utility reports the following financial information:

Allowance for funds during construction (AFC) credit	$ 540,000
Net income	1,100,000
Deferred increased fuel costs	250,000

A footnote discloses:

"The utility has borrowed $3,000,000 to finance plant construction."

"The policy of the company is to defer all increased fuel costs."

The industry norm for the ratio of AFC to net income is 19%.

The utility is using an 18% rate to accrue AFC but the analyst expects, based on past experience, that the regulatory commission will allow only a 16% rate.

The analyst determines that over the past several years the utility has received approval for about 85% of its increased fuel costs.

The utility's quality of earnings is deficient. The ratio of AFC to net income is high, namely 49% ($540,000/$1,100,000). Further, the ratio far surpasses the industry norm.

The analyst should downwardly adjust the AFC credit and net income for the unwarranted incremental AFC rate of 2% (18%—16%). The amount of the reduction is therefore $60,000 (2% × $3,000,000).

The deferred increased fuel cost account and net income should be reduced by $37,500 (15% × $250,000) representing the excess deferral of fuel costs that will probably not be approved for pass-along.

The restated earnings of the utility are:

Reported earnings		$1,100,000
Less:		
Overstated AFC	$60,000	
Excessive deferred fuel costs	37,500	97,500
Restated earnings		$1,002,500

---

[6] J. Bogen and S. Shipman, *Financial Handbook* (New York: Ronald Press Co., 1968), p. 720.

806.1 / Indicators of Poor Earnings Quality: A Checklist

☐ AFC is a high percentage of net income.

☐ AFC has been accrued at either a rate that is in excess of what the regulator commission will likely allow or at a rate that exceeds the utility's cost of capital.

☐ The deferral of increased fuel costs that probably will not be approved by the regulatory body to be passed on to consumers.

☐ A boost in earnings arising from a change in accounting policy from recording revenue and fuel costs on a "services billed" basis to a "services rendered" basis.

☐ Negative regulatory and economic factors affecting the utility.

807 / FRANCHISING

Franchise fee accounting is covered by FASB 45. According to it, franchise fee revenue from the initial sale of a franchise is to be recognized only when all material services have been substantially performed and there is an absence of intent to refund any cash received or forgive any unpaid receivables.

J. Hagler believes that sales of franchises are nonrecurring, and therefore detract from the stability of the earnings stream. He writes:[7]

> The recurring feature aspect of revenue is important. It is questionable whether the sales of franchises are recurring transactions. Within a defined area, only a limited number of franchise units can operate. In addition, competition will limit expansion.

The above comment must be qualified. Franchise revenue may show stability when the franchiser has a unique reputation and the franchisees are financially sound.

808 / HOME BUILDING

Home builders are able to manage earnings by assigning different values, ranging from high to low, for different plots of land; utilizing second mortgages to overstate the sales price of homes and plots sold; exchanging plots of low-cost land with other firms at inflated prices; and overestimating the degree of completion on home contracts accounted for under the percentage-of-completion method. The analyst must be on guard against such income management ploys.

---

[7] J. Hagler, "The Franchise Fee," *Management Accounting*, (July, 1974), p. 49.

Some builders have in the past sold property to charitable organizations at unusually high profits. These transactions were coupled with contracts stating that the builder would reacquire the property at a subsequent date at an agreed-upon price, leaving significant income for the exempt entity. This fictitious profit should be omitted from the home builder's reported net income.

Problems also exist with respect to the allocation of revenues and earnings on major projects that involve a number of independent efforts. Some builders have used the "packaging concept," where they develop and sell projects to unaffiliated third parties. In some instances, a "developing profit" is recognized before construction has commenced, or before it is completed, on the assumption that the transaction consists of a number of separate efforts. Development profit results in lower quality of earnings because substantial performance on the construction project has not occurred. Such profits should preferably be deferred.

In conclusion, earnings manipulation by some home builders results in the reporting of net incomes that do not reflect economic reality but rather allow the masking of the performance of the home builders for the period. The artificial shifting of income makes it difficult to compare performance from period to period.

The building industry is cyclical in nature, and hence home builders often experience fluctuating earnings.

808.1 / Things to Be Wary of: A Checklist

- ☐ The arbitrary assignment of different values for alternative plots of land
- ☐ The use of second mortgages to overstate the sales price of homes
- ☐ The exchange of low-cost plots of land
- ☐ The overstatement of the degree of completion on homes
- ☐ The recognition of "developing profit" prior to the commencement of construction

809 / INSURANCE

The AICPA audit guide titled "Audits of Stock Life Insurance Companies" provides for the deferral of costs incurred in obtaining new business when they vary with, and are directly related to, the production of new business. Amortization of these deferred charges will be made against income in proportion to premium revenues recognized. A problem arises as to which acquisition costs are truly direct and variable and therefore eligible for deferral. Management may have some ability to classify the types of acquisition costs to best meet its desired earnings trend. The analyst should assure herself that the acquisition costs that have been deferred are proper. If not, for analytical purposes, she should reduce the deferred amount and net income for such questionable costs.

A. Briloff criticizes the use of the sum-of-the-years' premium method in amortizing acquisition costs and develops a superior method based on the present value of premiums. His illustration follows:[8]

Illustration

Assume a life insurer incurs $5,000 in acquisition costs to obtain an expected premium flow of $10,000 in the first year, $8,000 in the second year, and $7,000 in the third year. If we assume an earnings rate of 6%, we would have the following comparative data:

(1) Year	(2) Premium expected on 1/1	(3) Expense Allocated based on Col. 2	(4) PV* Factor 6% Table	(5) PV* of Premium Cols. 2 × 4	(6) Expense Allocated based on Col. 5
1	$10,000	$2,000	1.0	$10,000	$2,103
2	8,000	1,600	.943	7,544	1,587
3	7,000	1,400	.890	6,230	1,310
	$25,000	$5,000		$23,774	$5,000

*PV = Present Value

The table demonstrates that allocating acquisition costs on the basis of the sum-of-the-years' premiums (which appears to be a common practice) produces a less than equitable charge to the initial year's operations, and a correspondingly greater than equitable deferral to be absorbed in subsequent years.

It is significant to note that each of the amounts shown in Column 6, when extrapolated for the compound interest factor, stands in the same relationship to the premium expected to be collected in the corresponding year (21.03% of each year's anticipated premiums).

A deficiency of the Audit Guide is that it enables firms to recognize in current income that income which applies to future years. This has the effect of front-loading profits, thus resulting in lower quality of earnings.

---

[8] A. Briloff, "SLIC GAAP," *Financial Analysts Journal*, (March/April, 1974), pp. 82–83. Reprinted with permission of the *Financial Analysts Journal*.

809.1 / Interest Assumption

A life insurance company may smooth earnings and reserve balances by changing its actuarial interest rate. For instance, an increase in the assumed interest rate on investments or an improvement in the mortality rate will cause the insurance provision to decline with the resultant increase in earnings.

Capital gains and losses on the sale of investments show less stability than underwriting income. The former source of earnings is of lower quality.

809.2 / Lines of Insurance

Certain lines of insurance (e.g., medical malpractice) require management to make very difficult estimates of future costs. Inflation as well as changing social attitudes makes it difficult for companies to estimate reliably future malpractice awards. Under these circumstances, the adequacy of the reserve provision is very uncertain. Inadequate or excessive reserves result in lower quality earnings.

Certain lines of insurance such as property and liability are highly cyclical in nature, and thus detract from earnings stability. More stable lines of insurance are life and health. The analyst should therefore look at the trend in the percentage of total revenue derived by each major line of insurance.

An article in the *Wall Street Transcript* (August 11, 1975) stated:

> The quality of earnings of fire and casualty companies is not too good. 1975 pre-tax underwriting loss approximately equals pre-tax investment income, and the only way that companies showed earnings was because of the tax loss credit which has a very low value.

Illustration

An insurance company provides the following financial data:

Deferred acqusition costs	$ 780,000
Revenue	12,000,000
Net income	4,500,000
Expense provision for future malpractice and claim payments	1,300,000

A footnote states: "Because of rapidly changing attitudes as evidenced by recent court decisions, it is difficult to estimate the provision necessary for future costs and losses associated with potential settlements on the company's major lines of insurance."

The analyst believes that about 20% of the deferred acquisition cost account does not relate to the generation of new business.

The company's expense provision for future malpractice and claim payments has averaged about 13% of total revenue in prior years. The industry norm is approximately this.

The deferred acquisition cost account and net income should be reduced by $156,000 (20% × $780,000) because of the overstatement in the deferred account.

The firm's expense provision of 10.8% of revenue ($1,300,000/$12,000,000) is too low. It should be $1,560,000 (13% × $12,000,000). Therefore, net income should be downwardly adjusted by $260,000 ($1,560,000—$1,300,000). Further, earnings quality is low because of the uncertainty associated with estimating future costs and losses as evidenced by the company's footnote.

The restatement of net income follows:

Reported earnings		$4,500,000
Less:		
Write-down of deferred acquisition cost account	$156,000	
Understatement in expense provision	260,000	416,000
Restated net income		$4,084,000

---

810 / LAND DEVELOPMENT

In response to accounting practices of land development companies that resulted in fictitious earnings, the AICPA issued an accounting guide entitled "Accounting for Retail Land Sales." The deficient accounting practices included the recognition of profit on retail land sales contracts long before it was reasonably evident that the purchaser would meet his payment obligations. Prior to the accounting guide, many companies immediately recognized the entire contract price, less related costs, even though only a nominal down payment (as low as 2 1/2%) had been made by financially insecure purchasers and the payment period extended long into the future. This accounting practice resulted in lower quality earnings.

The provisions of the accounting guide follow:

1. Revenue may be recognized under either the deposit, installment, or accrual methods.

2. Until it is certain that a project will meet the terms of the sales contract, revenues are to be accounted for on the installment basis. When it appears that the company is in a position to meet its obligations, the firm will be allowed to use the accrual method.

3. A customer's payment must be recorded as a deposit until it is evident that he is likely to meet the contract provisions. The company must defer recognition of a sale until the payments of the customer (including interest) are at least 10% of the agreed contract price.

• The 10% revenue recognition rule is a questionable one. The "earnings cycle" is not necessarily complete at the time the accounting guide suggests revenue can be realized. In most cases, the seller is obligated to complete improvements in future years so that the lots are in a usable state to the buyer. The "earnings cycle" is not complete then until the obligated improvements have been made. Furthermore, an exchange has not occurred when only 10% of the sales price has been collected. An exchange does not take place until the purchaser has received consideration commensurate with the cash payments he has made. Partially completed lots then should only justify a partial realization of revenue.[9]

The analyst should therefore eliminate from reported earnings the income that has been recognized prior to the completion of what he considers the "earnings cycle."

E. Deakin and M. Granof write:[10]

As a result of the accounting guide, in the event that a firm will switch from the installment to the accrual method in the middle of a project's life, its earnings pattern may be highly erratic.

810.1 / Cash Flow from Operations

Some land developers have very low percentages of operating cash flow to net income. *A significant disparity between the two is a low earnings quality indicator.*

---

[9] R. Lytle, "Accounting for Retail Land Sales," *Financial Analysts Journal,* (January/February, 1973), p. 98.

[10] E. Deakin and M. Granof, "Accounting for Retail Land Sales Under the New Accounting Guide," *The CPA Journal,* (November, 1973), p. 973.

810.2 / Source of Earnings

With respect to retail land sales, B. Graham, B. Dodd, and S. Cottle write:[11]

> The current "fair value" of real estate holdings is difficult to determine. *The analyst must separate the profits on real estate sales from the recurrent earnings realized through rentals.* He is unable to state with confidence what the "true earnings" of such a company have been over a period of years, since the relationship between "earnings" and increases in property values—realized and unrealized—must be a cloudy one. Real estate operations in periods of rising or fluctuating values do not lend themselves to the concept of an established or continuing earning power.

Another accounting guide issued by the AICPA is entitled "Profit Recognition on Sales of Real Estate." It applies to all real estate transactions except for retail land sales. Before a company can recognize the entire profit on sales contracts, the seller must be rid of ownership risks in the property, and a down payment of 25% of the sales value must be made.

———————— 811 / MOTION PICTURE ————————

Of prime concern is the realizability of the deferred costs of making a movie because of the high rate of movie failures and the reluctance of the company to recognize such. The overstatement of the deferred charge account results in the overstatement of earnings because of the failure to write down the asset.

- A motion picture company discloses: "In 19X3, the company recorded a $26 million write-down of its film inventories."
- An auditing firm declined to predict in its report on company A's fiscal 19X4 results whether the company would recover deferred costs of a movie venture.

———————— 812 / PETROLEUM REFINING ————————

Full cost accounting involves the capitalization of all exploration and development costs without consideration of the success of any particular project. The full cost method may overstate current reported earnings because it permits companies to stretch over a period of years such costs as unsuccessful exploration and drilling expenses. It is possible, in some cases,

---

[11] B. Graham, B. Dodd, and S. Cottle, *op. cit.,* p. 113.

that the amount capitalized could exceed the value of the firm's reserves. Under such circumstances, the deferred account is overstated. Earnings are of lower quality since they do not reflect charges necessary to write down the account to its proper amount. For analytical purposes, the analyst should reduce both the deferred account and net income for (1) unsuccessful exploration and development costs and for (2) the excess of the deferred account balance over the present value of the firm's reserves.

Some companies have retained capitalized costs on their books even though exploration activity has ceased. Therefore, the write-off policy used by full-cost companies should be carefully evaluated. If costs are capitalized until reserves are found, when does the company commence writing off these costs if no reserves are discovered?

A petroleum company has higher earnings quality if it uses the successful efforts method. Under this method, successful exploration costs are deferred and unsuccessful costs are expensed. This approach is conservative and realistic.

One must be wary of companies that change to the full-cost method because it creates "instant earnings."

• In 19X2, Basin Petroleum adopted full-cost accounting, and increased earnings from a $700,000 loss to a $750,000 profit.

During the energy shortage, oil companies showed substantial earnings due to the liquidation of low-cost inventories. As previously discussed, these inventory profits represent low quality of earnings elements.

812.1 / Qualitative Considerations

An integrated oil company that performs functions both of extracting and refining oil has greater earnings stability than does a nonintegrated company which is involved solely in the refining process. The latter company is highly dependent upon other firms to provide unrefined oil in times of energy shortage. It is also susceptible to highly fluctuating crude oil prices.

An oil company with a high petroleum reserve level has greater earning potential than a competitor with a low reserve level.

Illustration ─────────────────────────────────────

A petroleum refiner reports the following information:

Deferred exploration costs	$4,000,000
Net income	3,800,000

A footnote discloses:

"The company uses the full cost method. A number of exploration projects have not succeeded."

"Inventory profits are approximated at $350,000."

"The firm is only involved in refining oil."

The analyst approximates that 25% of the company's exploration efforts fail.

The deferred exploration cost account and net income should be reduced by $1,000,000 (25% × $4,000,000) based upon the estimated failure rate of exploration activity. The inventory profits of $350,000 should also be subtracted from net income.

The restated net income is:

Reported earnings		$3,800,000
Less:		
Write-down of deferred exploration costs	$1,000,000	
Inventory profits	350,000	1,350,000
Restated earnings		$2,450,000

Since the oil company is a nonintegrated one, it is subject to the risk of oil shortages and rapidly rising crude oil prices.

812.2 / Questions to Be Answered: A Checklist

- ☐ Is full cost accounting being used?
- ☐ Has the company changed to the full cost method from the successful efforts method?
- ☐ What is the relationship between the deferred exploration and development cost account and the value of the company's reserves?
- ☐ What is the write-off policy regarding deferred costs if no reserves are found?
- ☐ What is the magnitude of inventory profits?
- ☐ Is the oil company a nonintegrated one in that it is involved only in the refining process?
- ☐ Is the petroleum reserve level excessively low?

813 / PHARMACEUTICAL

The earnings quality of pharmaceutical companies is enhanced because of the stability of their earnings arising from inelastic product demand. Further, they have operations in low-tax foreign areas.

D. Saks writes:[12]

The real earnings of drug companies are close to reported earnings because of the fact that depreciation is a relatively minor cost item. Further, the amount of inventory profits is rather small due to high turnover rates.

814 / REAL ESTATE INVESTMENT TRUST (REIT)

REITs have experienced significant financial problems such as that evidenced by the following disclosure of M Trust of America:

Extremely depressed conditions in the real estate market in 19X4 seriously weakened the ability of many borrowers to meet their financial obligations. The decision was therefore made to add approximately $4 million to the allowance for possible losses account.

Non-earning investments increased from $10,215,000 at November 30, 19X3 to $43,618,000 at November 30, 19X4.

Some REITs with very high debt-to-equity ratios were paying substantial cash dividends while their earnings were declining, thus creating potential cash problems because significant funds would be needed to meet the principal and interest payments on the debt obligations.

REITs have engaged in numerous accounting practices that have rendered their quality of earnings suspect. These practices relate to the accrual of interest, commitment fees, and loan loss reserves.

814.1 / Problem Loans

The accrual of interest by REITs on problem loans to land developers should be closely scrutinized. Many construction loans are made on a discount basis, with both interest and principal due when the loan matures. In many cases, the collectibility of interest and principal are doubtful.

Some REITs are reluctant to identify poor loans, and continue to accrue interest on such loans.

• Cabot, Cabot & Forbes Land Trust continued to accrue rental or interest income on three bankrupt or foreclosed properties because management felt that the loans could be worked out.

---

[12] D. Saks, *Accounting Questions of Particular Importance to the Drug Industry*, (New York: Drexel Burnham, February 18, 1975), p. 24.

Trusts should stop accruing interest when the first signs of difficulty appear. This is the point at which the value of the real estate or building used as collateral declines sharply (the property is worth less than the principal and interest on the loan), and the developer has incurred significant cost overruns. Under such circumstances, REITs should reflect interest income only when it is received.

814.2 / Statement of Position

In 1975, the Accounting Standards Executive Committee of the AICPA had prepared a position paper titled "Accounting Practices of REITs." It states that "recognition of interest revenue should be discontinued when it is not reasonable to expect that the revenue will be received." It enumerates conditions under which the recording of such interest should be discontinued.

Many trusts recorded commitment fees on loans immediately as income at the loan record date or shortly afterward. This resulted in overstating current period earnings. The AICPA paper states that "commitment fees should be amortized over the combined commitment and loan period."

Many trusts consistently underestimated their loan loss reserves, thus overstating earnings. The AICPA's position paper provides that trusts would have to accrue in their loan loss provisions an amount equal to the cost of holding a problem asset. An REIT would be required to estimate the final sales price of the property on loan and reduce it by the estimated cost to complete, the estimated costs to dispose of the property, and estimated costs to hold the property.

As a follow-up to its 1975 Statement of Position, the AICPA issued another one in 1978. Its purpose was to recommend how REITs should conform to the requirements of FASB 15 titled "Accounting by Debtors and Creditors for Troubled Debt Restructurings." When it is probable that an REIT will engage in a troubled debt restructuring with a debtor that will result in a loss in excess of the allowance provided for under FASB 15, a provision should be established for the excess loss.

814.3 / Questionable Accounting Practices

First Mortage Investors engaged in certain accounting practices which rendered its earnings quality suspect. One practice was the use of letters of intent by which the trust would promise to finance a forthcoming project subject to the builder meeting in essence impossible requirements. The trust would recognize the fee as current income even though it knew that further financing would not occur, and the borrower would use the letter to borrow from banks. Further, the trust created fictitious "shell" companies to buy poor loans. For instance, in 1971, one of its $15 million loans went into default. Management wanted to do something prior to fiscal year-end, January 31, 1972. First Mortgage Investors created a shell corporation called World Land and Investment. The new company bought out the original developers for approximately $470,000, the funds supplied by the trust in a new and bigger loan. The danger of default was transferred to the future. The deal was closed approximately two weeks prior to FMI's year-end.[13]

Fidelity Mortgage Investors is a good example of an REIT that was forced to adjust its books because of fictitious profits previously recorded:[14]

• After a loan-by-loan portfolio analysis Fidelity Mortgage Investors announced early in February that it had paid out $4.7 million more than came in. And, it was ceasing to accrue interest retroactively to Oct. 31, 1973 on loans totaling some $40 million . . . Translated, this means that the company was wiping these "earnings" off its books, and the funds already paid out were being treated as a return of capital to shareholders.

Such incidents undermine the faith of the investor in the earnings determination process of REITs.

Illustration

An REIT provides the following financial data:

Total debt	$300,000
Stockholders' equity	130,000
Net income	20,000
Cash flow provided from operations	12,000
Cash dividends	60,000

A footnote discloses:

"Because land developers are having problems, it is anticipated that future write-offs of receivables will be necessary."

"It may be difficult to engage in further bank financing because of the weakened state of the real estate market."

Relevant computations follow:

Debt-to-equity ratio	231%
Dividends to net income	300%
Dividends to cash flow provided from operations	500%

---

[13] "Horror Story," *Forbes*, (February 1, 1975), pp. 28–30. Reprinted with the permission of *Forbes*.

[14] "The Numbers Game: When Is a Lemon a Lemon?" *Forbes*, (March 15, 1974), p. 63.

The company's cash dividends are excessive as evidenced by both the ratios of (1) dividends to net income and (2) dividends to cash flow provided from operations. In light of the excessive debt-to-equity ratio, the potential write-off of receivables, the difficulty in getting further credit, and the problems of the industry, it may be extremely difficult for the REIT to meet its obligations.

When a company has the financial problems and risks indicated here, it should not pay, or pay only minimal cash dividends. The high dividend-payout ratio in this case is a very poor financial management decision.

---

815 / SAVINGS AND LOAN (S&L)

In light of the current high interest rates offered by money market institutions, the high rate of inflation, and the recessionary environment, it is clear that S&Ls have much instability associated with them. However, a positive aspect of S&Ls is that they have minimal international exposure. In addition, the quality of assets is high due to the large underlying equity that most homeowners currently enjoy, due to past inflation.

815.1 / Earnings Stability

The earnings stability of an S&L is better when there is a low percentage of fee income to total revenue. A low percentage reduces the potential impact on earnings of possible changes in yearly loan production, which varies with the business cycle. Also, there should be a low percentage of construction loans in the S&L's loan portfolio because the potential exposure to bad loans is reduced.

Penalties for premature conversion of certificates that add to earnings are volatile in nature since they vary with changes in the market interest rates. The conversions also reduce long-term deposits and have an adverse impact on long-term profitability.

Capital gains and losses associated with disposing of foreclosed real estate are volatile earnings elements because they vary with the state of the economy.

- Financial included gains of $1.8 million in the first quarter of 19X5 from this source.

"Day of Deposit to Day of Withdrawal" accounts result in more earnings instability than do "Regular" accounts. The analyst should therefore determine the percentage of Day of Deposit to Day of Withdrawal accounts to total deposits.

815.2 / Loan Portfolio

The quality of the S&L loan portfolio can be evaluated thanks to regulatory practices. An S&L is required to report periodically to the Federal Home Loan Bank on (1) slow loans (90 days past due), (2) foreclosed real estate, and (3) loans applicable to the sale of foreclosed properties. The total of these three categories is stated as a percentage of total loans and is termed the scheduled-item ratio. A high ratio indicates that the loan portfolio has high realization risk.

Illustration

The analyst is evaluating the earnings quality of two S&Ls. Relevant data for 19X1 follow:

	S&L A	S&L B
Day of Deposit to Day of Withdrawal accounts	$2,000,000	$2,100,000
Regular accounts	1,000,000	800,000
Fee income	100,000	250,000
Total revenue	1,400,000	2,000,000
Capital gains and losses from the sale of foreclosed real estate	10,000	17,000
Net income	200,000	230,000
Construction loans	500,000	750,000
Total loans receivable	4,000,000	5,000,000
Scheduled-item ratio	2%	3%

Relevant computations follow:

	S&L A	S&L B
Day of Deposit to Day of Withdrawal accounts relative to Regular accounts	2.0x	2.63x
Fee income as a percentage of total revenue	7.1%	12.5%
Capital gains and losses from the sale of foreclosed real estate as a percentage of net income	5.0%	7.4%
Construction loans to total loans receivable	12.5%	15.0%
Scheduled-item ratio (given)	2.0%	3.0%

S&L B has lower quality of earnings than S&L A for the following reasons:

1. It has a higher degree of Day of Deposit to Day of Withdrawal accounts.
2. Its fee income is a higher percentage of total revenue.

3. There is a higher percentage of capital gains and losses from the sale of foreclosed real estate to reported earnings.

4. It has a higher realization risk in its loan portfolio as evidenced by the greater mix of construction loans and the higher scheduled-item ratio.

815.3 / Indicators of Low Earnings Quality: A Checklist

☐ A high ratio of fee income to total revenue

☐ An excessive scheduled-item ratio

☐ A high percentage of construction loans to total loans

☐ A high ratio of Day of Deposit to Day of Withdrawal accounts to total deposits

☐ Premature conversion of certificates

—— 816 / SUMMARY CHECKLIST OF KEY POINTS ——

816.1. The quality of earnings of a firm is affected by the accounting, financial, economic, and political factors associated with the industry it is in.

816.2. We should be on the lookout for questionable accounting policies, susceptibility to economic influences, vulnerability to foreign and domestic government controls, and trends in the industry.

816.3. / Airline

1. Earnings tend to fluctuate because of the combined effect of high operating and high financial leverage.

What to Do

☐ Determine the trend in the ratio of fixed costs to total costs.

☐ Determine the trend in the ratio of total debt to stockholders' equity.

2. Unearned Transportation Revenue Account

What to Watch Out For

☐ Improper adjustments to the account

What to Do

☐ Adjust net income for the effect of unrealistic adjustments to the account.

3. Accrual for Expected Labor Contract Settlements

What to Watch Out For

☐ Underaccrual or overaccrual of the expense provision.

What to Do

☐ Restate earnings for the underaccrued or overaccrued amount.

4. Nonoperating Aircraft

What to Do

☐ Determine the trend in the percentage of nonoperating aircraft to total aircraft.

5. Fuel Cost

What to Watch Out For

☐ An airline that has to pay open market prices for fuel

816.4. / Automobile

1. Special Tools

What to Watch Out For

☐ Excessive amortization period for special tools

816.5. / Banking

1. Hidden Reserves

What to Watch Out For

☐ Assets being carried at amounts significantly below their value Examples are:
   a. Marketable securities at cost when market value is higher
   b. Loans written down below their probable recovery value
   c. Real estate acquired through foreclosure recorded below market value

What to Do

☐ Reduce net income for the earnings increment due to the recognition of a "hidden reserve."

2. Management of Earnings

What to Watch Out For

☐ Accelerating or deferring mortgage closings and/or foreign losses to manage closing and/or commitment fees

What to Do

☐ Revise net income as it would have been without income smoothing.

3. Risky Loans

What to Watch Out For

☐ Accrual of above-average interest rates on high risk loans without making an adequate provision for higher anticipated loan losses
☐ Loan loss provision rates based on outdated historical averages
☐ Modification of interest rates on delinquent loans coupled with the accrual of interest at such lower rates
☐ A long delay in placing questionable loans on a nonaccruing interest basis
☐ Failure to write off high risk loans
☐ Commitments to lend additional funds to "problem" borrowers
☐ Recognition of interest income on loans to low quality borrowers
☐ A carrying value of the loan less than the collateral value of the property
☐ Loans to risky industries such as REITs and owners of shipping vessels
☐ Loans to industries that are positively correlated
☐ International loans to politically and economically unstable foreign countries

What to Do

☐ Determine the adequacy of the loan loss provision.
   a. Compare the ratio of the loan loss provision to actual loss charge-offs.
☐ Restate net income for the difference between the reported loan loss provision and what the provision should be.
☐ Reduce net income for accrued interest income on delinquent loans.
☐ Determine the trend in the ratio of noninterest-paying loans to total loans.

☐ Consider commitments to lend further money to financially deficient companies an unrecorded liability.

☐ Determine the trend in the percentage of interest income on low quality loans to total interest income.

☐ Determine the diversification of the loan portfolio.

4. Long-Term Loans

What to Watch Out For

☐ Long-term loans at unrealistically low fixed interest rates (CAP loans) such as mortgages

What to Do

☐ Determine the trend in the ratio of CAP loans to total loans.

5. Earnings Growth

What to Watch Out For

☐ Growth in earnings that cannot be sustained
   a. Liquidity has been severely reduced.
   b. The growth in loan volume has been excessive compared to deposit growth.

816.6. / Broadcasting

1. Income Management

What to Watch Out For

☐ Improper basis of allocating costs to television programs

☐ The purchase of film packages at lump-sum prices where a sliding scale is established for the cost of each film

What to Do

☐ Restate earnings as they would have been reported if income management had not taken place.

2. Deferral of Costs

What to Watch Out For

☐ The deferral of costs for outdated or unsuccessful films

What to Do

☐ Reduce the deferred charge account and net income for deferred costs associated with obsolete or low quality films.

3. Interest Charges

What to Watch Out For

☐ The deferral of interest charges on borrowed funds needed for existing programs

What to Do

☐ Reduce the deferred charge account and net income for the deferred interest expense applicable to existing programs.

4. Record Returns and Discounts.

What to Watch Out For

☐ Underaccrual or overaccrual of the expense provision for record returns and discounts

What to Do

☐ Compare over time the expense provision to the actual costs incurred.
☐ Adjust net income for the underaccrued or overaccrued expense provision for record returns and discounts.

5. Programming Expenses

What to Watch Out For

☐ Improperly accelerating or deferring the recognition of programming expenses

What to Do

☐ Restate net income as it would have been without the artificial change in programming expenses.

816.7. / Consumer Finance

1. Deferred Income

What to Watch Out For

☐ Unrealistically assigning a high rate to deferred income for acquisition charges

☐ The use of the sum-of-the-years'-digits method in accounting for deferred income

What to Do

☐ Downwardly adjust net income for the incremental earnings arising from the use of an unjustified high rate.

2. **Capital gains derived from insurance subsidiaries are a low quality of earnings source.**

816.8. / Electric and Gas

1. Allowance for Funds During Construction (AFC)

What to Watch Out For

☐ AFC representing a high percentage of net income
☐ AFC being accrued at an unrealistically high rate
   a. The accrued rate exceeds that which is likely to be approved by the regulatory body.
   b. The accrued rate is greater than the utility's cost of capital

What to Do

☐ Determine the trend in the ratio of AFC to net income.
☐ Reduce net income for overaccrued AFC.

2. Fuel Cost

What to Watch Out For

☐ The deferral of increased fuel costs when it is probable that the regulatory commission will not permit all or part of such costs to be passed on to consumers in the form of higher rates

What to Do

☐ Reduce the deferred charge account and net income for the excessive deferral of fuel costs.

3. Delays in new plant construction and/or excessive start-up costs

4. A change in accounting from the recording of revenue and fuel costs on a "services billed" basis to a "services rendered" basis

5. Adverse regulatory and economic conditions affecting the utility

816.9. / Franchising

1. Franchise Fee Income

What to Watch Out For

- ☐ The immediate recognition of the full franchise fee without an adequate provision for future losses
- ☐ Financially poor franchisees

What to Do

- ☐ Examine the financial soundness of franchisees.
- ☐ Reduce net income for the overstated franchise income.

816.10. / Home Building

1. Income Management

What to Watch Out For

- ☐ Assigning varying values for different plots of land
- ☐ The use of second mortgages to overstate the sales price of homes and plots sold
- ☐ Exchanging low-cost plots with other companies at inflated prices
- ☐ Overestimating the degree of completion on home contracts when the percentage-of-completion method is used

What to Do

- ☐ Restate net income to the way it would have been reported if income management had not occurred.

2. Developing Profit

What to Watch Out For

- ☐ Income recognition prior to the commencement of construction

What to Do

☐ Downwardly adjust reported earnings for "developing profit."

816.11. / Insurance

1. Acquisition Costs

What to Watch Out For

☐ The deferral of acquisition costs *not* related to the generation of new business

☐ The use of the sum-of-the-years' premium method in amortizing acquisition costs

What to Do

☐ Reduce the deferred account and net income for acquisition costs that have been improperly deferred.

2. Actuarial interest rate assumption

What to Watch Out For

☐ Unrealistic assumptions

☐ Unjustified changes in the actuarial interest rate

3. Capital gains and losses on the sale of investments show less stability than underwriting income.

4. Lines of insurance

What to Watch Out For

☐ Lines of insurance that necessitate difficult estimates of future costs such as medical malpractice

☐ Lines of insurance that are cyclical in nature such as property and liability insurance

What to Do

☐ Restate net income for an underaccrued or overaccrued loss provision.

☐ Determine the trend in the revenue derived from each major line of insurance to total revenue.

816.12. / Land Development

1. Ten percent revenue recognition rule in retail land sales

What to Watch Out For

☐ Recognition of revenue before the earnings cycle is complete (obligated improvements have been made)

What to Do

☐ Reduce reported earnings for the income that has been recognized before the completion of the earnings cycle

2. A low percentage of cash flow from operations to net income indicates poor earnings quality.

What to Do

☐ Determine the trend in the ratio of operating cash flow to reported earnings.

816.13. / Motion Picture

1. Deferred Movie Costs

What to Watch Out For

☐ Movies that have failed; the costs of making them remain deferred on the books

What to Do

☐ Reduce the deferred charge account and net income for the overstatement in deferred charges.

816.14. / Petroleum Refining

1. Full Cost Method

What to Watch Out For

☐ The deferral of unsuccessful exploration and drilling costs
☐ The deferred charge account exceeds the value of the company's reserves.
☐ There is a long delay in writing off capitalized costs if no reserves are found.

☐ "Instant earnings" created by switching to the full cost method

What to Do

☐ Downwardly adjust the deferred charge account and net income
for:
a. Unsuccessful exploration and development costs
b. The excess of the deferred account balance over the present
value of the company's reserves

2. **The use of the "successful efforts" method results in
higher earnings quality.**

3. **Inventory profits arising from the liquidation of low-cost
inventories result in low quality of earnings increments.**

4. **An integrated oil company that is involved in both
extracting and refining oil has better earnings stability
than a nonintegrated firm solely involved in the refining
process.**

5. **A company with a high petroleum reserve level has
better earning potential than one with a low reserve
level.**

816.15. / Pharmaceutical

1. **Earnings stability is enhanced because of the inelastic
demand for drugs.**

2. **There is a favorable tax aspect since operations are
primarily located in low-tax foreign areas.**

3. **Earnings quality is enhanced because of low
depreciation and low inventory profits.**

816.16. / Real Estate Investment Trust

1. **Problems in the Industry**

What to Watch Out For

☐ Depressed conditions in the real estate market
☐ A tight money market

2. Investments

What to Watch Out For

☐ Nonearning investments in real estate

3. Financial Characteristics

What to Watch Out For

☐ High debt-to-equity ratio coupled with a high ratio of cash dividends to net income

☐ The use of letters of intent by which the trust promises to finance an upcoming project if the builder meets impossible demands

4. Accounting Policies

What to Watch Out For

☐ Accrual of interest income on problem loans

☐ Underestimated loan loss provision

☐ A trust adjusting its books because of overstated profits reported in a prior year

What to Do

☐ Reduce net income for:
  a. Accrued interest income on high risk loans
  b. The understatement in the loan loss provision

816.17. / Savings and Loan

1. Signs of Poor Earnings Stability

What to Watch Out For

☐ A high percentage of fee income

☐ Premature conversion of certificates

☐ Capital gains and losses arising from the disposal of foreclosed real estate

☐ A high ratio of Day of Deposit to Day of Withdrawal accounts to Regular accounts

What to Do

☐ Determine the trend in the ratios of:
  a. Fee income to total revenue
  b. Capital gains and losses to total revenue
  c. Day of Deposit to Day of Withdrawal accounts to total deposits

2. Loan Portfolio Risk

What to Watch Out For

☐ Construction loans
☐ Loans that are past due
☐ Loans applicable to the sale of foreclosed real estate

What to Do

☐ Determine the trend in the ratio of construction loans to total loans.
☐ Compute the scheduled-item ratio.

Index